Adult Learning and Social Change in the UK

Adult Learning, Literacy and Social Change

SERIES EDITORS:
Anna Robinson-Pant (University of East Anglia, UK)
Alan Rogers (University of East Anglia, UK and University of Nottingham, UK)

This series explores the complex relationship between adult learning and social change. Instead of the common focus on adult literacy as kick-starting development, the series considers how adult learning and literacy can also emerge from processes of social change. Each volume introduces new theoretical and methodological lenses to investigate insights into adult learning and literacy based on original empirical research by the authors. Recognising that Governments from the Global North as well as the Global South have recently signed up to the Sustainable Development Goals, this series brings together research conducted in a wide range of countries, including Malawi, Nepal, China, the Philippines and the UK.

ADVISORY BOARD:
Dennis Banda (University of Zambia, Zambia)
Lesley Bartlett (University of Wisconsin, USA)
Maria Lucia Castanheira (Federal University of Minas Gerais, Brazil)
Mostafa Hasrati (Seneca College, Canada)
Li Jiacheng (East China Normal University, China)
Judy Kalman (CINVESTAV, Mexico)
Simon McGrath (University of Nottingham, UK)
Tonic Maruatona (University of Botswana, Botswana)
Tony Mays (Commonwealth of Learning)
Hendrik Nordvall (Mimer, The Swedish Network for Research on Popular Education, Sweden)
Mastin Prinsloo (University of Cape Town, South Africa)
Anita Rampal (University of Delhi, India)
Bonnie Slade (University of Glasgow, UK)

Also available in the series:
Literacies, Power and Identities in Figured Worlds in Malawi, Ahmmardouh Mjaya
Migrant Workers' Education in China, Fusheng Jia

Adult Learning and Social Change in the UK

National and Local Perspectives

Edited by
Jules Robbins and Alan Rogers

BLOOMSBURY ACADEMIC
LONDON • NEW YORK • OXFORD • NEW DELHI • SYDNEY

BLOOMSBURY ACADEMIC
Bloomsbury Publishing Plc
50 Bedford Square, London, WC1B 3DP, UK
1385 Broadway, New York, NY 10018, USA
29 Earlsfort Terrace, Dublin 2, Ireland

BLOOMSBURY, BLOOMSBURY ACADEMIC and the Diana logo are trademarks of Bloomsbury Publishing Plc

First published in Great Britain 2023
Paperback edition published 2024

Copyright © Jules Robbins, Alan Rogers and Contributors, 2023

Jules Robbins, Alan Rogers and Contributors have asserted their right under the Copyright, Designs and Patents Act, 1988, to be identified as Authors of this work.

For legal purposes the Acknowledgements on p. xvii constitute an extension of this copyright page.

All rights reserved. No part of this publication may be reproduced or transmitted in any form or by any means, electronic or mechanical, including photocopying, recording, or any information storage or retrieval system, without prior permission in writing from the publishers.

Bloomsbury Publishing Plc does not have any control over, or responsibility for, any third-party websites referred to or in this book. All internet addresses given in this book were correct at the time of going to press. The author and publisher regret any inconvenience caused if addresses have changed or sites have ceased to exist, but can accept no responsibility for any such changes.

A catalogue record for this book is available from the British Library.

ISBN:	HB:	978-1-3502-6212-6
	PB:	978-1-3502-6216-4
	ePDF:	978-1-3502-6213-3
	eBook:	978-1-3502-6214-0

Series: Adult Learning, Literacy and Social Change

Typeset by Integra Software Services Pvt. Ltd.

To find out more about our authors and books visit www.bloomsbury.com and sign up for our newsletters.

This book is dedicated to Professor Alan Rogers, an optimistic and dedicated researcher, author and practitioner in the field of adult education.

Sadly, Alan Rogers, the co-editor of this volume and of this series, passed away on 5 April 2022, as this volume was being finalized. He will be greatly missed by his family, friends and colleagues and by the many students, researchers and practitioners around the world who were informed and inspired by his teaching and writing.

Contents

List of Tables	viii
Contributors	ix
Preface	xii
Acknowledgements	xvii
Series Foreword	xviii

1. Being part of the social change: adult education and lessons from history *Sharon Clancy* — 1
2. Radical adult education practitioners in the UK: the International League for Social Commitment in Adult Education 1984–94 *Alan Tuckett* — 21
3. Adult learning and social justice: health, well-being and the inequalities of power *Lyn Tett* — 41
4. Learning English in a hostile environment: a study of volunteer ESOL teachers of refugees and asylum seekers in the UK *Lauren Bouttell* — 59
5. A refugee third sector learning ecology for social change: 'covert activism' *Mary-Rose Puttick* — 75
6. Discussion groups with older people: an interface of participatory ageing and social change *Kathleen Lane* — 93
7. Tales of adult learning, relationships and social change within the National Citizen Service *Natasha Rennolds* — 107
8. The achievements of informal adult reading group talk through vernacular expression: challenging the dominant discourses of literary study *John Gordon* — 127
9. Learning through the Covid-19 pandemic: how the pandemic has affected the ways in which adults experience learning in the UK *Karen Fairfax-Cholmeley and Clare Meade* — 147
10. Learning to live sustainably? A case study of a community gardening scheme in Norwich *Mahesh Pant* — 167

Concluding reflections *Alan Rogers and Jules Robbins* — 187

Index — 209

Tables

8.1 Literary study talk in 'Literature's Lasting Impression'   131
8.2 Positioning affordances of spoken quotation, and their effects on readers   137

Contributors

Lauren Bouttell is a PhD researcher at the University of East Anglia's School of Education and Lifelong Learning, UK. She has previously worked as an ESL teacher in South-East Asia and as a volunteer ESOL teacher in Glasgow and Norwich. She completed the Erasmus Mundus International Masters in Adult Education for Social Change at the University of Glasgow. Her PhD research explores the relationship between adult learning and social transformation with sanctuary seekers in the UK.

Sharon Clancy is Assistant Professor in educational leadership at the University of Nottingham, UK. Her PhD, writing and research focus on adult education, historical and contemporary, particularly issues of class, culture and social justice. Sharon was Head of Community Engagement at the University of Nottingham between 2007 and 2013 and Senior Research Fellow on ENLIVEN between 2016 and 2019. A voluntary sector leader before entering academia, she was previously CEO of Mansfield Council for Voluntary Services.

Karen Fairfax-Cholmeley is a freelance researcher and consultant and has worked in community and adult education for over thirty years. She has worked nationally and internationally to develop family and intergenerational learning, English as a Second or Other Language (ESOL), literacy and work-based learning including teacher training. Her work at National Institute of Adult Continuing Education (now The Learning and Work Institute) involved a variety of research and development projects and publications. She completed an MA at the Institute of Education, London, in education and international development in 2013 where her dissertation explored the part family stories and memories play in the development of identity and belonging and how this relates to concepts of citizenship for Palestinian Christian children living in the Occupied Palestinian Territories.

John Gordon is Professor of Education at the School of Education and Lifelong Learning, University of East Anglia, UK. He worked as a high school teacher of English and Media before becoming a researcher and teacher educator in

UEA's School of Education and Lifelong Learning. He leads a professional master's course in Shared Literary Reading, working and researching with teachers of reading in primary, secondary and higher education. John's research explores responses to literature through conversation in classrooms and adult reading groups. John is author of *Researching Interpretive Talk around Literary Narrative Texts: Shared Novel Reading* (2020) and *A Pedagogy of Poetry* (2014).

Kathleen Lane is a qualitative researcher whose main focus is on older people's well-being and participation. Her research has been conducted in clinical, community and residential settings. Since 2020 she has conducted research on the impact of Covid-19 in older people's care homes. Kathleen is Research Fellow in the School of Health Sciences, University of East Anglia, UK. She has conducted discussion groups in sheltered housing since 2002, first in Cambridge and later in Norwich where the group has run for ten years.

Clare Meade is a visual artist, freelance researcher and consultant with a focus on family and intergenerational learning, informal adult and community learning. She completed her Doctorate in Education in 2012 at the UEA. Clare has worked in Adult and Community Learning for over thirty years with both local authority and voluntary sectors. She worked for the National Institute of Adult Continuing Education (NIACE) and has contributed to a wide range of educational research and publications.

Mahesh Pant is the founder of Grow Our Own, a community gardening scheme in Norwich, UK. He is experienced in social research and community development and has worked in Nepal and the UK. His PhD thesis applied Sen's capability approach in studying the nature and extent of poverty in East Nepal.

Mary-Rose Puttick is Research Assistant in the Centre for the Study and Practice of Culture in Education (CSPACE) at Birmingham City University, UK. She previously worked for twelve years in the adult and community education sector in Manchester, teaching English for Speakers of Other Languages (ESOL) and Family Learning. Her doctoral research, 'Reimagining Family Literacy: Co-creating Pedagogies with Migrating Mothers in the Refugee Third Sector', took as a starting point her practice in government-funded family literacy provision to consider new possibilities for family literacy education in non-government-funded contexts, using a postcolonial feminist and new literacy studies approach.

Natasha Rennolds is a PhD Researcher at the University of East Anglia, UK. She has worked for over twenty-five years in fields related to young people, informal learning and safeguarding, delivering as part of both local community and school-based provision. She worked extensively with young people and in doing so experienced the importance of and difficulties in building sustainable relationships for learning and change. Her research builds on this experience in exploring the nature of relationships and engagement for learning outside of formal schooling. She is, also, the Independent Chair of a multi-agency Workforce Development Group and Independent Scrutiny for a Local Safeguarding Children Partnership.

Jules Robbins is a teacher and a senior educational assessor with over twenty-five years of experience in secondary, primary and adult education. For many years, she was a tutor for Norfolk County Council and the WEA on a range of adult education programmes including functional skills, ESOL and cultural leisure courses for adults in literature and creative writing.

Alan Rogers was Visiting Professor of Adult Education in the Universities of East Anglia and Nottingham; university tutor-organizer of extramural classes, Nottingham University, 1957–79; Director Institute of Continuing Education, Londonderry, Northern Ireland 1979–85; freelance adult educator and Director of *Education for Development* (based at University of Reading), 1985–98; teacher, trainer and author in the field of adult education and international development with many years' experience of working in Asia and Africa.

Lynn Tett is Professor Emerita at the Universities of Edinburgh and Huddersfield, UK. She has published extensively in the field of adult learning in journals, edited books and chapters in books. Her recent publications include Duckworth, V. and Tett, L. (2019), 'Transformative and Emancipatory Literacy to Empower', *International Journal of Lifelong Education,* 38 (4) pp. 366–78, and Tett, L. and Hamilton M. (2019) (eds.), *Resisting Neoliberalism in Education: Local, National and Transnational Perspectives.*

Sir Alan Tuckett is Emeritus Professor of Education at the University of Wolverhampton, UK, and an Honorary Fellow of UNESCO's Institute of Lifelong Learning. From 1988 to 2011, he led the National Institute of Adult Continuing Education in the UK. He was President of the International League for Social Commitment in Adult Education 1986–7 and President of the International Council for Adult Education 2011–15 and 2017.

Preface

The changing world

As we write, the world is changing before our eyes.

Change is, of course, happening all the time – it is a constant feature of life, individual and social. The historian Fernand Braudel distinguished between several different 'levels' of change – the immediate (events such as wars or volcano eruptions); the middle-term changes (e.g. population changes) and what he called *la longue durée*, those very long-term changes hardly perceptible to individuals but nevertheless calling for adaptations which are based on learning (see Lee, 2012).

But the speed and scale of change today is unusual. In February 2022, Russia invaded Ukraine and began a war of oppression which at the time of writing has displaced an estimated ten million people. Coronavirus (Covid-19) has wrapped itself around the planet and as yet we can only guess at the long-term implications of this and the social changes which will follow. Alongside the pandemic, climate change is coming to a crisis point, there is a cost of living crisis and migration on a scale never seen before is taking place in many parts of the world. In addition, groups of people have raised their voices to bear witness to some major inequalities and problems within our global society. These have included the Black Lives Matter movement, #MeToo and Extinction Rebellion. At an individual level, in many countries it has become socially acceptable for people to choose how they identify themselves, to select their own pronouns, and thereby dissolve one of the previously established differences between human beings. In so doing, they aim at eradicating some of the old barriers between themselves, others and the people they might one day become.

It is the relationship between forms of adult learning and education on the one hand and social change on the other hand which is the key theme of this book. The term 'social change' is often used interchangeably with other terms such as 'social transformation' and 'social development'. The view taken in this volume – and indeed in the series of which it is a part – is that social change is just that: any form of change in the sociocultural patterns of life of the peoples under discussion, irrespective of agency. By 'social transformation', while there is in many instances some hint of agency ('social transformation' is in this case planned and intended, whereas much social change is not planned or intended), we prefer to use the term 'transformation' to mean a more wide-ranging and longer-lasting (i.e. deeper) social change than may be implied by the term 'social change'. On the other hand, we see 'social development' as planned and intended change with specified outcomes.

The relationship then between all these varied kinds of social change and adult learning is complex. On the one hand, adults will learn to help themselves cope with the changes they meet in their everyday lives, to assimilate – this is adaptive learning. Alternatively, they may learn to be able to take more control of the changes – directive learning. They may do this learning individually or collectively (in, for example, social movements). Educational programmes aimed at supporting specific kinds of social change are often referred to as radical adult education. One of our aims in this volume is to give examples of different kinds of adult learning in relation to social change. The book is partly intended as a review, based on a number of case studies, which will perhaps provide the tools to analyse other forms of adult learning and education in relation to social change.

Adult learning and education

We need to define what we mean by the terms we use, for there are many different constructions which can be put upon these words. By 'adult learning and education', we draw a distinction between the many informal ways in which adults learn and the many forms of education, formal and non-formal, through which some of that learning is facilitated. This book includes some formal adult education provision and some very non-formal forms of adult learning. All this is against a background of everyday informal learning, lifelong and life-wide – mostly unconscious and unintentional but yet highly effective in terms of everyday living (Rogers, 2014).

One of the possible outcomes which could emerge from the current situation in the UK is an overdue re-evaluation of the importance of the role played by 'unskilled' workers. It seems that at last there is a shared societal appreciation of the fact that state-of-the-art hospitals can operate only when the cleaning team is as well managed as the theatre team. There's a growing understanding that many of the job areas which have sometimes been considered as *simply* 'unskilled' – public transport, supermarket checkout/delivery work, care work in homes for older people and the disabled – are in fact crucial to the success of society as a whole. Might the future provide a route for workers in those areas to increase their sense of enfranchisement and agency in their working lives through different forms of adult learning and education?

Continuing professional development suffers as a concept because of the inclusion of the word 'professional'. We still tend to distinguish the professions as jobs which require the individual worker to invest their time and brain power into studying upfront in order to later reap the benefits in terms of esteem and financial reward. A shift in this thinking, combined with a response to the changing demographics of the UK workforce, could lead to the normalization of provision of lifelong, meaningful, beneficial training and upskilling for workers in all areas.

Already in the UK, in recent times, adult education has become increasingly focused around bankable skills and the acquisition of certificates in valued qualifications such as functional skills in English, maths and ICT. Funding is currently provided within strict parameters and is generally based on the success of individual students being moved through the levels of functional skills at an agreed pace. However, many tutors recognize that the true value of what they are providing cannot be measured in SMART targets or reduced to certificates. To be in a classroom is to be in a safe and welcoming environment. It shows willing. It may lead to something. But most importantly, it allows the learner a voice, a position within a group, albeit sometimes marginal; it enables mixing with people not ordinarily encountered in everyday life. It opens doors, it opens minds and it broadens horizons.

During the UK Covid-19 lockdowns, many people were busy teaching themselves new skills. Home baking flourished, blankets were crocheted, garden ponds were dug, seeds were sown and book groups went online. Walking group members posted photos of their individual walks on social media. Meanwhile, the various impacts of Covid-19, including lockdowns, shielding and social distancing, meant that mental health issues were discussed more openly; during the first lockdown, over half a million people accessed an online course about suicide prevention (https://www.bbc.co.uk/news/uk-52702048). A sense of community, a need for connection, was evident in many places.

This volume

It will be observed that many of the case studies in the current volume come from the Norwich area of the UK. That is deliberate. For one thing, several of the authors of individual chapters, plus both of the editors, came together in 2018 as part of the AdultEducation100 initiative in Norfolk. Additionally, over the last twenty or so years, the School of Education and Lifelong Learning at the University of East Anglia, in association with other parts of the university and with the city and county, has developed a strong adult learning dimension – despite the dismantling of its former extramural programme of community-based, rather than campus-based, 'continuing education'. This new adult learning programme is both academic and practical (with active involvement with Norwich as a City of Sanctuary, for example). UEA's School of Education and Lifelong Learning is also international as well as regional. This volume is intended to draw on the strengths of this programme but at the same time to locate it in a wider setting of adult learning in the UK.

The first two chapters of this volume add historical perspectives through an examination of the 1919 Adult Education report (Clancy, Chapter 1) and a review of the 1984–94 work of ILSCAE (the International League for Social Commitment in Adult Education) (Tuckett, Chapter 2). The impact of adult education on well-being and health (Tett, Chapter 3) is considered, plus the impact of discussion groups on older people (Lane, Chapter 6). Two chapters are largely concerned with the provision for asylum-seeking (Puttick, Chapter 5) and refugee learners (Bouttell, Chapter 4). Chapter 7 critiques the UK's National Citizenship Programme for older teenagers (Rennolds), and Chapter 8 discusses the literary achievements of participants in informal reading groups (Gordon). The impact of the pandemic on adult learners and their providers is discussed in Chapter 9 (Fairfax-Cholmeley and Meade), and the final chapter provides a case study of a community gardening scheme in Norwich (Pant, Chapter 10). The editors draw together themes and ideas in a reflective conclusion which will also seek to suggest a way ahead.

We are conscious that we have included only England and Scotland among the nations of the UK – an indication (we suggest) of the strength of Scottish 'community education' rather than of bias. But the aim is to demonstrate something of the great diversity of forms of adult learning rather than stress the limitations of current provision. Adult education in the UK – like all other aspects of life – is constantly changing and adapting, 'ducking and diving', as one author has recently put it (Bowl, 2016), in order to survive. It is perhaps in some places rather healthier than some analysts have suggested, taking many different forms. And it will continue to develop new agendas and activities to fulfil its role, to help all women and men, irrespective of class, race, gender, colour or any other form of distinction, to flourish individually and collectively in times of change.

The book was planned before the pandemic broke up the existing patterns of social life, with the resulting increase in 'self-directed learning'. It is impossible to see clearly what forms of social life and what forms of adult learning and education will emerge from the current crisis; if this volume contributes towards the new normal by encouraging new thinking about forms and programmes, it will have served its purpose. There is much which is not covered in this volume but what is here is suggestive of the direction of travel.

Jules Robbins
Alan Rogers

References

Bowl, M. (2016), 'Ducking and Diving', Adult Educator Agency in Testing Times: Insights from England and New Zealand, in M. Milana, J. Holford, and V.A. Mohorčič Špolar (eds.), *Adult and Lifelong Education: Global, National and Local Perspectives*, 32–50, Abingdon: Routledge, 2016.

Lee, R. (2012), *Fernand Braudel, the Longue Duree, and World Systems Analysis*, Albany, NY: State University of New York Press.

Rogers, A. (2014), *The Base of the Iceberg: Informal Learning and Its Impact on Formal and Non-formal Learning*, Leverkusen Opladen: Verlag Barbara Budrich.

Acknowledgements

No person is an island. I would like to acknowledge the deep and lasting influence of my parents, my brother Alan and especially my loving and patient family – Ade, Tee and Liam – without whom nothing is possible.

I would also like to say a heartfelt thanks to the friends who have supported me, prodded me and kept me company during this book's journey, especially Heather M-S, James T, Rachel M and Rex.

Finally, I would not have been in a position to work on this volume had it not been for the many inspiring learners, learning support assistants and tutors whom it has been my privilege to meet along the way. They have generously shared their ideas, insights and life stories and have hugely enriched my working life.

Jules

Series Foreword

Adult Learning, Literacy and Social Change

This series explores the complex relationship between adult learning, literacy and social change through empirical research conducted within and beyond educational programmes in a wide range of countries in the Global North and South. Since the launch of the 2030 Sustainable Development Goals, there has been growing interest in how adult literacy – sometimes referred to as 'the invisible glue' (LWG, 2007) – connects the seventeen goals. Much research has focused on how to measure literacy progress quantitatively (through literacy rates) against such development indicators and assumed that most literacy learning takes place formally within institutions or educational programmes. Rather than taking this instrumental approach, this series investigates the 'why' and 'how' of the assumed relationship between adult learning, literacy and social change.

The UNESCO Chair in Adult Literacy and Learning for Social Transformation (based at University of East Anglia, UK) has strongly shaped the approach and stance of this series. Aiming to develop understanding about how adult literacy and learning – particularly for women and young adults – can help address inequalities in the poorest communities of the world, the UNESCO Chair brings together university departments specializing in adult literacy and community learning in the UK, Ethiopia, Nepal, Malawi, Egypt and the Philippines. Several of the books in this series emerged from in-depth qualitative research studies conducted by researchers within this international partnership.

Providing a much-needed critical perspective on adult literacy and development, the series challenges the usual starting point of international and national policy discourse and research in this field. First, the shift to consider social change rather than development offers a broader, holistic lens, since 'development' implies a limited perspective on social change as predetermined, planned, staged, and often with an envisaged endpoint (Castles, 2001). Conceptual debate on 'social transformation' (defined as 'big' social change by Haas et al., 2020) informs this analysis – particularly the notion that 'social transformations are deeply political in nature, an insight which dominant, "technocratic" development theories and ideologies ignore and actively try to conceal' (ibid.: 7). This alternative lens provides a way to step outside development frameworks that focus only on literacy and development outcomes, in order to recentre attention onto people's lived experiences of social change.

Second, this series is grounded on an 'ideological', rather than an 'autonomous', model of literacy (Street, 1984). In contrast to much international development policy and research which has drawn on an understanding of literacy as decontextualized skills learned in a classroom, the series takes a 'situated' approach (Barton, Hamilton and Ivanic, 2000) to investigate literacy and adult learning in everyday life. Researching informal and non-formal learning – both within and beyond educational institutions and development programmes – the authors offer original insights into how adults are engaging with an ever-increasing diversity of literacies, languages, cultural values and technologies. Resisting the common tendency to conflate literacy, learning and education, they explore the complex relationships around power, knowledge and identities that are shaping people's lives and social change.

Third, this series accepts the now widely held view of adult learning as comprising formal, non-formal and informal elements (UNESCO, 2009: 27); not necessarily as discrete activities but often inextricably mixed in a lifelong and life-wide process of interaction between social members. Learning can no longer be seen as the sole prerogative of educational institutions in time-limited activities; it takes multiple forms and occurs in multiple locations throughout life. The volumes in this series will explore how such adult learning is inspired by and at the same time contributes to social change.

As the world now grapples with the devastating effects of the global Covid-19 pandemic, climate change, conflict, migration and widening inequalities, the focus of this series is particularly relevant. More than ever before, social change is seen as unpredictable, and new educational challenges are emerging. The authors in this series do not set out to advocate solutions for policymakers or educational providers. However, these in-depth research accounts share rich first-hand experiences, observations, analysis and voices that are often unheard, thereby introducing new ways to understand adult learning, literacy and social change.

Anna Robinson-Pant
Alan Rogers

References

Barton, D., Hamilton, M., and Ivanic, R. (2000), *Situated Literacies: Reading and Writing in Context*, London: Routledge.

Castles, S. (2001), Studying social transformation, *International Political Science Review*, 22 (1): 13–32.

Haas, H., Fransen, S., Natter, K., Schewel, K., and Vezzoli, S. (2020), *Social Transformation*, International Migration Institute Working Papers, Paper 166, July 2020, Oxford: IMI.

Street, B.V. (1984), *Literacy in Theory and Practice*, Cambridge: Cambridge University Press.

University of East Anglia UNESCO Chair Available at: https://www.uea.ac.uk/groups-and-centres/unesco-chair-programme.

UK Literacy Working Group (2007), Literacy and International Development: The Next Steps, LWG Position Paper. Available at: http://balid.org.uk/pdfs/LWG%20Position%20Paper%20Final%20June07%20CD%20final.doc.

UNESCO (2009), *Global Report on Adult Learning and Education*, Hamburg: UIL.

Being part of the social change: adult education and lessons from history

Sharon Clancy University of Nottingham

The 1919 Adult Education Committee's (AEC) *Final Report* on Adult Education (Cmd 321, 1919) was conceived during a time of great change and turmoil, in the immediate aftermath of the Great War. This chapter will examine the 1919 Adult Education report, as a lens on adult learning needs for our own contemporary world of contestation, movement and turbulence, marked by climate pressures, Covid-19 and a rise in fake news and demagoguery. It will focus on the Report's resolute belief in the necessity of twin strands in adult education, defining itself explicitly beyond the 'vocational': the 'Humane', understood as 'the satisfaction of intellectual, aesthetic and spiritual needs', and the 'Civic', in which education is a vehicle for collectivism, social responsibility and giving voice to the ignored and excluded. This chapter argues that critical thinking and embracing social movements for change to counter the rise in anti-democratic sentiment is of pressing urgency for a functioning and relevant adult education movement. It articulates the need for a re-politicization of adult education through an exploration of the complex relationships between adult learning and the impetus for social change, in line with the original political courage of the 1919 Report. It argues that adult education must strive to be, in the words of Raymond Williams, not merely 'the bottle with the message in it, bobbing on the tides and waves of history', but must urgently emerge from the 'the desire to make learning part of the process of social change itself' (Williams, 1983, in McIlroy, J. and Westwood, S. eds. (1993)).

Background to the 1919 Report

In 1919, as Britain recovered from the devastating effects of the First World War and the Spanish flu pandemic, the Ministry of Reconstruction for Adult

Education published a powerful report, visionary in its scope and practical in its detail, on the key role adult education had to play in fostering an active democracy, enriching communities and nourishing curiosity and a love of learning. Adult education, it argued, was 'a permanent national necessity' (Ministry of Reconstruction Adult Education Committee (1919: 5). The authors of the 1919 Report, the Ministry of Reconstruction's Adult Education Committee (AEC), were drawn from a spectrum of those with an interest in rejuvenating the economy and society after the devastation of world war, along with those with experience in delivering adult education. The AEC was chaired by A. L. Smith, Master of Balliol, Oxford, and included R. H. Tawney, the historian and social critic, and Albert Mansbridge,[1] founder, in 1903, of the Workers' Educational Association (WEA). Tawney and Mansbridge conceived of adult education as essentially democratic. Tawney stated that 'adult education is not put on like varnish. It springs like a plant from the soil and the fragrance of the earth is upon it' (Tawney, 1914/1973: 81). He believed that adult education emerges from the grassroots upwards and acts as an emancipatory space for individual and community challenge and transformation. The WEA, led by Mansbridge, initiated an approach which focused on giving people the tools to improve their own circumstances, building capacity at a community level, tackling social and economic disadvantage and promoting values of citizenship and democratic engagement. In the words of the 1919 Report, adult education should help people to develop 'an open habit of mind, clear-sighted and truth-loving, proof against sophisms, shibboleths, claptrap phrases and cant' (Ministry of Reconstruction Adult Education Committee, 1919: 5).

Adult education – philosophy and vision

At the heart of the AEC's bold vision was a direct attempt to critically reflect on the nature and purpose of adult education – and also its method of delivery – by whom and by what means. They examined these issues head on, including a close examination of the role of the state and civil society in delivering adult education. As Kuk and Tarlau (2020: 598) argue, 'the field of adult education ... boasts a rich tradition in critical pedagogy as well as internal debates on the educational aspects of social movements', and the AEC embodied this debate. They did not shy away from the political or from challenging the establishment, and this audacious clear-sightedness is pivotal to their vision – and is the focus of this chapter.

In 1961, in *An Open Letter to WEA Tutors,* Raymond Williams argued that there has been no single central mobilizing theory, vision or philosophy of adult education, due to its huge breadth and range, its myriad manifestations and its protean quality. Consequently, he argued, it has been shaped and moulded by the vicissitudes and demands of different periods in history. Williams argued that it has been variously perceived as a simple response to social change – 'the bottle with the message in it, bobbing on the tides and waves of history' (Williams, 1989: 157) and, conversely, as central to movements for change – 'part of the process of social change itself' (Williams, 1989). He stated that because adult education lacked a grand central theory, much of his own thinking was focused on reflecting on what it should be. Williams's *The Long Revolution* (1961) can be read as an examination of the true purpose of education and as a paean to the importance of learning for life. In this work, Williams described adult education as a struggle between three traditions, all battling for supremacy. These were 'the old humanist' tradition, 'the industrial trainer' and 'the democratic educator'.

In Williams's definition, the 'industrial trainer' concept is associated with the need for skilled, pliant workers operating in a marketplace, a strictly vocational approach which is mirrored everywhere in contemporary rhetoric and policy, such as the recent White Paper on further education and skills (January 2021) *Skills for Jobs: Lifelong Learning for Opportunity and Growth*. The 'old humanist' concept is perhaps the more traditional conception of adult education, particularly associated with university education and the extramural departments, with a greater focus on high culture, intellectual rigour and anti-utilitarianism. The sociologist Michael Rustin described it in the following way: 'The "old humanist" conception aimed to preserve the values of "culture" against both industrial materialism, and the corruptions and dilutions of commercial mass culture' (Rustin, 2016: 148). Finally, the 'democratic educator' concept, associated most closely with the political Left, the post-war labour movement and the social democratic welfare state, called for education for as many people as possible, through numerous public means, both independent of, and supported by, the state.

Williams's framework is helpful for critically considering how adult education has evolved and also for recognizing how very farsighted the AEC 1919 Report was. Adult education has also been a place in which the spiritual and the material come together through the liberal arts, a means of promoting the best in culture and thought for all classes. This is closer to Williams's 'old humanist' conception. Liberal arts education has also sometimes been a means of controlling and calibrating what 'good culture' should look like. It has been linked with what might be described as a 'missionary' approach to education, with a strong emphasis on fostering morality and spiritual enrichment, through the efforts of church or state agencies, and through the work of philanthropic organizations. This sustained interest in the spiritual and moral well-being of the nation has peaked during periods of national uncertainty and social change, with the 'democratic educator' and 'industrial trainer' concepts of adult education butting up against the 'old humanist' tradition in a series of 'pendulum swings', which are suggestive of the tension between adult education as a tool for enlightenment and for social control:

> Public Knowledge and Public Education have historically been subject to recurrent pendulum swings between the emancipatory/enlightenment vision and the darker forces of subordination and social control. From the point of view of public intellectual life, Thomas Paine expresses the high optimism of the enlightenment when he argued, 'I am a farmer of thoughts and all the crops I raise I give away'.
>
> (Goodson, 2003: 1)

Arguably, Williams's 'democratic educator' concept and Tawney's vision of grassroots emancipation are close to the concept of 'popular education' or 'educación popular' which evolved in Latin America from the mid-twentieth century onwards, and sits at the intersection of politics and pedagogy. As Kane argues, this tradition espouses three key beliefs – a recognition that education must eschew notions of political neutrality; it must side with those most marginalized and it must question existing structures:

> What distinguishes popular education from 'adult', 'non-formal', 'distance', or 'permanent education', for example, is that in the context of social injustice, education can never be politically neutral: if it does not side with the poorest and marginalised sectors – the 'oppressed' – in an attempt to transform society, then it necessarily sides with the 'oppressors' in maintaining the existing structures of oppression, even if by default.
>
> (Kane, 2001: 9)

Farsighted and bold

The AEC took these issues – and many of Williams's concerns – as central. First, the AEC had a number of specific objectives which related to promoting democratic engagement and active citizenship. Democracy, the AEC argued, meant ensuring voluntary agencies and social movements were central in shaping and delivering adult education. The AEC sought to bolster the likelihood of this through a range of democratic institutions and mechanisms to enhance the influence of voluntary organizations ('an integral part of the fabric of national education') in the adult curriculum. Their ambition was to oversee rebuilding 'the national life on a better and more durable foundation'. The result was a network of adult education institutions and provision strongly linked to social movements (see list identified in the 1919 Report below[2]).

They also held a particular understanding of non-vocational education which embraced elements of both the 'old humanist' and the 'democratic educator' models. They identified both the importance of 'Humane' adult education, chiefly defined as life-enhancing learning through the arts, music, crafts, literature to meet the human need for personal development and self-expression – 'the satisfaction of intellectual, aesthetic and spiritual needs' (Ministry of Reconstruction Adult Education Committee, 1919: 54) – and for 'Civic' education, specifically education conceived through a lens of collectivism and social responsibility which focuses on the importance of social movements to effect change, particularly for working-class people:

> They demand opportunities for education in the hope that the power which it brings will enable them to understand and help in the solution of the common problems of society. In many cases, therefore, their efforts to obtain education are specifically directed towards rendering themselves better fitted for the responsibilities of membership in political, social and industrial organisations.
> (1919: 54)

They argued not only that adult education is 'a permanent national necessity' but is also 'an inseparable aspect of citizenship, and therefore should be both universal and lifelong' and that it 'should be spread uniformly and systematically over the whole community'. In other words, any sense of cultural elitism was swiftly rebutted.

They were also motivated by the need to seek out new pedagogical approaches which engaged the adult, recognizing that this must both address specifically adult learning needs and approaches and encourage citizenship: 'We need to think out educational methods and possibilities from the new point of view … of the adult learning to be a citizen.' Foremost, the Adult Education Committee articulated their task as being 'to consider the provision for, and possibilities of, Adult Education (other than technical or vocational) in Great Britain, and to make recommendations'.

Additional research on the AEC and the Centenary Commission

In 2018, a group of adult educators, recognizing the historic importance of the AEC's Final Report, set up the Adult Education 100 campaign. The campaign sought to encourage a programme of activities, centred on the centenary of the 1919 Report, which would both recover and re-evaluate the twentieth-century history of adult education, and set out a vision for life-wide adult lifelong education for the twenty-first century through their report. The Centenary Commission on Adult Education Report: *Adult Education and Lifelong Learning for 21st Century Britain* (2019)[3] was published in pre-pandemic times. But, like its predecessor, it recognized that Britain was facing a critical time, and a series of social, political, economic, health, technological and demographic challenges. One of its key chapters, 'Fostering community, democracy and dialogue through adult lifelong education' (Centenary Commission, 2019: 19–28), begins with the following quotation from the 1919 Report – 'An uneducated democracy cannot be other than a failure'.

In late 2018, I was able to secure some funding under the aegis of the Centenary Commission from the Society for Educational Studies (SES) for a detailed survey and analysis of records in the National Archives relating to the Ministry of Reconstruction's AEC and some scrutiny of related Board of Education papers. This historically focused work was supported by a series of project meetings of the Centenary Commission which allowed me to test out the ideas and insights gained from the archival research. It was further supported by a series of twenty interviews over July and August 2019 with key contemporary practitioners/activists in adult, political and community education and new and emerging radical social movements, who gave critical insights into contemporary relationships with the state and incidentally into funding connected with their work. This included colleagues from The World Transformed, Arts Emergency, a charity working with sixteen- to nineteen-year-olds in further education from diverse backgrounds who are least able to access higher education in the Arts, Humanities or Social Sciences, User Voice, which is a government-funded charity run predominantly by ex-offenders with the aim of reducing offending through peer-to-peer learning, and Common Wealth theatre company, amongst others.

Two workshops followed in the autumn of 2019, in Oxford and Nottingham, with those seeking to shape adult education today, including historians of adult education, policymakers, managers, practitioners and activists engaged in the provision and development of adult education. The workshops sought to influence important contemporary policy debates about the social and economic conditions which most effectively support adult learning and helped to situate and explore the significance of the empirical findings in the context of the broader social, economic and political history of the First World War and the 1920s, a turbulent period of change, as well as reflecting on the implications for adult education, democracy and systems of work today at another critical political and democratic juncture.

The AEC had not been researched for some time and the research grant allowed for a renewed focus on the origins of, and thinking behind, the 1919 Report at a time when adult education is no longer a 'fixture', ideologically or structurally, as it was when last explored in depth in the 1970s (Jennings, 1980; Kelly, 1973; Taylor, 1976). It is essentially in deeply troubled times. Since the 1980s, despite rhetoric about 'lifelong learning' for a 'learning society', opportunities for, and institutions of, formal adult education have been largely swept away. With some exceptions, what remains formally focuses on training young adults in workplace skills, migrant education and social skills. However, grassroots, informal education and community activism, and 'horizontal movements' connected to important societal issues (such as climate collapse, gender politics, economic breakdown and industry, big business capitalism) have become new sources of spontaneous and responsive learning. Funding, however, remains a critical point of contestation; much of the old Local Authority grant aid monies, which were part of the funding fabric for 'innovative', and often less restricted, voluntary sector work, have disappeared, with this process accelerating over the recent years of austerity-focused policy and the strictures of the (short-lived) Big Society which catalysed numerous enduring tensions about the role of the voluntary sector, the nature of voluntarism and the ongoing withdrawal of the state from civil society.

The interim and final reports I created for the SES focused on the 1919 Report's relationship with the state, specifically the role of non-vocational education, state intervention, politics and grassroots activism. The research allowed for an exploration of the histories relating to both the Report's evolution and its impact over time and to draw policy attention to the focus of the *Final Report* on the importance of placing engaged democracy and community at the heart of a renewed or re-imagined adult education system.

Emerging themes from the research

The 1919 Report gave detailed consideration to the ethos of state independence and the non-vocational on the AEC's mode of work and considered the tensions and compromises inherent in state leadership in adult education at the time. This has been a point of contestation throughout the twentieth century; some independent organizations have refused state funding to avoid being compromised; others have taken it as a social right: it is complex issue. A consideration of the long-term impact of state intervention, juxtaposed with the alternative, informal connections that emerge from grassroots adult learning in the twenty-first-century context, enables us to ask how the state should relate to the world of adult and community learning and whether there is room for both voluntary sector-led and state sector-led adult/community education.

From the start the AEC took a more sceptical view of the capacity of Local Education Authorities (LEAs) for shaping (adult) education and, given this scepticism, examined how it should itself develop strategies and approaches to ensure the vitality of non-vocational adult education in an educational system organized around LEAs. It examined the response of the Board of Education to the Adult Education Committee's reports and, in particular, how the Board was influenced by the Committee's view of the significance, or otherwise, of the voluntary sector and social movements in the development of (adult) education, and particularly the relationship between labour market conditions and their framing of adult education in relation to democracy, voluntarism and civil society.

The 1918 Education ('Fisher') Act was clear that education, for all ages and of all types, should be supported and managed through state infrastructure, and its primary focus was upon education for children and adolescents. What little indication there was of government interest in adult education was primarily of a vocational nature. However, as a letter from the Board of Education, dated 12 February 1918, outlined, even the apparently simple distinctions of 'vocational' and 'non-vocational' education proved problematic:

> subjects such as Modern Languages may have either a vocational or a non-vocational object, and the mere naming of the subject in a programme of work will leave this object uncertain. Again, a subject may be included in a course which is primarily designed for a particular vocation, but an individual student may attend the instruction for individual non-vocational purposes ... Much

depends on the way in which a given subject is taught, and the object with which it is taken by the individual student.

(L. Welby Briggs, Board of Education letter, 12th February 1918)

Welby Briggs then went on to acknowledge that 'the volume of non-vocational education for adults is comparatively small, and that much of it is not provided by Local Education Authorities'. Certain measures for improvement were proposed:

> The Board are impressed with the present unsatisfactory state of education in this direction, and in the draft of the proposed new Regulations for Continuation, Technical and Art Courses, they have included a paragraph in the Prefactory Memorandum, stating that one of the main ideas of educational administration on which the proposed changes in the Regulations rest is 'the importance of continuing general education side by side with technical instruction, particularly by means of Grouped Courses for younger students, and of providing facilities for disinterested studies making for wise living and good citizenship.
>
> (L. Welby Briggs, Board of Education letter, 12th February 1918)

Furthermore, Welby suggested that the proposed new Local College infrastructure ('the coping stone of local education' – Ministry of Reconstruction Adult Education Committee, 1919: 111) 'should provide facilities for disinterested intellectual development by means of Classes in Literature, History, Economics, and other humane studies which make for wise living and good citizenship' (L. Welby Briggs, Board of Education letter, 12 February 1918). The letter did at least suggest that there was government awareness in 1918 of the importance of non-vocational adult education, even if it was not explicitly expressed in the Fisher Act. It is also interesting that Briggs placed a strong focus upon non-vocational adult education as being conducive to 'wise living and good citizenship', a correlation that was also specifically emphasized in the 1919 Report.

The AEC doubted that LEAs would promote a broad, life-wide, adult education curriculum which looked beyond the vocational: 'We do not think that Local Authorities will, generally speaking, take bold steps for the provision of non-vocational subjects. Indeed, we believe that they are more likely to provide vocational studies' (Ministry of Reconstruction Adult Education Committee, 1919: 108). The AEC specifically argued that 'by far the greater bulk of the work of Local Education Authorities in Great Britain is concerned with the children in the Elementary Schools', and consequently that the state should act as only as 'a medium for encouraging and assisting the activities of Universities and Local Education Authorities, and the educational work of voluntary bodies. This we regard as the main function of the State so far as education is concerned' (Ministry of Reconstruction Adult Education Committee, 1919: 119). The 1919 Report stated: 'In England and Wales by far the greater proportion of the provision made by Local Authorities for further education is primarily vocational in character' (Ministry of Reconstruction Adult Education Committee, 1919: 206). The authors of the Report wrote that this was due to a combination of the LEA focus upon education amongst children and adolescents and of 'a certain shamefacedness [amongst adults] about "going to school"'. The primary, and perhaps most telling concern, however, was ideological and specifically political in that they outlined that

> There is still a number of education committees who are unable to understand a desire for education of no direct utilitarian value, unless it be for purposes of personal accomplishment, and who suspect dark motives in the minds of those who desire such education. More especially is this so where the demand is for the study of problems which are controversial. It is within our knowledge that there are even today town councillors to whom the term "economics" is synonymous with "socialism". The majority of those who desire to study do so probably because of the interest they have already taken in industrial or other public affairs [trade unionists] ... This is presumably the basis for the charge sometimes made by Local Authorities and even by some members of universities, that the classes 'encourage discontent and socialism'.
> (Ministry of Reconstruction Adult Education Committee, 1919: 206–7)

Upon requesting a room for educational meetings, one tutor was reputedly told by a Local Authority official, 'If we let you have a room you will make the place a den of anarchists' (1919 Report: 207). This tension and lack of trust was mutual in that the Report identified that some of the 'workers' demonstrated a similar level of suspicion 'towards such facilities for classes as are offered by the Local Authorities' (1919). Elsewhere in the Report, it was also recorded: 'The fact that there has been little demand made upon Local Authorities by adults for classes in non-vocational subjects is attributable not so much to lack of desire as to lack of knowledge as to the possibilities of obtaining suitable educational facilities from Educational Authorities and lack of confidence in their established methods' (Ministry of Reconstruction Adult Education Committee, 1919: 105). This statement appeared to reinforce the sense of inappropriate pedagogical approaches, ideological tensions and an unconducive atmosphere in Local Authority-led educational courses for adults such that 'non-vocational adult education has not in the past thriven in it' (1919). The Report was clear that competency in teaching technical education, described as primarily 'utilitarian', particularly with a focus on children and adolescents, did not make for good teaching of 'humane adult education'.

The emphasis on the non-vocational in the 1919 Report was clear. It was equally evident that the AEC's understanding of non-vocational education was nuanced and consistent with their perspectives on who was best placed to offer it and how it should be funded. Given the political dynamics described above, it is important to comment that the AEC argued that there should be no restrictions placed on how monies for adult education were utilized, in that learners, they argued, should be allowed to talk about political or complex issues and that the state 'should not ... refuse financial support to institutions, colleges and classes, merely on the ground that they have a particular "atmosphere" or appeal to students of this type or that. All that it ought to ask is that they be concerned with serious study' (Ministry of Reconstruction Adult Education Committee, 1919: 172). This is in stark contrast to the attitudes demonstrated by some Local Authorities, as we have seen. This remains a persistent source of concern today for many voluntary bodies, in that charities/not-for-profit organizations who receive state funding for their work (including educational) may campaign but are not allowed to engage in any activities which have a political purpose or undertake political activity that is not relevant to the charity's charitable purposes.

Though the 1919 Report did list certain LEAs which were supporting the development of adult education activities, it nonetheless concluded that 'the most important agencies for the promotion of adult non-vocational education are to be found amongst voluntary organisations' (Ministry of Reconstruction Adult Education Committee, 1919: 210). The report underlined the importance of such voluntary bodies still further, at various points, for instance: 'It will not ... be denied that adult non-vocational education has owed its main inspiration to voluntary organisations, and particularly those established for educational purposes' (Ministry of Reconstruction Adult Education Committee, 1919: 112).

Critical to this central role of voluntary organizations for the AEC was their ability to create the right kind of socially responsive, flexible learning opportunities in tune with the interests of adults at a local level: 'Voluntary organisations, by their spontaneity and responsiveness to local needs, by their elasticity and the enthusiasm they evoke, are a safeguard against over-organisation and formalism and an encouragement to the growth of the social spirit' (Ministry of Reconstruction Adult Education Committee, 1919). The importance of an overt move beyond 'over-organisation and formalism' is emphasized throughout.

There is some suggestion in the 1919 Report that the 1918 Education Act offered opportunity for greater co-ordination of education, including for adults, as well as a systematized national infrastructure: "'In England and Wales, the Education Act of 1918 opens up new possibilities of growth and co-ordination. It enacts that 'with a view to the establishment of a national system of public education available to all persons capable of profiting thereby, it shall be the duty of the council of every county and county borough … to contribute thereto by providing for the progressive development and comprehensive organisation of education in respect of their area …'. Whilst the Act imposed no new statutory duties upon Education Authorities so far as adult education was concerned, the clause quoted may be reasonably interpreted as requiring them to 'take within their purview all forms of education'" (Ministry of Reconstruction Adult Education Committee, 1919: 107). The AEC clearly saw this development as an indication of positive change, while recognizing that there was insufficient concrete or practical evidence to support it. This appears to have been disappointing for them, as they argued that 'The field of adult education is so large that the active co-operation of LEAs is a vital need, and non-vocational adult education should be regarded as an integral part of their activities' (Ministry of Reconstruction Adult Education Committee, 1919: 108).

Having examined the archives more closely, and specifically sub-committee work and reports which informed the Final Report, it was evident that the evolution of the Final Report was neither straightforward nor uncontroversial. There were numerous instances which demonstrated state and establishment anger and concern from senior government ministers/officials that the AEC had overstepped the mark and was flouting convention. To illustrate this issue, it is worth quoting from perhaps the boldest of all the individual reports which focused on work and education – 'Notes on Industry and Education', by James Morton, who was described as an Employer of Labour (Textiles). Morton started out with a damning indictment on 'degrading' work conditions and how this drives the worker to seek satisfaction not from his work but only outside it:

> It is only too evident in modern industry that there is little pleasure in work for work's sake, that the doing of it does not satisfy the worker, that his chief concern is to get as big wages as he can for the least amount of time spent, and that he seeks his chief interest and pleasure outside his ordinary work. This is probably the main cause of the unrest and discontent so prevalent today.
>
> (Notes on Industry and Education: 1)

Morton continued this theme and emphasized the need for education for the senses and the mind, the humane and the imaginative:

> So that to the extent that the work of our factories and workshops is dull and uninteresting, does it not mean that it is we ourselves that are dull, that we have not been educated to know the pleasure of interesting and beautiful things, and that until we reverse all this, and educate ourselves to feel and know, and want things of real interest, so long will the work that goes to the making of them be dull and monotonous?
>
> (Notes on Industry and Education: 3) and
> (Notes on Industry and Education: 8)

Morton berated school education for its slavish devotion to a cold bookish intellectualism which he believed did not attempt to engage with a child's real-world interests, his [sic] imagination or desire to make, shape and craft things: 'the work has not become part of his real life' (ibid.: 5). Instead, he argued that school should play an important role in stimulating interest in both the intellectual and the manual and craft-based, enabling adults to better utilize their leisure time later in life and stimulating new interests, and asserted that the distinction between vocational and non-vocational is a false one: 'Every kind of education, manual, intellectual, moral, should ultimately be of value in after life to a man's vocation, no matter what that vocation might be' (ibid.: 8).

Edward Troup, on behalf of the Home Secretary, expressed the Home Secretary's deep displeasure about both the AEC's interim report, and particularly the Industrial report, in a letter to the Secretary of the Ministry of Reconstruction. He identified that the Home Secretary saw the recommendations of the industrial report as anti-establishment and deeply prejudicial and would not be supporting the findings or conclusions of the Ministry of Reconstruction's interim report as a consequence:

> Sir George Cave[4] ... feels bound to express his regret that the Committee should have put forward a number of serious and far-reaching proposals on industrial matters outside the scope of their reference, without any consultation with the departments concerned and with little or no regard for the practicability of their recommendations. He feels that the Report may do much to embarrass the schemes which are now under consideration of the Home Office and other Departments for the improvement of industrial conditions, and, by the prejudice which it will tend to arouse against such methods as the shift system, may seriously interfere with production after the war.
>
> (Edward Troup, 9th July 1918, Whitehall)

Contemporary adult education – the state and social movements

As the AEC argued, adult education is political, ideological and experiential; it is also 'civic' and 'humane'. Learning through life is at the nexus of wider societal debates about the relationship of power over communities, who governs them and how, the role of the state in exercising organized control, how much communities can self-govern and how power and resources are ultimately organized. How much citizens know and understand, how much they are able to challenge – from a position of knowledge and understanding – are central to any concept of societal and individual change. It is both an exhilarating possibility to the community learner and a source of profound disquiet, fear and anxiety to those in power. As the historian and adult educationalist E. P. Thompson stated in his 1968 Mansbridge Memorial lecture, *Education and Experience*, adult education, by its very nature, is 'a relationship of mutuality, a dialectic' (Thompson, 1968: 1) because it brings together adults, with a wealth of differing life experiences, with educators, and involves an intellectual exchange based on equality of experience between both parties. So much of the legacy of adult education is based on relationships, shared history and community.

Coming back to the contemporary, in the workshops and interviews which I convened to support my SES research in 2019, there was a strong view that adult education still has a very important function to play in social, economic and personal development, despite mass compulsory education up to the age of nineteen. In personal development terms, it is seen to promote a sense of identity and high-level self-respect, relating to *thymos*, the human desire for recognition and knowing that your place in society is respected. This is beneficial not only to individuals but to society and the economy. Many participants argued that the contemporary schooling system can fail people due to its rigid systems and narrow curriculum which do not suit everyone, along with the increasing focus on employment and employability. Adult education, at its best, offers access to a broader range of subjects, connected to the individual's human experience (life-wide education) with employability as part of it but not its sole focus.

As Mark Johnson, CEO of User Voice, put it, in relation to his work with ex-offenders:

> English and maths are not fundamental in this environment, basic skills can only be addressed after the other vital issues have been tackled. Once you address

people's self-esteem and self-worth issues, you don't have to force people into learning – because they want to better themselves naturally.

Fundamentally, Johnson suggests that the urge to learn springs from freedom and innovation, and from celebrating lived experience; as Rhiannon White, Co-artistic Director, Common Wealth theatre company, argued:

> Common Wealth believe people can be artists and tell stories. We want people to have the power to represent themselves – telling our stories is an embodiment of power. In terms of adult education, I'm interested in what happened to places like Dartington College of the Arts, where I went to study but has closed now. It was very experimental – and that was a real opportunity for me to discover myself and so much came from there that I do now. So, I guess, I'm interested in seeing more adult learning that's like that – which gives people a bit more freedom and space to fail, experiment and break boundaries – it gave me options.
> (Rhiannon White)

Having a society actively using critical thinking means also having a society that encourages constant informed debate. This, as one of the workshop groups argued, is education's ultimate rationale, but this is constantly contested, as critical thinking implies challenge, as Neil Griffiths, Director and campaigner, Arts Emergency, suggested:

> It's what type of education people have a right to, and what type of education is enshrined in the European human rights. It's implied that it's the kind of education that makes you a functioning democratic citizen in some ways. It implies developing critical skills, and class function and historical knowledge, but … education doesn't really seem to mean that anymore.
> (Neil Griffiths)

Both workshop groups argued the case for universal and lifelong adult education for the good of society and economy, and for the well-being and improved mental health of the population. They perceived this as not simply the training of technical skills, but educating in a wide sense, acquiring knowledge, exchanging ideas and promoting independent critical thinking and judgement, encouraging greater awareness of how we are shaped by our social, political and economic circumstances. Generally speaking, the groups' view was that adult education's flexibility and creativity in terms of where it is offered and to whom are crucial strengths. Both workshop group participants argued that, ideally, opportunities for adult education should be accessible throughout the country, at any age and to people from all backgrounds. This mixing of people from all backgrounds was felt to be core to adult education's pedagogical values and its ability to stimulate understanding and empathy across disparate groups in society. This view was also articulated eloquently by David Anderson, who spoke of the enduring appetite for adult education, particularly for working-class people:

> I've been influenced by Jonathan Rose's book, *The Intellectual Life of the British Working Classes*, in which he shows that roughly a quarter of working-class adults were lifelong, committed and driven learners in different fields. I don't believe this impulse has disappeared, although much of the infrastructure that formerly supported this kind of informal life-long adult learning in working class communities has. The key question is what, in the 21st Century, needs to be put in its place?
>
> (David Anderson, Amgueddfa Cymru – Director General, National Museum Wales)

Both workshop groups argued that adult education's particular appeal is the group learning aspect and the collegiality. They asserted that learning communities are important and that adult education benefits from offering alternative spaces for learning, which was evidenced by the sheer range of user-led groups and self-initiated organizations who formed the workshop groups and who agreed to be interviewed.

Both workshop groups and many of the interviewees argued that, in terms of an overarching philosophy or approach, government-led adult education is problematic in contemporary society. From my own research, it is clear that, in the past, the state has funded some adult education infrastructure – buildings, teaching staff, materials/resources, etc. – and, as has been shown in my analysis of the 1919 Adult Education report, much of the course provision/services were offered by the voluntary sector, in the form of bodies such as the WEA. Voluntary sector–led provision has had the advantage of being able to deliver services which are flexible and are able to respond quickly to evolving needs at a local level. However, many of the interview and workshop respondents felt it unlikely that the state will provide much funding for adult education in the current social and economic context, despite a plethora of reports examining adult and lifelong learning, including the Centenary Commission Report, the findings of the Civic University Commission,[5] the Independent Commission on Lifelong Learning – convened by Vince Cable[6] – and others, many of which reported in 2019. With the demise of EU funding at government level, pressures are even greater on providing alternative education in disadvantaged areas. The lure of courses with accreditation or which can be assessed on observable results becomes more potent, and locally focused non-fee-paying, often highly creative but time-intensive, courses are the first to go.

Respondents felt that the voluntary sector – and evolving social movements – must retain a strong campaigning role if they are to be understood and recognized as genuinely independent and as having the power to challenge the state. To be courageous and creative in offering adult education/learning which may not follow a government line, which may be political and/or consciousness-raising, can be a dangerous space – as the AEC themselves experienced in 1919 and as is evidenced in contemporary adult education by the recent demise of the Union Learning Fund. Charlie Clarke commented on this:

> The squeeze on popular political education has come both in terms of the loss of adult education centres, but then also the other institutions that provide spaces for people to develop politically, like the Trade Unions and Labour Party, have – over the last however many years – stopped providing that for various reasons.
> (Charlie Clarke, The World Transformed Researcher)

Conclusion

The AEC's *Final Report* has proved to be an enduring and prescient template for adult education, committed to enriching the communities where people live and work, and to building community-led, democratically orientated forms of education. Through most of the twentieth century, such adult education in the UK played a vital part in the social fabric. This helped shape, and became embedded in, the post-1945 social-democratic welfare state. The AEC was deeply influenced by forward-looking appraisals of political, social and economic change – specifically, the extension of the franchise, industrial and occupational structures and emerging social movements.

New generations of younger activists are again seeking ways of re-energizing popular democratic education, in the Latin American sense, looking to movements such as Occupy, which directly challenged statism: 'the more immediate reference around more democratic forms of learning and also organising is the effect of the early 2000s anti-globalisation movement, and the horizontalist movements around that time. And the idea of pre-figurative politics, which obviously has a much longer history' (Charlie Clarke, TWT).

Such groups are seeking a re-politicization, not a pallid 'grassroots' community education which does not embrace links to local and national movements. The connections to real inequalities and the impulse to 'being the social change' are urgent. As Arthur Greenwood wrote, the 1919 *Final Report*'s 'main argument' was that 'responsible citizenship' would be 'impossible so long as the industrial and social conditions prevailing before the war remain' (quoted Goldman, 1995: 205). This remains an acute point of tension and one in which a critical, reflective and uncompromised adult education network should play an increasingly important role.

Notes

1. Albert Mansbridge, 1876–1952, co-founded the WEA and was its first secretary until 1915. The son of a carpenter, he was largely self-taught and a passionate advocate for adult education.
2. Connected with universities – Tutorial classes and Summer Schools, Extension lectures and Summer meetings; Local Authorities – Education Committees, Public Libraries, etc.; Voluntary Organisations – (a) Educational organisations: i/ The Workers' Educational Association, ii/ The Adult Schools, iii/ The Council for the Study of International Relations, iv/ The National Home Reading Union; (b) Organizations doing specifically educational work: i/ Religious Organizations, ii/ The Co-operative Movement, iii/ The Y.M.C.A and the Y.W.C.A (1919 Report, p. 2).
3. (https://www.centenarycommission.org).
4. George Cave, 1st Viscount Cave, GCMG, PC was a British lawyer and Conservative politician. He was Home Secretary under David Lloyd George from 1916 to 1919.
5. Civic-University-Commission-Final-Report.pdf (upp-foundation.org).
6. Independent Commission announces plans for up to £9000 in lifelong learning grants – FE News.

References

The Centenary Commission on Adult Education Report (2019), *Adult Education and Lifelong Learning for 21st Century Britain*, ed. J. Holford and J. Michie, Nottingham: School of Education, University of Nottingham.

Clancy, S. (2019), *Society for Educational Studies Interim Report and Final Reports*, Nottingham: University of Nottingham.

Goldman, L. (1995), *Dons and Workers: Oxford and Adult Education since 1850*, New York: OUP.

Goodson, I. F. (2003), *Life History and Professional Development: Stories of Teachers' Life and Work*, ed. U. Numan, Lund: Studentlitteratur.

Jennings, B. (1980), *The Reception of the 1919 Report*, ed. H. Wiltshire et al., *The 1919 Report*, Nottingham: Nottingham University.

Kane, l. (2001), *Popular Education and Social Change in Latin America*, Nottingham, UK: Russell Press.

Kelly, T. (1973), Two Reports: 1919 and 1973, *Studies in Adult Education*, 5 (2), 113–23.

Kuk, H. and Tarlau, R. (2020), The Confluence of Popular Education and Social Movement Studies into Social Movement Learning: A Systematic Literature Review, *International Journal of Lifelong Education*, 39 (5–6), 591–604.

McIlroy, J. and Westwood, S. eds. (1993), *Border Country: Raymond Williams*, London: NIACE, 255–64, From: Williams, R. (1983) *Adult Education and Social Change: Lectures and Reminiscences in Honour of Tony McLean*, WEA Southern District, pp. 9–24.

Ministry of Reconstruction Adult Education Committee (1919), *Final Report*. Cmd 321, London: H. M. Stationery Office.

Rustin, M. (2016), The Neoliberal University and Its Alternatives, in *Soundings – A Journal of Politics and Culture*, Issue 63, *Spaces of Resistance*, Summer 2016, 147–70, Dagenham: Lawrence and Wishart Independent Radical Publishing.

Tawney, R. H. (1914), *An Experiment in Democratic Education*, first published in Political Quarterly, reprinted in *R.H. Tawney and His Times* ed. R. Terrill, 1973, London: Deutsch, 70–81.

Taylor, F. J. (1976), The Making of the 1919 Report, *Studies in Adult Education,* 8 (2), 134–48.

Thompson, E.P. (1968), *Education and Experience: Fifth Mansbridge Memorial Lecture*, Leeds: Leeds University Press, 21–2.

Williams, R. (1961), The Common Good, *Adult Education,* 344 (November 1961).

Williams, R. (1961/1990), *An Open Letter to W.E.A. Tutors*, London: W.E.A.

Williams, R. (1961/2011), *The Long Revolution*, Swansea: Parthian Books.

Williams, R. (1989), *What I Came to Say*, London: Radius.

2

Radical adult education practitioners in the UK: the International League for Social Commitment in Adult Education 1984–94

Alan Tuckett, Emeritus Professor of Education,
University of Wolverhampton

In memory of Adnan Abdul Rahim

> The International League for Social Commitment in Adult Education (ILSCAE) ... taught me that some of the best, most sustaining learning we do does not require a shared language. It was through ILSCAE's activities that I came to see myself as part of an international educational movement, and that to make a contribution to struggles for social justice, the work of adult educators has to move beyond isolated pockets and classes to becoming a dimension of the work of wider social movements – working class, women's, disabled, environmental. Through conferences, workshops and study circles in ILSCAE, I learned about popular education in Latin America in the 1960s and 1970s, ... the political street theatre of Augusto Boal and the potential of drama and song to provide a more celebratory and joyful dimension to adult learning ... I learned too about education in social action in Zimbabwe and South Africa; about Aboriginal adult education work in South Africa, ... (and) the work of Myles Horton and the Folklander High School in the American South ... It was here I came to understand the meaning of 'dialogue' as an educational method and that the basic starting point for any democratic education is a deep respect for learners' life experiences – to 'start from where they are' and to discover with them 'where it's worth going'.
>
> (Barr, 1999: 45–6)

This chapter tells a story of big ideas and tiny budgets, of the excitement and solidarity engendered when people with common values but dramatically different working contexts across the globe meet and work intensively together, and of the fragility of the support arrangements that make such collaborations possible. It tells the story of the relatively short-lived International League for Social Commitment in Adult Education, and what British radical adult educators brought to its work. It starts with a brief overview of some radical adult education responses in twentieth-century Britain to a field that was otherwise liberal in values, broadly sympathetic to social change, but better at meeting the educational needs of those who have already enjoyed initial education than the needs of adults failed by, or excluded from, the school system.

Liberals and radicals

From the creation of the Workers' Educational Association (WEA) in 1903, to the Ruskin College students' strike in 1909, and subsequent foundation of the Central Labour College, there has been tension between an aspiration to teach the best of liberal thought, as preserved by universities, and a curriculum developed from and relevant to the experience of workers themselves (Fieldhouse, 1996: 242–3; Simon, 1965: 12). Albert Mansbridge, the WEA's founder, was keen throughout his leadership of the organization to keep it at a distance from organized labour, but the guild socialist G. D. H. Cole argued, 'The WEA is nothing, or worse than nothing, unless it is based firmly in the support of the working class movement' (Cole, 1925: 6), and argued against the dangers of well-meaning educators, committed to their subject, with no desire to help trade unionists who seek education for a practical purpose, who offered education 'as an opiate for social discontent … I want to serve the live-wired practical worker, who wants guidance in facing the practical problems of living' (Cole, 1925: 8; Jennings, 2002: 65–6, cited in Fieldhouse, 1996: 175).

In a different vein in the immediate post–Second World War period, the engagement of Raymond Williams and Richard Hoggart in university extramural education led through dialogue with learners to the emergence of cultural studies, and Edward Thompson's work led to an explosion of interest in working class history (Hoggart, 1957; Thompson, 1963; Williams, 1958, 1965). Taken together, and along with a range of colleagues, they forged a transformation of the intellectual landscape, bringing attention to the lives and circumstances of ordinary people, and pointed to the possibility of adult education as a site for major innovation and reconfiguring of the intellectual landscape, a possibility later paralleled in the emergence of women's studies as part of second-wave feminism.

If cultural studies emerged from university extramural provision, the 1970s reshaping of adult education began outside formal educational institutions, with adult literacy work initiated first in the voluntary social services, Industrial Training Boards playing a large role in the start of English as a Second Language programmes, alongside migrant resettlement initiatives, and community development initiatives inspiring the development of strategies to engage working-class adults in Liverpool, Coventry and elsewhere. A 1973 social survey of adult participants in education in the Inner London Education Authority (ILEA) led the authority to a recognition that working class adults and minority communities were excluded from current provision, and outreach activities, the development of women's studies, Black and anti-racist studies, and strategies to reach disabled adults were developed in response. Outside London, the residential adult colleges played an active role in supporting community struggles, and in opening opportunities to return to study. Access to higher education programmes followed, as did educational guidance services for adults, and renewed energy in trade union education (Lovett, 1975; Newman, 1975, 1979; Thompson, 1980, 1983). These developments created a cohort of practitioners, paralleled by community-focused workers in higher education looking for links in other countries to enrich and challenge their experiences.

While the WEA had strong international links, and literacy initiatives like Pamoja, developed by Action Aid and others, and engaged practitioners inspired by the writing of Paulo Freire, in the main, British adult education had, overwhelmingly, focused on domestic debates, and community-based practitioners had few opportunities to engage internationally. The World Association for Adult Education, founded in 1918, had been an early attempt to create an institutional context for international interchange. Oxford University supported extramural provision in West Africa after 1945 which acted as an inspiration for education beyond colonialism for much of Anglophone Africa. In 1961, the Secretary of the British National Institute of Adult Education wrote in the *Australian Journal of Adult Learning*, arguing that any global organization for adult education was just not possible:

> It is the typical hen and egg situation – without large funds pre-committed, no justifying activity is possible; without previous evidence of usefulness, no one is in fact likely to commit funds at all, and certainly on the scale necessary to make formal organisation viable.
>
> (Hutchinson, 2010 (1961): 586)

Against this background, the announcement of an International League for Social Commitment in Adult Education seemed an exciting prospect.

ILSCAE

ILSCAE was a relatively short-lived (1984–94) and utopian organization with almost no resources, that mounted nine international conferences over eleven years bringing together liberal, social democrat and radical academics and practitioners, a preponderance of members from the Global North, but with increasing engagement of radical adult educators from the Global South. ILSCAE fired the imagination of its members, and created an invisible college and network that far outlived the organization's life. Over its life, the League shifted from a discourse shaped by the liberal norms of academic debate, to an increasing concern with practitioner engagement and international solidarity, with each meeting examining its governance and operational procedures afresh. ILSCAE's aspirations always outstretched its organizational and fiscal capacity, and the League closed when the narrow austerity and the neoliberal policies it critiqued closed down the spaces for the institutional gift economy on which it had relied.

ILSCAE was launched at a conference on 'Rekindling commitment in adult education' at Rutgers University, New Jersey, in June 1984. The event was attended overwhelmingly by academics, and their students, some of whom were practitioners, from North America, Scandinavia, Australasia, and with a smattering of other Europeans, including participants from the UK. The conference took place with Reaganomics ascendant in the United States and liberal academics in retreat, with social democracy securely supported in Scandinavia, and Thatcherism emboldened by the miners' strike and the memory of the Falklands in the United Kingdom. The common concern of participants was to reflect on how to share international perspectives in order to revitalize and reinforce strategies for adult education to contribute to the creation of a more socially just society. As the editorial of its conference report argued:

> Although in recent years the field of Adult and Continuing Education has grown significantly, there has been a decline in the social commitment and intellectual leadership that were once the heart of our profession. In many industrialized countries, focus on technique has replaced concern for the learner and for

society. Economic profit has replaced human and justice as the predominant professional value. In the developing world, issues of oppression and cultural imperialism stand out.

(Hoghielm, 1985: 1)

The format of the event combined academic papers presented in plenary and small groups, with town hall meetings – a process for democratic decision-making drawn from North American colonial communities – in which every member could attend, and every member had a voice; and at which the conference adopted a charter, drafted in an all-night session by Tom Valentine of the University of Georgia, which comprised a preamble and seven objectives:

Preamble

Our grave concern over the social inequality and social injustice which exist in nations throughout the world, coupled with our firm belief in adult education as a powerful force for social change, have led us to create the International League for Social Commitment in Adult Education, an organization dedicated to social equality, social justice, and collective and individual human rights.

(Hoghielm, 1985: 1)

Seven objectives were identified, the first of which captured the focus of its work:

Objective 1: To encourage all those involved in adult education to foster participation in dialogue on the critical social issues confronting humankind today, such as class inequality, environmental concerns, peace, racism, sexism and ageism.

Objective 2: To encourage all those involved in adult education to identify and act to overcome the social, political and economic forces which perpetuate the existence of poverty, oppression and political powerlessness.

Objective 3: To encourage all those in adult education to view and practise adult education as a vehicle to enable all adults to gain and exert control over their own lives.

Objective 4: To encourage all those involved in adult education to work with the poor, oppressed and politically powerless in learning activities which have social, political, economic, cultural and aesthetic import.

Objective 5: To encourage all adult educators to make explicit the ethics and values which guide their practice.

Objective 6: To encourage those responsible for the preparation of adult educators to provide not only for the enhancement of technical skills, but also for the critical examination of ethical and social issues.

Objective 7. To encourage the design, conduct and reporting of research and other forms of scholarship focusing on adult education as a force for social change (Svensson and Tuckett, 1987: 7).

In his keynote address to the founding conference, Ettore Gelpi identified the challenge faced in giving reality the League's goals:

> Today mankind does not need verbal declarations on international understanding or vague intercultural exchanges. It needs concrete scientific, technical, cultural, economic projects for self-development that reinforce the capacity for self-development of the countries on the periphery. For this very reason, education for the international co-operation has to be action oriented, rich in knowledge of concrete problems of national and international societies, but we are very far from this approach.
>
> (Gelpi, 1985: 8)

It was a challenge offered to a conference whose core structure relied on academic papers. It was only after the fourth conference in the Netherlands in 1987 that the League took on Gelpi's approach, and that decision, as will be seen below, had an impact on its active membership. Gelpi continued by highlighting the dissatisfaction in the East and West with dominant education ideologies, and argued:

> I have a strong impression that real educational innovations are the result of the creativity and personal risks taken by people fighting in their social and productive life to improve working and social conditions for their colleagues and for themselves.
>
> (Gelpi, 1985: 16)

Gelpi was scathing about the timidity, the caution and introspection of people who work as educators of adults:

> Ignorance, taboos and prejudices are more frequent among adult educationists than, for example, among atomic scientists: look at their respective publications and you will be surprised at the difference.
>
> (Gelpi, 1985: 14)

These comments are in stark contrast to the conviction expressed by the League's founding members that saw 'adult education as a powerful source for social change'. Gelpi finished by questioning whether adult educators have a say concerning new values and models of development in our societies, to foster more courageous individual and collective action to address inequality, to address the need for jobs, the need to eradicate illiteracy – 'for life and peace against death, prisons, camps, starvation' (Gelpi, 1985: 18).

A feature of all of the early ILSCAE conferences was that process and governance were as central as the papers delivered. In response to Gelpi's challenges, the League responded in equally ringing tones:

> The structures and activities of the League will reflect, without exception, its espoused goals of social equality and social justice, as well as a determination to preserve its international identity.
>
> (Svensson and Tuckett, 1987: 8)

Despite this rhetorical commitment, the League faced a series of practical challenges in establishing itself as an international organization. The cost of conference participation was such that community literacy organizers from the Bronx were inhibited from attending, while participants included many who could call on academic institutions for assistance with fees and fares. Representation from the Global South was limited mainly to exiles and refugees living in North America or Scandinavia, and Eastern Europe and socialist Asia were absent. And the issue of the languages of the organization – and resultant inclusion and exclusion of communities – was not addressed at all in the decisions of the first meeting.

What they did decide was that conferences should happen every two years, although in practice they happened annually until 1989, and then after a three-year gap annually from 1992 to 1994. The founding event also agreed that membership should be individual or institutional, yet despite renewed encouragement at the third annual meeting, no institutions joined (Svensson and Tuckett, 1987: 16). The League hoped to mount programmes involving adult educators from as many countries as possible, and 'work towards resisting all the forces which threaten to undermine the efficacy of adult education for social change' (Hoghielm, 1985: 3). Yet this proved hard to fund solely through its individual membership. Nevertheless, the League benefitted from the support and nurturing of successive host organizations for its events.

Among the range of papers with practical accounts of engagement with marginalized groups were two from British participants. Paul Fordham presented the work of Southampton University in a working-class housing estate in Portsmouth, and Tom Lovett provided an analysis of work, centred on the Ulster People's College. His paper 'Adult Education and Social Change in Northern

Ireland' focused on issues of exclusion and strategies to overcome them. Lovett outlined the scale of the challenges faced by its divided communities, and the response of adult educators to it:

> Northern Ireland has been described as a society under siege, a society where there is a problem for every solution. The usual picture is one of violence and sectarianism. However, it is in fact a society facing all the problems of modern industrial nations **plus** armed conflict and community division.
>
> (Lovett, 1985: 102)

Focusing on work in impoverished communities makes clear that the challenges of social and economic change confront people across the community divide, and the challenge for adult educators in finding effective ways to address them. Lovett offered a typology of initiatives undertaken, focused on individual or community empowerment; community action or mediation between marginalized groups and existing power structures, arguing that each presents challenges, in engaging with communities, but also in operating within the framework of institutional regulations and culture. He concluded that educators must be clear about the questions they ask, reflect on the success and failures of their initiatives, and work effectively to create radical alternatives. However, it was important to remember that not all alternative education was necessarily radical.

The issues raised by Lovett – how best to square community action with the limitations posed by institutional support; where the boundaries lie between action and learning; how best to stimulate the emergence of organic intellectuals – resurface throughout the life of the League, influencing and influenced by the discrete and sometimes radically different experiences of educators working in very different circumstances.

The extent of cultural difference was highlighted at one of the Town Meetings at the second conference in Sweden. A Polish Solidarity refugee academic, Michael Bron, stood and said, 'I have been insulted, we have all been insulted,' citing a local newspaper interview given by a New York inner-city community educator, who had suggested that we would need to look out for the spies at the conference. Bron suggested that such an approach eroded the trust needed for international co-operation and understanding. Yet it was clear, given the history of American radical organizations, that the community educator's views had been shaped by prior experience. In the end the meeting agreed with Michael that to work together we need to trust one another, but that if the League were at all successful, it would surely attract attention from people concerned to preserve the status quo. Much of the rest of the Swedish event was spent on a search for common understandings – with values shared despite different contexts. The Swedes had been successful in raising considerable funds to secure participation from a much wider range of countries, including participants from Africa, the Caribbean, Latin America, Israel and Palestine. Still Scandinavians were the largest contingent and English the only language used in the sessions.

Jack Mezirow gave the keynote presentation in Sweden on transformational learning, with its grounding in humanistic psychology and focus on individual transformation, while in many of the papers the focus was rather on community change and Freire was a recurrent influence, as was the body of ideas associated with Grundtvig and the Scandinavian folk high school tradition. In her paper on 'Puerto Rico, Adult Education, and the U.S. Education System', Sonia Nieto described the effects of American colonization on Puerto Rico, the resultant migration of Puerto Ricans to the United States, where the education system replicates the existing class structure, and identified the problem of whether to 'refuse to participate in a system which is inherently unequal or to advocate for yet more programs' (cited in Svensson and Tuckett, 1987: 10). There were no other papers looking explicitly at colonialism and displacement, yet the numbers of refugees and asylum seekers in attendance highlighted the need to balance a concern with place and geographically bounded structures with a need to recognize that migration was a key transnational issue ILSCAE would need to develop much clearer perspectives on.

At the end of the event, as an evaluation process, John Benseman introduced a process drawing on Maori traditions not dissimilar to Quaker services, opening with everyone sitting in a circle, a period of shared silence, sharing 'from the heart', and expressions of appreciation. Only when everyone has had the chance to speak does the session end.

Nottingham University hosted the third conference, and saw a major influx of British adult education practitioners, who brought with them perspectives shaped, as in part the Lovett paper had been, by community-based activism, like that developed in Liverpool, adult literacy work, heavily influenced by Freire, by the History Workshop, and worker writer movement, by second-wave feminism, by the experiences of Black Britons and people who spoke English as a Second Language, and in particular by a discourse developed strongly by activists working in the Inner London Education Authority, in which identity and power were central foci. For many, as a respondent to the survey of past members on ILSCAE, undertaken seven years after its closure, made clear, the space provided by ILSCAE was in striking contrast to their normal working context:

> We feel that it was especially relevant to adult basic education workers, and that in (our country) we are not encouraged to acknowledge or explore our own political motivation or to work politically in an upfront or direct way. ILSCAE was both a good forum in which to explore the politics of education and a safe place in which to express our own political views.
>
> (Mohorcic Spolar and Payne, 2002: 71)

Another European participant observed that the debates in the early conferences focused on 'the tyranny of dominant languages ... the reconciliation of competing truths, and the co-existence of differently expressed endorsements of (the) purposes (of ILSCAE)' (Mohorcic Spolar and Payne, 2002: 70). The report of the Nottingham conference, which was edited by practitioners working in the Inner London Education Authority, reflected a more sharply self-critical exploration of the League's work. John Payne's reflection on 'The Language Question' illustrated this:

> To conclude that English is unproblematically the ideal language for international communication between socially committed adult education workers is our equivalent of adopting Freire's "oppressor mentality". When Third World members of ILSCAE confront the problem of the use of the English language, they confront a part of their own oppression.

Delegates who do speak English as a first language need to think carefully about speed of delivery, clarity of diction and communication is essential for real sharing of ideas and experiences to take place at our conferences.

Ruud van der Veen wrote from Holland:

> Listening in unofficial situations (like dinner, small talk in groups) is a problem because there is often a lot of noise, two or more people sometimes talk at the same time, all types of unofficial English are used. Even when you understand what is going on, the concentration needed makes you very tired. Even when your discussion partner is of good will, you often see that it is a problem for him to listen to your slow bad-pronounced English. He probably understands but it is difficult for him to enjoy. So, after some time, both try to escape the discussion.
>
> (Payne, 1987: 18–19)

Payne concluded with a series of practical recommendations – calling for simultaneous translation of English, French and Spanish; the advance circulation of a Council of Europe glossary of the terminology of adult education in different contexts; advance deadlines on papers, so that translated synopses could be prepared; and at least the publishing of synopses of all papers in these three languages. Given the poverty of the League's organizational capacity, and of its funding for translators, none of these recommendations was implemented, but self-help processes were developed, to ameliorate at least some of the behaviours identified.

Jenny Scribbins's paper, 'Gender issues – A perspective on the ILSCAE conference 1986', contrasted the organization's aim to foster dialogue, and to contest sexism with the experience of the event, in which women's voices were marginal, the papers presented included just two on women's education, where in the Town Hall meetings 'the men talked more often and at greater length than the women – they were also the officers who presided'. She continues that this was no surprise, 'but it would have been good if the League had been able to surprise us. It sounded like an organisation that might – that still could, if it began to take these issues seriously'. Scribbins contrasted the public plenary discourse with the more informal spaces of the conference, where gender issues were more explicitly addressed, and noting on the whole that women at the conference were lower paid, in more vulnerable employment, and more likely than men to be at the 'caring service end of the profession':

> The autobiographies and other histories that lay behind the papers – sometimes becoming overt in the workshops, and more often in the informal spaces of the conference, formed a very important part of the sharing and learning experience – and one which met issues of gender more explicitly ... The story of how they had raised money for the journey, how they had made arrangements for substitute cover, how they felt about coming to such a conference, formed a graphic parallel with the experience of many students on adult education courses. Discussion was often informal – but very intense. Women from Chile, Scotland, U.S.A., Australia, Sweden, U.K. and so on, finding that, as women, they had a great deal to share. In one of the 'spaces' in the formal programme, a discussion group for women was announced and took place – (as in many conferences, an 'add on', an optional extra to the 'real' business) – and discussion centred around how the processes of the League, and of this particular conference, could be influenced to take account of women's experience and perspective; also on whether any of the women present had enough energy to spare from their work, their families, their attempts to make some space in their lives for themselves, to commit to make this happen.
>
> (Scribbins, 1987: 22)

This paper reflected the increased energy in League debates on how the politics and processes of the League took account of its core aspirations, how far the

League's practice was alive to diversity and difference, and how far international conferences reverted to business as usual. Voice, and whose voices are heard, and on what terms came to be a central issue in the fourth and subsequent events.

While its conferences were the most visible element of ILSCAE's work, chapters were formed in different countries (notably in Australia, Sweden and in London in the UK); from 1985 to 1987 there were regular newsletters – posted to members in a pre-e-mail age – and a host of international one-to-one communications and exchanges.

If the tone of the conference exchanges had been strong on mutual respect, listening and at least surface tolerance in the early meetings, despite the imbalances in voices heard and privileged, things took a sharply different turn at the fourth event in Bergen, the Netherlands, in 1987. A large cohort of radical practitioners from inner London, shaped by critical debates around literacy, English as a Second Language, migration, gender, ethnicity, inclusion for disabled adults, and gay rights, changed the balance from academic-led to practitioner-led discourse. This was reinforced by the visits to local projects, and workshops introducing participants to Augusto Boal's Theatre of the Oppressed.

A flashpoint emerged around the issue of anti-apartheid strategies. A South African student activist studying in the United States had had her application to attend the conference denied, as the Dutch maintained an academic boycott on links with South Africa, despite her opposition to apartheid. Yet, at a cultural evening during the conference, the organizers invited a South African exile and storyteller living in Amsterdam, who was 'verbally excoriated for his appropriation of back African stories' (Payne, 2010: 90). There were loud and disruptive objections to this, as evidence of double standards, and the heat of the argument spilled over into the Town Meetings. Mohorcic Spolar and Payne argued:

> The objectives of ILSCAE speak of oppression. Personal experience of such oppression (based on gender, ethnicity, class, disability) varied between ILSCAE delegates. This led to impatience and animosity, with people only too willing to speak out about oppression (theirs and/or other people's) but less willing to listen to those with different understandings.
>
> (Mohorcic Spolar and Payne, 2002: 73)

Mohorcic Spolar and Payne also highlight the analysis of William Dowling, a member from the United States, in the 1989 conference report:

> All of us need to learn from one another. ILSCAE can provide a forum for that learning, but not if significant portions of the membership are alienated

by behaviour that does not tolerate divergent views, or, worse yet, actively puts down with ill-concealed scorn, the evolving concepts, ideas being developed by those whose learning is at a more beginning level.

(ILSCAE, 1989: 79)

In the final reflective session of the Bergen conference, a Swedish delegate pointed out that in Swedish the word ILSCAE is halfway between the Swedish for love and anger, not a bad reflection on the week's events. But the Bergen conference did lead to splits. After the event American academics overwhelmingly withdrew from the League, alienated by the tone of the discourse, but also because of a decision to shift away from academic papers to exploration of the social commitment practices in the local contexts in which meetings took place. Many turned their allegiance to the fledgling educational research network, the Standing Conference of University Teaching and Research in the Education of Adults (SCUTREA), which had a distinct academic and transatlantic focus.

An academic respondent to the 2001 survey of past members commented:

Things changed dramatically in Bergen. There were lots of divisions over liberal/radical positions, South Africa, university/non-university and just plain personal animosity ... One problem was that given different cultures and different conflict resolution styles, we never did establish norms and structures that enabled us to work together towards common goals ... Finally, although ILSCAE had a clear purpose, the meaning of democratic social change varied substantially among us.

(Mohorcic Spolar and Payne, 2002: 74)

Bergen was a key turning point for ILSCAE. The meeting agreed that after the 1988 conference outside Toronto, future meetings would be more focused on an in-depth engagement with the local context, and that the League should meet in the Global South, and that efforts should be made to hold the 1989 event in Nicaragua, where the Sandinistas had embarked on an impressive literacy campaign for adults while at war with the US-backed Contras in the country's north.

The decision to move away from research-based papers, towards a focus on supporting project-focused activity and support for community-based practitioners (a move incidentally paralleled at the beginning of the 1990s by the Asian Pacific Bureau for Adult Education), meant that academics could no longer claim support for travel, accommodation and fees from their institutions. Nor could they offer their graduate students credit for attending the conference.

The decision to visit Nicaragua also contributed to the withdrawal of many academic participants from the United States. As Mohorcic Spolar and Payne comment, 'There is no doubt that the difficulty experienced by ILSCAE in dealing with issues of tolerance in personal and interpersonal relations had consequences for the League itself' (2002: 73).

This was apparent in fundraising as well as in attendance at the fifth event in Canada. The League sought to raise funds for participants from the Global South to attend, and at the same time issued a call for papers (academic- or practice-focused). Of the twenty-two papers proposed, nineteen came from the Global South, yet at the event itself just four were from the south. Nevertheless, despite dramatically smaller numbers in attendance, there were creative engagements with indigenous groups from across Canada, further explorations of the role of Boal's Theatre of the Oppressed and visits to Toronto-based literacy, women's education and refugee provision, to the Ontario Institute for the Study of Education, and the headquarters of the International Council for Adult Education. The challenges were, nevertheless, ever present. As the author of this paper commented in the report of the Toronto conference: 'The difficult issue is how an organisation without staffing, resources, or even regular continuity of attendance maintains a sufficient sense of its own direction and development' (ICAE, 1989: 3). While David Deshler, the convenor of the Toronto event, felt it had been a failure overall, the conference did secure passionate engagement combined with a renewed civility – a willingness to listen to different and divergent voices, and a return to a discourse that was sharp in its critical analysis and debates, yet struggling for the maximum shared understanding.

The Sandinistas invited the 1989 conference participants to come three weeks early and to work alongside literacy and wider education projects around the country. That experience changed the focus of discussions during the event. How far was it possible for ILSCAE members, and the organizations in which they worked, to offer practical and continuing support following their engagement? To what extent could the League avoid being radical tourists? How far did the experience of the central and Latin American people, in escaping the oppression of a tiny landowning class, have space to shape their own futures when it was clear that US foreign policy was antipathetic to radical democratic government in central and Latin America? One Puerto Rican delegate working in environmental education highlighted the limits of educational support in the face of people's need to feed their families. His case study showed how chemical spillage from a large multinational soft drinks factory was poisoning the water supply of communities living close to it, with dramatic consequences on health and morbidity in the communities. Puzzled why the analytical work did not lead activists to fight for change in the factory's emissions, he was told, 'We know the longer term impact, but have to feed our families now. If the factory leaves, many will die.'

Delegates left the conference fired with a determination to turn project plans into practice, but many failed to find the necessary resources, or in many cases the time, to sustain practical solidarity work in the way they had hoped. Nevertheless, League members brought their experiences back to their work and wider communities, and maintained dialogue with their hosts.

The three-year hiatus between Managua and the next conference was, in part, shaped by an absence of a host organization with the will and resources to support ILSCAE. However, members sustained the will and commitment to continue as a network, and in 1992 a meeting was held in Derry, Northern Ireland, during the Northern Ireland troubles. Delegates met groups, overwhelmingly of women, seeking cross-community dialogue, and in the case of one of the Palestinian participants with years of exposure to the Middle East conflict, a narrow escape from a nearby car bombing on a site visit to Belfast. The 1992 conference also took the time to revisit the League's purposes, to assert a focus on adult educators 'to learn about oppression from the oppressed, to name their oppression, and to make explicit their ethics and practice ... to encourage all those involved in adult education to direct resources towards the exploited, the oppressed and politically powerless, and to work in solidarity in developing learning activities with social, political, economic, cultural and aesthetic content', and to encourage all in adult education to view and practise adult education 'as a vehicle to enable all adults to gain and exert control over their lives as part of the community and environment' (ILSCAE, 1993). This last commitment is the first evidence of ILSCAE taking environmental concerns into its goals, perhaps influenced by the emergence of Latin American thinking about Pachamama, the rights of mother earth.

The following year the League met as guests of the Palestine Liberation Organization (PLO), on the prompting of long-term Palestinian members of the League, at its headquarters in Tunis, during the run-up to the Oslo accords in 1994. It explored the challenge in organizing effective education programmes for Palestinians in Gaza and the West Bank, in the dozen countries of the Palestinian diaspora, and the different challenge in securing that Palestinians inside Israel had access to the history and culture of their inheritance. This was, it turned out, an issue too for Palestinians in many of the dozen states that were home to Palestinian refugee communities. How could education for young people and adults be developed with a distinctive Palestinian focus while observing the legal and curricular requirements of the host country? The search to create a coherent national education programme for all Palestinians provided a sharp focus for the new goals the League had set itself. Following the conference, League members did work with the newly declared Palestinian National Authority to convene a seminar on women's education, held in Gaza and involving Palestinians from the West Bank, Gaza and from Israel. Israeli authorities would not allow Palestinians from the diaspora to attend. One modest practical outcome was the creation of a Women's Educational Centre in Ramullah, focusing on skills that would support women to earn independent income.

The League's last meeting was at Lake Bled in Slovenia in 1994, at a time when Slovenia was seeking entry to the European Union, while to the south Balkan wars unleashed the most bitter and violent ethnic struggles. The report of the Slovenian conference had sections on gender issues; race, ethnicity, refugees and nationalism; economic power and citizenship; civil society and voluntary organizations. Each, as Mohorcic and Payne point out, began with the same words:

> Most adult education does not change society. It confirms the powerful in their positions of power (people with more initial education get more adult education and training) and confirms the powerless in their positions.
> (ILSCAE, 1996, cited in Mohorcic and Spolar, 2002: 75)

Each then went on to say how that was not inevitable, and to argue what could be done about it. Nevertheless, despite its best intentions, doing something about it was not, after this, something ILSCAE itself could take forward. Its members and conference participants, however, continued to draw on the radical ideas and practices of the League, taking them into their own working practice, to the work of other networks and organizations, collaborating with each other where possible, and through maintaining rich and imaginative dialogue with one another across countries and contexts.

The League then went into abeyance in 1994, forced by the impact of the early 1990s recessions on the freedom of institutions to offer help from their discretionary funds, by its own organizational weakness and its reliance on voluntary labour increasingly constrained by New Management practices at work. For Europeans, the accelerating dialogue that led to the creation of regular European programmes for interchange took away some energy, as did the work of civil society organizations leading to the 1997 CONFINTEA V, World Conference on Adult Education, which was perhaps the high water mark of adult learning and education policy-making globally. The emergence of the World Social Forum took some activists' energies, as did the more successful global alliances in the International Council for Adult Education. A survey respondent summed up:

> I still support the aims and am pursuing them in my own way. But I think our practice in ILSCAE did not, and perhaps could not, match the grand ambitions of the aims because we were all institutionally and individually part of the 'forces of oppression'. This is not a criticism so much as a sociological observation ... Really meeting these aims involves life challenges which are greater than most of us are honestly willing to accept.
>
> (Mohorcic Spolar and Payne, 2002: 69–70)

Nevertheless, while clearly the League's aspirations were not matched by its ability to bring them all into practice through its own endeavours, it did have a major impact on the lives and experience of many of those who participated. Respondent after respondent found exciting and invaluable the chance to debate issues around social change with others from different contexts, and took back to their practice an invisible college of friends and colleagues on whose experience they could draw well beyond the end of the formal organization. ILSCAE created a forum for new kinds of international dialogue in adult education and no other international body has had quite its distinctive range of purposes. While it is possible to see its eleven-year life as a catalogue of failures, its collaborations and the community of thinking and practice it fostered can also be seen as impressive achievements, given its limited capacity. For this writer as for so many others, ILSCAE offered solidarity, critical friendships and a rich vein of insight into effective strategies, policies and practice to contest inequalities, and sharpened and enriched a commitment to social justice far beyond its short existence.

References

Barr, J. (1999), *Liberating Knowledge*, Leicester: NIACE.
Cole, G. D. H. (1925), The Task Ahead, *Yorkshire Bulletin*, 20 Leeds, 2–14.
Fieldhouse, R. ed. (1996), *A History of Modern British Adult Education*, Leicester: NIACE.
Gelpi, E. (1985), International Relations, Lifelong Education and Adult Education, in R. Hoghielm (ed.), *Rekindling Commitment in Adult Education: Conference Report 10–14 June 1984 at Rutgers State University, NJ*, Stockholm: Stockholm Institute of Education Department of Educational Research, 6–18.
Hoggart, R. (1957), *The Uses of Literacy*, London: Chatto & Windus.

Hoghielm, R. ed. (1985), *Rekindling Commitment in Adult Education: Conference Report 10–14 June 1984 at Rutgers State University, NJ*, Stockholm: Stockholm Institute of Education Department of Educational Research.

Hutchinson, E. (2010 (1961)), The International Importance of a National Association, *Australian Journal of Adult Learning*, 50 (3), 580–91.

ILSCAE (1989), *Finding Our Voices ... Seeing with New Eyes: Themes from the 1988 ILSCAE Conference, Toronto, Canada*, Sydney: Institute of Technical and Adult Education.

ILSCAE (1993), *Leaflet Outlining Aims and Purposes Prepared for 1993 Conference*, London: ILSCAE.

ILSCAE (1996), *Adult Learning and Power: The 8th Annual ILSCAE Conference, Bled, Slovenia, June 26 to July 3, 1994*, Ljubljana: Slovene Adult Education Centre.

Jennings, B. (2002), *Albert Mansbridge: The Life and Work of the Founder of the WEA*, Leeds: University of Leeds with WEA.

Lovett, T. (1975), *Adult Education, Community Development and the Working Class*, London: Ward Lock.

Lovett, T. (1985), Adult Education and Social Change in Northern Ireland, in R. Hoghielm (ed.), *Rekindling Commitment in Adult Education: Conference Report 10–14 June 1984 at Rutgers State University, NJ*, Stockholm: Stockholm Institute of Education Department of Educational Research, 101–15.

Mansbridge, A. (1920), *An Adventure in Working Class Education*, London: Longmans, Green.

Mohorcic Spolar, V. and Payne, J. (2002), Adult Education and Social Purpose: The Work of the International League for Social Commitment in Adult Education 1984–1994, in J. Field (ed.), *Promoting European Dimensions in Lifelong Learning*, Leicester: NIACE, 66–77.

Newman, M. (1975), *Adult Education and Community Action*, London: Writers and Readers Publishing Co-operative Community Publishers.

Newman, M. (1979), *The Poor Cousin*, London: Allen & Unwin.

Payne, J. (1987), The Language Question, in ILSCAE (ed.), *About a Week in Nottingham: Themes from the 1986 Conference of the International League for Social Commitment in Adult Education*, London: Clapham-Battersea Adult Education Institute, 18–20.

Payne, J. (2010), Is Adult Education an International Movement? Alan Tuckett and the International League for Social Commitment in Adult Education (ILSCAE) 1984–94, in Derrick et al. (eds.), *Remaking Adult Learning*, London: Institute of Education, 86–92.

Scribbins, J. (1987), Gender Issues: A Perspective on the ILSCAE Conference, 1986, in ILSCAE (ed.), *About a Week in Nottingham: Themes from the 1986 Conference of the International League for Social Commitment in Adult Education*, London: Clapham-Battersea Adult Education Institute, 21–3.

Simon, B. (1965), *Education and the Labour Movement*, London: Lawrence & Wishart.

Svensson A. and Tuckett, A. (1987), The International League – Its Background, Organisation and Structure, in ILSCAE (ed.), *About a Week in Nottingham: Themes from the 1986 Conference of the International League for Social Commitment in Adult Education*, London: Clapham-Battersea Adult Education Institute, 6–17.

Thompson, E. P. (1968), *The Making of the English Working Class*, London: Victor Gollancz.

Thompson, J. ed. (1980), *Adult Education for a Change*, London: Hutchinson.

Thompson, J. (1983), *Learning Liberation*, Falmer: Croom Helm.

Williams, R. (1958), *Culture and Society 1780–1950*, London: Chatto & Windus.

Williams, R. (1965), *The Long Revolution*, Harmondsworth: Penguin.

3

Adult learning and social justice: health, well-being and the inequalities of power

Lyn Tett, Professor Emerita,
Universities of Edinburgh and Huddersfield

Health inequalities, and the poverty that drives them, are increasing in the UK (JRF, 2020). Research shows (Bambra and Payne, 2020: 266) that the poorer someone is, the less likely they are to live in good quality housing, have time and money for leisure activities, feel secure at home or work, be employed or afford to eat healthy food. So, although ill health may be experienced as a private trouble, it is embedded in broader social and political processes and should be seen instead as a public issue (Mills, 1959). This means that, as Marmot and colleagues (2020: 5) have pointed out, the health of the population is not just about how well the health service functions but is closely linked to the conditions in which people are born, grow, live, work and age and the resulting inequities in power, money and resources. These social determinants of health are also associated with feelings of lack of control over one's life leading to greater levels of stress and anxiety at the individual level and lack of social cohesion and trust at the community level. On the other hand, to experience well-being means having sufficient resources, living in a vibrant community where cultural diversity is respected, being able to balance work and other important things in life, such as time with family and friends, and not feeling isolated and lonely.

This chapter explores how adult learning can help to reduce inequalities in health and increase well-being with a particular focus on its ability to improve feelings of self-efficacy and belonging (see Tett and Maclachlan, 2007). To do this, it draws on three different case studies from community-based programmes in Scotland – a family literacy programme (reported on in Tett, 2019), a support project for homeless adults and recovering substance abusers (reported on in Duckworth and Tett, 2019) and a 'Health Issues in the Community' course (reported on in Jones, 2021). I begin by considering the links between policy, conceptualizations of equality and approaches to pedagogy before moving on to describe the case studies. These case studies are then analysed using Nancy Fraser's (2003) conceptualization of social justice that comprises three areas – redistribution, recognition and participatory parity. *Redistribution* focuses on the equal distribution of educational, health and economic opportunities, *recognition* on respect for people's identities and their cultural diversity, and *participatory parity* on equality of participation in decision-making about the things that are important in people's lives. This framework enables me to analyse how power can be challenged at the individual and collective levels especially through experiences of making decisions that are respected and lead to positive change.

Policy, equality and pedagogy

Policies at both the national and international levels are underpinned by the assumption that labour markets work rationally and efficiently, and consequently that there are causal links between education systems and the economy. As part of a neoliberal hegemony (Harvey, 2005) education systems have been mandated to develop efficient, creative and problem-solving workers for a globally competitive economy leading to the neglect of education's social and developmental responsibilities (Tett and Hamilton, 2019). Such policies conceptualize equality as about *opportunities,* so the focus is on the achievement of equality of access to, and participation in, education. The underlying assumption is that education is meritocratic, and we live in a fair society that ensures that people will progress according to their ability. From this perspective, socio-economic adversity can be overcome by enabling access to a wide range of educational opportunities that individuals can take up or decide not to, according to their own motivation.

An alternative approach to equality is *social justice* where not only the economic but also the cultural aspects of justice are seen as vital. From this perspective, remedying injustice requires not only the redistribution of opportunities but also equality of condition, which encompasses recognition of people's identities and their cultural diversity. Nancy Fraser (2003) argues that issues of distribution and recognition interact causally and so it is important to be attuned to both dimensions. Treating every injustice as both economic and cultural, all must be assessed from both outlooks without reducing one to the other. Key to this approach is what Fraser calls the 'status model' of recognition. This model views misrecognition as a matter of *social status*, where: 'patterns of disrespect and disesteem are institutionalized, for example, in law, social welfare, medicine, public education, and/or the social practices and group mores that structure everyday interaction' (Fraser, 1998: 25–6). Fraser points out that some groups are subjected to both types of discrimination, particularly those from racial minorities, because they are 'discriminated against in the labour market [whilst simultaneously] ... patterns of cultural value privilege some traits ... [meaning that they] are constructed as deficient and inferior ... [people] who cannot be full members of society' (Fraser, 2003: 23). This conceptualization of inequality is invaluable for exploring how adult education and learning might contribute to social justice because its comprehensive view means that inequalities can be interrogated, and responded to, by researchers and practitioners.

Conceptualizations of equality also have an impact on pedagogy, which can be broadly defined as the theory and practice of education and their combined impact on learning. Pedagogies are not neutral because they emerge from different economic, social, political and cultural contexts and are thus strongly influenced by policy (Freire, 1972). Burke (2015: 391) has pointed out how 'pedagogies are formed through intersecting and embodied classed, gendered and racialised subjectivities ... [that conceal] the ways that educational encounters form subjectivities, ways of being and doing'. One form of subjectivity relates to how minorities are constructed as a problem and are positioned as lacking aspiration, motivation, confidence and so on rather than as people that have important knowledge and experience to offer. This deficit approach also underpins the focus on the economic worth of an individual because it ignores that person's knowledge and instead emphasizes their limitations and can lead to a conceptualization of the purpose of adult education as the provider of 'employment ready' workers (Allatt and Tett, 2019). This leads to a curriculum that is focused on delivering the information-processing skills claimed to be necessary for employment and the outcomes that are prioritized are about narrow employability-related skills and take no account of the social and emotional aspects of learning.

González, Moll and Amanti (2005) claim that the pedagogical approaches that are most effective are those based on the view that people have important 'funds of knowledge' to contribute to education. Their research shows that this approach is successful because it focuses on the resources and practices learners bring and so builds on, rather than denigrating, their expertise. When an 'inquiry method of teaching' (González et al., 2005: 19) is used, where participants are actively involved in developing their lived experiences, these become validated as legitimate sources of knowledge both inside and outside of programmes. Moreover, when participants can influence the curriculum to make it relevant, this can provide valuable resources for their emotional and social development (Baquedano-López et al., 2013). This funds-of-knowledge approach shifts more agency to learners as meaning-makers rather than receivers of expert instruction. As a result, programmes that build on learners' own knowledge lead to increasing skills, confidence and self-respect (Tett, 2019). The approach also has a positive impact on learners at the 'cognitive dimension of knowledge and skills, the emotional dimension of feelings and motivation, and the social dimension of communication and cooperation' (Illeris, 2004: 82).

To illustrate how pedagogical approaches impact on equality, health and well-being, I now turn to my case studies.

Case study 1: Family literacy

The aim of this programme was to involve parents and to support them to become more engaged in both their own and their children's learning through breaking down the barriers between the home and the school and helping to close the attainment gap. Twelve parents (all mothers) met twice a week in their local school for a ten-week programme. One session each week involved both parents and their children, and the other session was solely for the parents.

The family-literacy worker (FLW) promoted the value of the everyday learning opportunities that parents engage in, so that their needs and interests were central to the learning process. She worked from the parents' strengths by asking them how they had dealt with any difficulties they had, so that their experience could be used. A key value was being focused on the assets that the participants brought, rather than their deficits, and they were asked to share their knowledge with each other. By finding out what skills the mothers had to offer, the FLW was able to illustrate the ways in which they supported their children and that what happened in the home was important. At the heart of this practitioner's resistance to a narrow interpretation of family literacy was being clear about her professional values coupled with a commitment to ensuring that the learners' goals were at the centre of the provision. The approach meant that it took longer to negotiate the curriculum, but it resulted in a course that was owned by the participants and created a positive atmosphere because the mothers knew that they had an influence on the content of the programme.

The programme used authentic assessment situated in real-life contexts, which is done *with*, not *to*, participants and was based on the extent to which they had been able to change their literacy practices from their own baselines – the distance that they had travelled. This process-oriented focus involved participants developing a portfolio of examples of their literacy work as evidence of what they had learnt. Portfolios included the titles of books that the mothers had read with their children; stories that they had created about their own family life; texts and emails written to friends and families; examples of reading and writing from a variety of contexts including church, neighbourhood meetings, work; as well as photographs of writing that had interested them. This type of assessment helped them to reflect on what and how they learned and gave them opportunities to test out their newly acquired skills, knowledge and understanding. Reflection was enhanced when the portfolio was brought along to the group and formed part of a 'show and tell' session that could also be shared with the children. This approach was empowering to both learners and the FLW tutor. For learners, it enabled them to have an equal say in the direction the programme should take that was based on their own goals. For the tutor, it provided feedback on the course design, content and delivery and the strengths and weaknesses of her approaches.

As a result of these approaches, many participants talked about the way they thought about themselves: 'here they build you up and help you to think positively'. In addition, because participants felt their knowledge of their children was valued, they considered, as one put it, 'that education was probably something that I could go back to as an adult. It just made me see things in a different light'. Others spoke about being respected for example, a learner from the Traveller community commented: 'in this programme you're respected as a person that has a lot of knowledge that others can learn from' after her ability to tell stories had been recognized by her peers as an asset rather than a deficit. A culture of respect was enhanced through learners feeling that their issues, circumstances and concerns were both acknowledged and valued. For example, another participant said: 'I used to just go to the shops and back to the house but now I'm out doing lots of things and I'm not isolated any more.' Learners found that their progress made them feel differently about what they could achieve: 'I felt more confident. It made me a more confident parent with my daughters ... [and] in what I could achieve myself.'

Using a 'funds of knowledge' pedagogy that focused on what learners *could* do increased confidence: 'the tutor helped me to work out what I could do and then, once I was happy about that, I worked on what I couldn't do.' It also involved participants valuing their own skills in ways that reduced their social isolation. For example, one found that her ability to tell stories from her Traveller culture meant that she had a much better oral memory than other people, but this skill had not been recognized before. For many being part of a group helped with learning: 'you're in with the group, so you get involved ... we've worked together on making books for the children and it's very satisfying.' Several learners suggested that it was the tutor that made an impact: 'she [tutor] brings stuff out of me and stretches my mind' and 'it motivates me to really try because the tutor is working so hard.'

An atmosphere had been created where learners were treated with respect within relationships of trust (Feeley, 2014). For example, 'here you don't get judged on what you can't do. Instead, the tutor helps you to find what you can do.' Having a caring ethos not only enabled participants' strengths to be recognized but also helped to create supportive social networks. The curriculum was based on the learners' concerns and aspirations about their own and their children's learning and relationships to their teachers, so that education was seen as a co-operative activity involving respect and trust. This approach provided an incentive for learning because it concentrated on what really mattered to the participants. It also helped the mothers to value their strengths: 'learning can open your eyes to what you are good at and means that you are willing to take risks in trying to make changes for your children and in the community.' Some participants had also become more confident about challenging the social injustices they had experienced: for example, 'I speak out more at home if I think things are not fair', and 'I'm more confident in challenging the teachers' negative views about my child.'

Good relationships between and among the tutor and the learners created an atmosphere where support, encouragement and constructive feedback helped people to take risks. For example, 'being part of the group has helped me to keep going even when things were really difficult at home' and 'I was afraid that the others might be racist, so I kept Khurshid in but now I've learned to trust them, and she has made friends with the other children'. Being in a positive environment also gave people the scaffolding to stretch their understanding beyond what they currently knew, to see learning as valuable and develop the ability to use their own judgement regarding the quality of their work. For example, 'the first version of my letter to the council about the racist graffiti was all muddled up, so I rewrote it four times before I was satisfied it said what I wanted.' Gaining confidence in their ability to learn also enabled some of the parents to move on to more formal provision, and the project tutor developed relationships with other providers so that individuals could easily go to the local Further Education College and take courses that led to accreditation.

Marmot and colleagues (2020: 184) have pointed out that a sense of control over one's own life is a key factor for well-being and health. In this project, the participants had positive experiences of equality of decision-making that they were able to use in their family and community lives. This ability to take more control helped to reduce stress and anxiety at the individual level and increase a sense of trust and belonging at the community level. Similarly, well-being was increased when opportunities for participation and self-determination were taken up and participants' voices were heard. Being part of a cooperative group also reduced isolation and loneliness because people's strengths were recognized whereas before they had been unacknowledged.

Case study 2: Homelessness project

This project was designed for adults that were homeless and had problems with addictions. Fifteen people participated and it was staffed by an advice worker, a rehabilitation worker and a literacy tutor. The programme lasted for three months and provided holistic support for the participants to enable them to recover from their addictions, improve their material and social circumstances, overcome personal isolation and low self-esteem, and become active members of their communities. The literacy provision was designed to support these aims, so the advice worker built on the newly acquired literacy skills that participants had gained in helping them to apply for housing, and the rehabilitation worker used the oral competencies that learners had developed to discuss their plans for their future. This meant that the skills, knowledge and understanding participants had gained were immediately and practically helping them to deal with real tasks in their lives. Conversely, these achievements in form filling, talking, reading and writing were fed back to the literacy tutor in a mutually re-enforcing cycle that enhanced progress and achievement.

The learners brought with them a diverse range of life experiences and circumstances but, despite this diversity, they shared a negative sense of themselves. A second commonality was a marginalization from mainstream society and the loss of self-esteem that this produced. At some stage in the past, their experiences of addiction, mental health issues and worklessness had caused them to identify themselves as outsiders, and their engagement in learning was part of their efforts to counter this. Several participants commented on the effect of this alienation on their skills and competencies because they had lost abilities that had previously been easy for them. One learner began drinking heavily when his company crashed, and he lost all his investments and then: 'I went downhill very fast, my health was bad, and I did nothing apart from vegetate. I didn't read a newspaper or add 2 and 2 in eight years and was brain dead.'

The tutor said that group work was valuable in overcoming some of these negative feelings. She also saw it as promoting learning because she found it encouraged participants to offer their opinions, especially if they were asked to give examples from their lives as illustrations. She said:

> With this group I have done some pair and small group work, but they prefer to work as a whole group. They know each other's strengths and weaknesses and are supportive of each other because they have faced the same homelessness and addiction issues.

The learners' reflections showed how group-work built confidence and reduced isolation.

> You're in with the group so you get involved. When there's three or four of us together, you must work out tasks, you're communicating with each other and it's very satisfying.

Learners also valued peer support because the 'whole group gets on well together and there are no cliques.' Peer and tutor support led to the building of self-esteem and confidence and helped the learners to think positively. As a result, one said: 'I feel much more confident about what I can do, as now I know I'm not thick, but I used to think I was.' The pace of learning was responsive to the learning abilities of the participants, so participants were supportively challenged to extend themselves by taking small steps with the scaffolding provided through the help of their tutor and their peers. As one learner said, 'they let you do things that you can manage because they know your boundaries, but they push a bit to get you to try more things like the couple of sentences I'm saying in the play we are putting on.' And the literacy tutor reflected:

> Everyone here is encouraging and wanting them to do well in every aspect of their lives. Most people here are quite negative about themselves and don't think they can achieve anything, so we need to help them see that small steps are important, and they need to acknowledge that for themselves too.

Several learners suggested that it was the staff that made a difference: 'it makes me feel motivated that the tutors are working so hard to help me'; and 'all the staff here help you, they will never see you struggle.' Enthusiastic and encouraging staff helped because 'if you've got somebody encouraging you to say you can do these things, you're not the bottom of the rung. You are able to do something'.

Tutors were able to create warm, welcoming and informal learning environments that put learners at ease and therefore encouraged more engagement in learning. Learners themselves frequently spoke of their appreciation for their tutor and the commitment and support they received from them. They reported that they had changed their attitude to learning and altered their practices partly because of the positive tutor–learner relationships. For example: 'It's safe here and that makes it easy to talk to the workers who understand how I feel and if you trust a person and they say try this [learning activity] then you do it.'

Creating a positive educational experience involved learners feeling that their issues, circumstances and concerns are both openly acknowledged and valued. For example: 'I just feel so comfortable in here. I mean you don't get judged, criticised, everybody does care about everybody else, even though we've got our own problems.' Another participant pointed out that 'in this group they're saying, you can be capable. They're not just saying, "you do this, you do that." It's down to us where we want to go and what we want to do'.

The pedagogical practices that contributed to the formation of this positive environment were holistic. This created strong communities where the affinities between members, be they tutors or learners, helped them to continue to engage and persist through difficult times. The frequent references learners made to the value of the group and the tutor, and the importance of a safe environment, demonstrate that they no longer felt out of place in educational environments. The learners' narratives also showed the importance of the individual's wider experience and how the activities they had engaged in could be used outside of their programme. For example, 'I'm more able to judge my own work now and know when I've done a good thing, whereas before I thought that I was a failure.' Confidence increased, not only because of changing experiences but also because of the dialogue that took place around those experiences in ways that promoted social awareness and critique. For example, 'I've learnt to take a few risks because if you only stick to what you know you're never going to achieve anything.'

Within the programme, the participants had been recognized as competent, learnt how to engage with others, communicated effectively and gone about their activities in ways that had given them a positive sense of themselves. They had acquired valued knowledge and demonstrated their competence by building on and extending what they thought, based on their needs and interests when support, encouragement and constructive feedback were offered by both the tutor and their peers.

As in the previous case study, participation has given the learners back a greater sense of control over their lives as well as greater trust in others, and this had resulted in an increase in their health and well-being. It has also reduced participants' isolation and loneliness because of the supportive community that was formed. In this project, learners have been enabled to adopt and maintain more healthy behaviours, especially in relation to their addictions, but also in other ways. For example, one learner said: 'I have improved on my old self where I was an angry wee man all the time and always fighting. I am getting better at walking away from things rather than trying to get fights started because I now want to get on with my life.' The participants' improved communication skills had also enabled them to access experiences and material resources such as getting housing that would help them out of poverty and so break the link between inadequate incomes and poor health. As Marmot and colleagues point out (2020: 70), 'having too little of anything, for example money, food or time – affects mental processes, in effect narrowing mental "bandwidth", resulting in people making decisions that go against their long-term interests.' This project created time for reflection that enabled the participants to be more effective in their decision-making and helped them to make changes that would have a long-term benefit on their health and well-being.

Case study 3: Health Issues in the Community

Health Issues in the Community (HIIC) is a sixteen-week course run by tutors across Scotland. It comprises a pack of materials that guide tutors in helping participants understand what affects their health and the health of their communities (https://www.chex.org.uk/health-issues-community-hiic). The course aims to help participants gain a broad understanding of the social model of health, health inequalities, power and participation and community development approaches in health – and how they can use these to make positive change happen in their communities. HIIC is focused on helping participants to widen and deepen awareness of health issues through communicating their findings into their communities by using presentations, discussions or other creative methods. It also encourages people to act by engaging with their elected representatives and others to push for change.

The assumption underpinning the course is that damaging social experiences produce ill-health and that remedial action needs to be social. This view of health focuses on the socio-economic risk conditions such as poverty, unemployment, pollution, poor housing and power imbalances that cause ill-health. The perspective taken by HIIC is that an important way that inequalities in health can be tackled, and social exclusion reduced, is to find ways of strengthening individuals and communities so that they can join together for mutual support.

The HIIC course draws on the philosophy and approach of transformative popular education espoused by Paulo Freire. Freire (1972) argues that it is not enough for people to come together in dialogue to gain knowledge of their social reality. Rather, they must act together to reflect upon that reality and so transform it through further action and critical reflection. Based on this philosophy, the aim of the HIIC tutor is to help participants identify what they wish to change, to identify the problems, find the root causes of these problems and work out practical ways in which they can change the situation. This involves the tutor developing a strong relationship with the group so that the design of the programme takes account of the influences that impact on them. The tutor then provides opportunities for people to express their own views, and to question everyday assumptions and explanations, particularly where they differ from their own experience.

The course I am focusing on took place in a disadvantaged community in a town in the Central Belt of Scotland and had eight participants. The health issues initially identified by the group were those they had personal experience of, but these acted as triggers for wider discussion of the bigger issues at the root of their individual, family and community concerns. The learners then enriched and extended this by interrogating the issues using local surveys, interviews, meetings and visits to groups and organizations. Through this ongoing dialogue between themselves and the wider community, the detailed way in which issues were impacting locally, and the causes of them, were brought to light. The learners reported that

> what we learned about our community came first from other community members and then we researched various sources to find out if the local statistics supported their views. The methods we used included face to face surveys, finding local health and employment statistics, and small group discussions. We also questioned some organisations that we invited to come and talk to us.

The health issue the group unearthed was the shame people felt about being unemployed or unable to earn enough to live on. The group thought that the shame arose from the labelling of people who become unemployed as 'shirkers' by sections of the media and politicians over the last decade. The effect of this was stigma, loss of dignity and shame, and this damaging emotional and social impact on their community was uncovered in their critical enquiry. The learners said that 'this culture of silence in the community means that the issues are not being addressed and as such people are suffering'.

The group then worked with the tutor to identify how this issue might be tackled in the local community and this provided an opportunity to increase their self-determination through collective organization and action. They then went on to create a more public debate and discussion about this previously unaddressed issue that not only enabled them to find their voice as active citizens but also to formulate a proposal that had the backing of the whole community. As a result, a proposal to establish a Community Hub in the local Community Centre was made to local politicians, the Health Board and regional welfare organizations. The HIIC group argued that having the Hub would give the community access to the services they needed and the privacy they wanted. After a great deal of discussion, it was agreed by the Council that an advice worker would be based in the Hub as this would help to ensure individuals could discuss their financial issues and be advised about their entitlement to financial and socio-emotional support in ways that protected their right to privacy. As one HIIC participant pointed out, 'The right to privacy protects you against intrusion into your personal life – including unnecessary, heavy-handed state surveillance.' This meant that the group achieved real changes to the way local services were provided and created dialogues with local, regional and national decision-makers.

Research (Layte et al., 2010) has shown that the stigma of poverty not only causes distress to the individuals on the receiving end, but also leads to social isolation as people try to avoid situations where they might be labelled. The shame that follows creates a sense of powerlessness and lack of agency that cannot be overcome by the individual but needs to be seen as a structural issue. Building organizations, taking action to redistribute resources, ensuring that community voices are heard all have direct health benefits. This is because lack of control over one's own destiny promotes a susceptibility to ill-health for people who live in difficult situations where they do not have adequate resources or supports in their day-to-day lives. Clearly the people who participated in this course have involved themselves in action that has enabled them to have their voices listened to about the health and well-being issues that are important to them. At the individual level this has raised their self-esteem and confidence, and this in turn has enabled them collectively to have an impact on decision-making and the use and distribution of resources in relation to health and well-being. The people in this community have been involved in decisions that affect them, and that decision-making has been improved by drawing on their lived experience of inequality.

Redistribution, recognition and participatory parity

The case studies have shown the ways in which a funds-of-knowledge pedagogy increases participants' self-efficacy leading to a reduction in health inequalities. In this section, I consider the impact of this on the achievement of social justice.

There is evidence that participation in these programmes brought about changes in the recognitional aspect of Fraser's (2003) model of social justice and, as a result, there are also examples of the redistributive aspect. The learners clearly saw the recognition of their expertise, derived from the critical interrogation of their knowledge, as a step towards greater self-efficacy. They were also able to challenge some of the patterns of cultural privilege that had constructed them as 'inferior others who cannot be full members of society' (Fraser, 2003: 23). For example, the learner from the Traveller community that had her culture of storytelling recognized by her peers as an asset rather than a deficit (case study 1). In case study 2, participants' common experience of homelessness and addictions became a shared asset that enabled these experiences to be viewed positively. In case study 3, instead of seeing unemployment as an individual problem, people were able to see that it was caused by structural forces. These changes came about because the activities the participants engaged in enabled them to develop their ability to speak out, take risks and think differently about themselves.

The recognition of participants' strengths and cultural diversity also led to some economic redistribution because, for example, 'the tutors trusted us with important tasks like creating the children's book so that made me feel that I could get a job where I would also need to be trusted' (case study 1). It contributed to their well-being through reducing isolation – 'being part of the group has helped me to keep going even when things were really difficult at home' (case study 2). Finally, there is evidence that they had improved their access to health resources through having the services that were important to them recognized (case study 3). While most of the changes that the learners experienced in the redistribution of employment opportunities and access to health services were quite modest, this does demonstrate that the recognitive and redistributive aspects of social justice fold into one another and action needs to be taken in both spheres simultaneously to obtain greater equality.

I have now considered how participants in the case studies have experienced two of the dimensions of social justice, namely redistribution and recognition. Fraser also proposed a third dimension that she named 'participatory parity', because it focuses on equality of participation in decision-making. Its achievement requires that individuals participate on an equal footing in processes that give them a voice in public deliberations and democratic decision-making particularly over issues that directly affect them. So, this aspect of social justice involves making social arrangements that mean that *all* people are enabled to participate as equals in social life. This means that there needs to be a revaluation of the knowledge, skills and understanding of non-dominant groups, so that rather than providing an education that is good for them, we need instead to ensure that the curriculum is built around their views.

In the case studies, curriculum approaches were developed that operated to support the decision-making of the participants and were based on the learners' concerns and aspirations, so that education was seen as a co-operative activity involving respect and trust. The teaching was based on a group process, where the tutor and learners learnt together, beginning with the concrete experience of the participants, leading to reflection on that experience to effect positive change. As a result, the participants were able to add new and different knowledge and become the subjects of learning rather than the objects of educational interventions that were supposed to be good for them. As participants became more reflexive about their experiences, they found ways to reconstitute previously internalized injustices. As one participant put it: 'learning can open your eyes to what you are good at and means that you are willing to take risks in trying to make changes both for yourself but also for others that struggle with addictions' (case study 2). Participants had become more confident about challenging the social injustices they had experienced: for example, 'I speak out more at home if I think things are not fair' (case study 1) and 'I'm more confident in challenging people's views about what is means to be unemployed' (case study 3).

Engaging in participatory processes in implementing and evaluating programmes, being in a safe and open space to discuss, dissent and agree on the best courses of action, and integrating different views can foster dialogue and enable the recognition of difference and diversity (Baquedano-López et al., 2013). This form of education meant that participants were enabled to take these experiences of equality of decision-making and participation into their families and communities. In addition, in case study 3, participants were able to participate in the broader political arena, where the power imbalances and negative discourses they experienced could be most effectively challenged. For the HIIC group then, an issue that they had come to understand through sharing and critically reflecting on their experiences together had resulted in action that focused on the political level. Their intervention was driven by equity concerns enacted in solidarity that gave them a voice in resolving issues in their community that also had wider political implications.

Conclusion

As I have shown, what counts as important knowledge is one way in which inequalities of power are systematically reproduced. In a democracy, political representatives, public institutions and services, the activities of those who work for them (e.g. doctors, teachers, welfare workers), community organizations and groups must be accountable to the people they represent, or work for, if democracy is to become a way of life. Learning and education should, therefore, contribute towards enabling people to interrogate the claims and activities done on their behalf and encourage them to develop the skill, analysis and confidence to make their own voice heard. Education should also help people to engage in a wide range of political roles and social relationships that occur outside both the workplace and the marketplace. Stimulating and supporting lifelong learning for a more active and inclusive construction of citizenship involves recognizing marginalized people's capacity for generating really useful knowledge.

As Beresford (2021: 135) points out, it is only when people can speak for themselves and exert their own power that they are they likely to be treated equitably. Too often we are offered warm and seductive rhetoric that is guided by the logic of perceived self-interest of those who control it, rather than a commitment to real equality. Instead, we should be treating people as whole human beings rather than labelling them (as unemployed, mentally ill, etc.), and involving them in co-designing and delivering education and learning, if inequities in health and well-being are to be challenged. Rather than marginalized groups simply being consulted, tackling discrimination requires that they have a seat at the table when decisions are taken, and that decision-makers are held to account.

It is particularly important as the UK begins to recover from the Covid-19 pandemic that has exacerbated inequalities in education, health and well-being (James and Thériault, 2020) that the importance of adult learning and education is recognized. My research for the case studies was undertaken before the pandemic impacted on the provision of community-based adult learning, but research I conducted in the summer of 2021 demonstrated how the loss of face-to-face teaching exacerbated many learners' loneliness and isolation. Practitioners reported that the lack of regular contact led to many learners' feeling that they had lost a lifeline that kept them going in times of trouble. As restrictions eased, and online and small group classes were re-established, practitioners reported that learners said they now had something to get up for and look forward to doing. Many practitioners had responded to new social challenges and developed innovative ways of engaging with learners that helped to combat some of the worst effects of Covid-19. These included one-to-one help with digital skills, establishing small walking groups for English as a Second or Other Language (ESOL) learners to have conversations in English and creating online groups that prioritized mutual support for literacy and numeracy learners.

Learner-centred education is a resource that enables participants to identify inequalities, probe their origins and begin to challenge them, using skills, information and knowledge in order to achieve and stimulate change. Through this type of learning, the production of knowledge is put back into the hands of people, competing values can be thought through and their relevance to people's lives can be assessed. Clearly, while adult education alone cannot abolish social divisions, it can make a useful contribution to combating them by challenging the ways in which discrimination is reinforced through the very processes and outcomes of education. This will involve the nurturing of an education system whose function is not to reflect and reproduce existing inequalities in society but rather one that prioritizes provision for those whose earlier educational and socio-economic disadvantage should give them a first claim in a genuinely lifelong learning system.

References

Allatt, G. and Tett, L. (2019), Adult Literacy Practitioners and Employability Skills: Resisting Neo-Liberalism? *Journal of Education Policy*, 34 (4), 577–94.

Bambra, C. and Payne, G. (2020), Health, in G. Payne and E. Harrison (eds.), *Social Divisions, Inequality and Diversity in Britain 4th Edition*, 259–73, Bristol: Policy Press.

Baquedano-López, P., Alexander, R.A., and Hernandez, S.J. (2013), Equity Issues in Parental and Community Involvement in Schools: What Teacher Educators Need to Know, *Review of Research in Education*, 37, 149–82.

Beresford, P. (2021), *Participatory Ideology: From Exclusion to Involvement*, Bristol: Policy Press.

Burke, P. J. (2015), Re/imagining Higher Education Pedagogies: Gender, Emotion and Difference, *Teaching in Higher Education*, 20 (4), 388–401.

Duckworth, V. and Tett, L. (2019), Transformative and Emancipatory Literacy to Empower, *International Journal of Lifelong Education*, 38 (4), 366–78.

Feeley, M. (2014), *Learning Care Lessons: Literacy, Love Care and Solidarity*, London: Tufnell Press.

Fraser, N. (1998), Heterosexism, Misrecognition and Capitalism: A Response to Judith Butler, *New Left Review*, March/April, 140–9.

Fraser, N. (2003), Social Justice in the Age of Identity Politics: Redistribution, Recognition, and Participation, in Fraser and A. Honneth (eds.), *Redistribution or Recognition? A Political-Philosophical Exchange*, 7–109, London: Verso.

Freire, P. (1972), *Pedagogy of the Oppressed*, Harmondsworth: Penguin.

Gewirtz, S. (1998), Conceptualising Social Justice in Education: Mapping the Territory, *Journal of Education Policy*, 13 (4), 469–84.

González, N., Moll, L., and Amanti, C. (2005), *Funds of Knowledge: Theorizing Practices in Households, Communities, and Classrooms*, New Jersey: Lawrence Erlbaum Associates.

Harvey, D. (2005), *A Brief History of Neoliberalism*, Oxford: Oxford University Press.

Illeris, K. (2004), Transformative Learning in the Perspective of a Comprehensive Learning Theory, *Journal of Transformative Education*, 2 (2), 79–89.

James, N. and Thériault, V. (2020), Adult Education in Times of the COVID-19 Pandemic: Inequalities, Changes, and Resilience, *Studies in the Education of Adults*, 52 (2), 129–33.

Jones, J. (2021), *Writing about Health Issues, Volume 4*, Glasgow: Community Health Exchange.

JRF (Joseph Rowntree Foundation) (2020), *Poverty in Scotland*, www.jrf.org.uk.

Layte, R., Maître, B., and Whelan, C. T. (2010), *Second European Quality of Life Survey Living Conditions, Social Exclusion and Mental Well-Being*, Dublin: European Foundation for the Improvement of Living and Working Conditions.

Marmot, M., Allen, J., Boyce, T., Goldblatt, P., and Morrison, J. (2020), *Health Equity in England: The Marmot Review 10 years on*, London: Institute of Health Equity.

Mills, C. W. (1959), *The Sociological Imagination*, New York: Oxford University Press.

Tett, L. (2019), Transforming Learning Identities in Literacy Programmes, *Journal of Transformative Education*, 17 (2), 154–72.

Tett, L. and Hamilton, M. (2019), *Resisting Neoliberalism in Education: Local, National and Transnational Perspectives*, Bristol: Policy Press.

Tett, L. and Maclachlan, K. (2007), Adult Literacy and Numeracy, Social Capital, Learner Identities and Self–Confidence, *Studies in the Education of Adults*, 39 (2), 150–67.

4

Learning English in a hostile environment: a study of volunteer ESOL teachers of refugees and asylum seekers in the UK

Lauren Bouttell, University of East Anglia

Learning English is regularly cited in political discourse as the most important adult learning that new migrants to the UK should undertake. For example, in July 2019, Boris Johnson stated, 'I want everybody who comes here and makes their lives here to be, and to feel British – that's the most important thing – and to learn English' (Halliday and Brooks, 2019). Alongside this political focus, studies have found that many migrants in the UK are also very keen to learn English (Bennett, 2018; Refugee Action, 2019). Learning English is also often presented as the gateway to 'integration' for new migrants to the UK. But this political rhetoric has also come alongside contradictory policy provision. Funding for ESOL (English for Speakers of Other Languages) has been cut repeatedly over the last twenty years (Foster and Bolton, 2018; Refugee Action, 2019). There has also been increasingly restrictive immigration policy put in place in the UK during the same time period. The UK government's proposed Nationality and Borders Bill in 2021 aims to make claiming asylum in the UK much more difficult, and proposes measures such as creating off-shore centres to house asylum seekers while their claims are being processed (Home Office, 2021). Shortly before the completion of this volume, the UK government announced a plan to deport asylum seekers to Rwanda (Home Office, 2022). This has been widely condemned as inhumane, as well as an evasion of the UK's responsibilities under the Refugee Convention by sending asylum seekers thousands of miles to a country in the Global South (UNHCR, 2022).

As this chapter will explore, this hostile policy context impacts on sanctuary seekers' ability to access adult education provision and to learn English. This chapter details a study of volunteer ESOL teachers from around the UK and their insights about ESOL provision for people who are refugees and asylum seekers. This study suggests that the current lack of funding and policy for community ESOL, particularly in England, means that the current provision is unsustainable. On the other hand, there is also an implication that volunteer ESOL teachers and learners are actively resisting restrictive UK government policy through community-based English classes. I will discuss volunteers' insights about adult ESOL provision for refugees in the UK, as well as some of the implications of what volunteering as a teacher can show about the relationship between adult education and social change.

Refugees in the UK

This chapter will explore adult education for people who are refugees and asylum seekers in the UK, so it is important to include a brief overview of the context of the UK government's approach to migration in recent years. In 2012 Theresa May, then the Home Secretary, laid out the UK government's 'hostile environment' approach to 'illegal migration' (Kirkup and Winnett, 2012). This was manifested in the Immigration Acts of 2014 and 2016. These acts included measures such as requiring landlords and medical providers to check the migration status of those accessing services (Webber, 2019). Individuals the government believed to be without the correct migration documentation were also contacted by the Home Office, barred from accessing services and in some cases were deported. The result of this became known as the Windrush scandal, in which Caribbean-born people who had been legally living in the UK, but did not have correct documentation, often because of errors the UK government had made, were threatened with deportation or lost access to healthcare and benefits (Craggs, 2018).

Refugees and asylum seekers were certainly impacted by 'hostile environment' policies. The UN Refugee Convention defines a refugee as 'someone who is unable or unwilling to return to their country of origin owing to a well-founded fear of being persecuted for reasons of race, religion, nationality, membership of a particular social group, or political opinion' (UNHCR (1), 2021). When the UK Home Office decides that an individual meets this definition, they are granted official 'refugee status'. Someone who has applied for refugee status but has not yet had a decision about their case is referred to as an 'asylum seeker' (UNHCR (2), n.d.).

The 'hostile environment' was ostensibly focussed on tackling 'illegal migration' (Kirkup and Winnett, 2012), but having the required documentation is not always easy for people who have migrated to the UK fleeing factors such as war or persecution. The political discourse often talks about 'legal' and 'illegal' migration, but this implies that there is a clear-cut distinction between these two terms. Legal discourse usually uses the terms 'regular' and 'irregular' migration, although even these terms could also be seen to be problematic. The Universal Declaration of Human Rights, article 14, states that 'Everyone has the right to seek and to enjoy in other countries asylum from persecution' (United Nations, 1948). But in recent years, the right to seek asylum has been contested, and what De Genova (2002: 419) refers to as 'the legal production of migrant illegality' has been heightened in recent years. In 2021, the Home Office produced what it terms the 'New Plan for Immigration' (HM Government, 2021), and later the Nationality and Borders Bill (Home Office, 2021), which at the time of writing is in its final stages. This has continued the trend of constructing illegality in migration. This legislation differentiates between people who have entered the UK and then claimed asylum, designating this as an 'illegal', illegitimate route. It wishes to distinguish these refugees from those whom the UK government has resettled in the UK as part of refugee resettlement programmes. Hundreds of charities supporting refugees in the UK have contested this, including the United Nations High Commissioner for Refugees (e.g. Refugee Council, 2021; UNHCR UK, 2021). In 2020, with the Covid-19 pandemic cutting off some routes for people seeking asylum in the UK, crossings across the channel have increased. Although in 2020 this accompanied a net fall in asylum claims, the visibility of channel crossings has led to increased government hostility, and a more militarized response towards asylum seekers arriving by boat (Davies et al., 2021).

People seeking asylum in the UK have not been allowed to work (with a few certain exceptions) since 2002 (Bales, 2013). Because of this, most asylum seekers are not able to financially support themselves, so the UK government provides accommodation and a living allowance of just under £40 per week for those who are destitute (Right to Remain, 2021). This amount is often not enough to live on, and many asylum seekers in the UK live below the poverty line and need to regularly use food banks and other support services (Bales, 2013). The asylum process itself has also been found to negatively impact the mental health of those going through the system (H. Rogers et al., 2015). Many applicants are left in limbo for months or even years, with no knowledge about whether they will be allowed to stay in the UK (Cortvriend, 2020). Even if refugee status is granted by the Home Office, there are still many challenges faced by refugees in the UK, and they are likely to experience many difficulties, including destitution, underemployment or discrimination. These factors mean that there are a variety of additional considerations regarding adult learning. Providers often need to be flexible and accommodating, offering a wide variety of services to encompass the complex and hectic lives of refugees and asylum seekers in the UK.

ESOL in the UK

ESOL (English for Speakers of Other Languages) features prominently in discourse surrounding integration of people who are migrants and is often the main kind of adult education discussed in policy for these groups. This is demonstrated by the chapter's earlier quote from the current Prime Minister Boris Johnson, asserting that migrants to the UK should 'feel British' and 'learn English' (Halliday and Brooks, 2019). However, this is contradicted by a lack of funding and specific policy for ESOL education, particularly in England. Funding for ESOL has been continually cut (Foster and Bolton, 2018; Refugee Action, 2019), with refugees in some areas of England facing long waiting lists for free classes. In contrast to England's approach, in 2007 Scotland introduced the Scottish Executive Strategy for ESOL, which secured an extra £5 million in funding for ESOL, leading to 4000 more classroom spaces, keeping a fee waiver for asylum seekers (Rosenberg, 2007: 256). Scotland's ESOL strategy, updated in 2015, commits to offering 'high quality English language provision' for people who do not have English as a first language (Scottish Government, 2015: 6). Scotland's approach has been perceived as less prescriptive and skills-based than England's approach to ESOL (Simpson, 2015: 209). Likewise, Wales has also tried to move away from the skills-based framework in England by introducing its own ESOL strategy in 2014 (Simpson, 2015). England does not yet have an ESOL strategy, and although one had been planned for autumn of 2019, this has not yet been published at the time of writing. People seeking asylum are barred from working and are not able to afford to pay for classes, so this means that many newcomers in the UK are left waiting for months, during which time they could be attending classes. There is also ring-fenced funding for specific groups of resettled refugees; for example, Syrian refugees, relocated to the UK by a specific resettlement scheme, have an allocation of funding for English classes which is unavailable for other refugees. This means that around the UK there are many people, particularly refugees and asylum seekers, who want to learn English but are not always able to access formal classes at colleges (Refugee Action, 2019). For this reason, there are many civil society organizations around the country who offer free classes, usually taught by volunteers. These vary around the UK, depending on the organizations themselves and the populations of refugees living in those areas, but these classes are usually non-formal in nature.

Organizations offering free ESOL classes around the UK vary, and free classes are offered by a range of charities, NGOs and faith organizations. Prior to the Covid-19 pandemic, there were usually other services and learning opportunities offered, such as community meals, access to food banks and clothing and signposting to other local support services for refugees (Dawson, 2017). Funding comes from a variety of sources, including local foundations, the National Lottery, local authorities, as well as small donations and fundraising, because most organizations are registered as charities, and funding can be precarious and short-term (Dawson, 2017). In the post-Covid-19 era, ESOL classes have moved online (Lewandowski, 2021). This has presented challenges for some learners to access classes, as well as presenting new opportunities with some learners preferring the added flexibility that online classes can provide (Lewandowski, 2021).

The study

This chapter is based on a study which was conducted as a part of my master's dissertation, completed at the University of Glasgow in 2019. I am also a volunteer ESOL teacher and was motivated by what I perceived as a lack of funding and policy interest in supporting learning for people who are refugees in the UK, which contradicted the rhetoric that migrants should learn English. I wanted to explore how sustainable the provision was, and was interested in how wider immigration policies like the 'hostile environment' may influence learning. Like some of the teachers interviewed as part of the study, I was motivated to volunteer by a desire to welcome people who were new arrivals in the UK, as a contrast to the government's hostile approach. Having volunteered in England and Scotland, I also noticed that as free classes were offered by small NGOs, there was a lot of variation in provision around the country, and some insight into this may be useful. I have identified findings from the study which are relevant to the themes of this book, and have consolidated some of the themes which I initially found in the original study, and will discuss them in the following sections.

I conducted semi-structured interviews with eleven volunteer ESOL teachers around the UK in the early part of 2019, including volunteers from Scotland, England, Wales and Northern Ireland. Most interviews were conducted on

Skype, although some were over the telephone and one was in person. It could be said that there are some limitations to telephone and video conferencing interviews as it is more difficult to read non-verbal cues (Creswell, 2012: 385), but the advantage of being able to speak to people from all around the UK made this worthwhile. Participants were recruited through an online mailing list in the ESOL sector, as well as through snowball sampling with contacts I already had in the field. The interview data was analysed using an inductive approach, from a critical perspective, using Thematic Analysis (Braun and Clarke, 2006).

This study was concerned with the motivations of volunteer ESOL teachers, their perception of the standard of ESOL provision, as well as ideas about what may happen in the future. The volunteers themselves and the organizations they volunteer with were anonymized using pseudonyms, which I have used in this chapter when using direct quotes from participants. The names of organizations were also omitted, because of the small sample size, and to help the volunteers feel comfortable in speaking about the spaces they volunteer in. In the following sections, I will explore some of the key themes identified in the study.

Funding for adult education

Unavailability and precarity of funding was discussed by many volunteers as dramatically impacting ESOL learners who are refugees and asylum seekers. In particular, the volunteers in England noted that factors like a lack of exercise books and other classroom resources were frustrating. More than one volunteer noted that the loss of funding which had been in place previously was detrimental to learners. Denise told me that the organization she volunteered with at one point had funding for bus tickets for learners; 'When that funding ran out, quite a few of the female participants stopped coming.' Female participants primarily stopped coming to classes because they could not afford the transport themselves, especially if they had to bring young children with them. Some of the male participants would walk the several miles to class, so were still able to attend, but even this is still a large burden for learners. This suggests that unstable funding can be particularly detrimental to women, by removing the means for them to access classes.

Gemma, a volunteer, expressed the frustrations behind enforcing ring-fenced funding schemes. In her area, the local council provided funding only for those with refugee status who had been in the UK for one year. This meant she had to turn away many people who were seeking asylum and did not qualify. She found this distressing and frustrating. She told me:

> We were only allowed to deliver those Functional Skills courses to refugees and migrants, not asylum seekers because it was funded by [a local government office] … um and any refugee taking the course had to have lived in the UK for twelve months to be able to be eligible, so that really frustrated me because I thought well surely the people who need English the most are those who have just got to the country but from the home office perspective, government's perspective, you have to prove that you're staying here long-term and that it's worthwhile investing in you.

This demonstrates that there are certain areas in which many people want to access ESOL classes but are barred because of their migration status. This seemed to be a particular problem in England.

Anna, another volunteer teacher, described the negative impact of funders asking volunteers to collect information about the types of trauma experienced by learners in classes so that they could try to demonstrate the impact of their services. This shows that although some funders may have good intentions, the need to show the impact of their work can have a detrimental effect on volunteers and refugees. The need to negotiate the desires of funders was distressing, and arguably prevented Anna from performing her role as a teacher effectively, by asking her to discuss her students' trauma. Consideration of the methods used to determine impact, and whether these are harmful for volunteers or learners, is a very important area for funders to consider.

Cooke and Peutrell (2019) have observed that ESOL teachers have recently needed to negotiate the UK government's agenda in delivering adult education for 'citizenship' and 'integration'. Although it was not common for volunteers to need to mediate who had access to the classroom like Gemma did, many did feel the impacts of low levels of funding for resources. This was most keenly felt by the volunteers from England and Northern Ireland, which potentially reflects the Welsh and Scottish Governments' greater support of ESOL provision. Hannah, a volunteer teacher in Northern Ireland, commented: 'you might have the room absolutely crowded and it was one room and there were maybe four teachers and we would just take a group at each table in this tiny room and somehow we all managed to all teach our students […] the noise level was horrific'. The lack of reliable funding, particularly for community ESOL in England, is keenly felt by volunteers and learners. The fact that some funding is ring-fenced and unavailable to people with different migration statuses means that there are groups of asylum seekers who do have little or no access to formal ESOL classes. If the government is concerned about integration for new migrants, it seems logical that ESOL classes should be available to *all* new migrants, regardless of migration status. This prevention of learning comes across as an attempt to annex ESOL teachers as an extension of the Home Office and hostile government policies. Community organizations often try their best to provide classes with limited resources, but volunteer teachers may struggle to help their learners without secure funding. Gemma also observed that the learners needed 'things like notebooks, something so simple as notebooks, because every week they come with a scrap piece of paper and you never see it again, where they can keep all of their English work in one book and you can see their progress.' More secure funding for community ESOL classes would be an important step in helping refugees and asylum seekers learn what they need to settle in the UK. However, deeper change at a policy level for immigration is needed.

Volunteer agency and social change

Although some volunteers do need to negotiate the ways in which the government may limit access to certain migrants, or create hostile policies, many cited their acute awareness of these policies. As Colin expressed, 'there is quite a worrying tide of populism, and scapegoating really, when people have problems with their lives, it's very easy to blame minorities'. Many volunteers directly cited the 'hostile environment' as a negative force in UK society in our interview, and some cited it as a motivation to begin volunteering themselves, with others discussing racism inherent in such policies. This shows that many volunteers are aware of the political forces affecting refugees and asylum seekers in the UK, and it could be argued that the very act of volunteering as an ESOL teacher is an act of resistance to 'hostile environment' policies for some volunteers. Some volunteers had also migrated to the UK themselves, had relatives who had been refugees or had experience of migration in the past. Julia, whose father had been a refugee, told me he used to bring her to his own community volunteer roles and that 'I sort of did the same thing with my children because they also volunteer'. For some that I spoke to, volunteering was a form of solidarity with people who are migrants, whom some volunteers viewed as being mistreated by the UK government.

Volunteering as resistance was also paired with a concern from some volunteers that their volunteering would not legitimize a lack of funding. Bernadette remarked, 'I've always made it a rule that I would not take a job if I was displacing a paid teacher ... I'm filling a gap in the provision.' This shows that some volunteers are negotiating the difficult terrain created by this 'gap' and their opposition to it. Tuckett (2015) has suggested that adult educators tend to see themselves as facilitators of social transformation and frequently target learning programmes to those who may be marginalized. He puts forward that adult learning alone 'is a necessary but not sufficient component in social change, and where the formal structures of adult education can engage with external social forces it can play a constructive and dynamic role' (Tuckett, 2015: 248). Volunteer teachers interviewed in this study were able to provide free ESOL classes, in defiance of the neglect of funding and the 'hostile environment', but greater social change is still limited by the wider structural factors like the limitations on funding and restrictive immigration policy. Volunteers were consistently aware of structural challenges which they felt they were unable to influence, but through the act of volunteering itself they were able to exercise agency.

Flexible, non-formal classes

Many of the volunteers interviewed expressed that the flexibility of non-formal English classes led by volunteers is mostly a positive thing for learners who are refugees and asylum seekers. Formal classes do not tend to be as flexible, often also due to limitations on funding and exams. Many volunteer teachers, the majority of whom were highly qualified and experienced, also enjoyed having the freedom as adult educators to plan their own classes and teach in the way that they wanted to, something which they told me is not always possible when teaching formal classes in a college or English school. Formal colleges tend to have exams and specific curriculum content, whereas community organizations may not, so there is more flexibility in planning learning activities. Volunteers often appreciated the freedom to be able to adapt materials to the specific topics their students asked to learn. Colin told me that he would ask the learners what they needed: 'well get it from the students, what do they need to say and try to assist them in those specific language needs, I mean the obvious first thing they need is an ability with English that's going to serve them well in their dealings with the home office, that's um and as we know, home office jargon, like legal jargon is quite special.' As discussed briefly in the introductory paragraphs, the UK asylum system is a stressful and uncertain process for applicants. Because of this, a flexible learning provision, which can accommodate areas they want to learn, does seem to be useful for people who are refugees and asylum seekers in the UK. Although it may be preferable to make the asylum system less hectic for those applying, non-formal, flexible classes are very important for both learners and volunteer teachers.

Although many volunteers wished to create a welcoming space for new migrants to the UK, some did express that they did not know much about the lives of their students, particularly with regard to the UK asylum system. Karen mentioned that 'I don't quite know much about immigration rules, […] I think like refugees, migrants, asylum seekers, I think they do have access to […] essentials, for example a place to live and things like that but I'm not entirely sure what the rules regarding immigration and then having ESOL classes … I'm not really sure though'. This suggests that this is a potential area for future training for volunteer ESOL teachers, if an organization does not do this already. Helping to prepare learners for their dealings with the Home Office would also be an important area for potential teacher training. It could also help teachers to know some of the wider needs of learners, such as hectic schedules, so they can be flexible to allow for lateness or missed classes.

The sustainability of volunteering

There was a division between volunteers who were retired and those who were not in terms of how they were motivated to volunteer. In studies of motivation, Deci and Ryan (2008) differentiate between extrinsic and intrinsic motivations. Extrinsic motivations are those that lead to some kind of material consequence such as a reward or avoiding punishment. Intrinsic motivations are those that come when the activity itself is satisfying, and Deci and Ryan (2008) suggest that these kinds of motivations are more sustainable in the long term. In this study, I found that retired volunteer ESOL teachers had more intrinsic motivations, and were able to choose to volunteer as English teachers because it was something they found inherently rewarding. On the other hand, volunteer ESOL teachers who were not retired had more extrinsic motivations, such as volunteering to gain vocational experience, and as part of study programmes such as master's courses. Although the non-retired volunteers certainly did have intrinsic motivations, Anna, a PhD student, noted, 'cos I'm funded for my PhD, it's a unique opportunity where I can actually work for free, because normally I can't afford to work for free.' Non-retired teachers had more extrinsic motivations, which retired teachers did not express. This is arguably related to financial stability and employment. It means that retired teachers are more likely to stay in their roles for a longer period of time because they are able to financially support themselves with their pension. I also found that non-retired teachers had more factors which meant they might stop volunteering. Others noted that they would not be able to continue with volunteering when they found full-time work, even though they would like to. In fact, some expressed that they wanted to volunteer permanently, but were not able to do so because full-time work did not leave them with enough time off to do so. This suggests that because volunteers who are not yet retired are not able to volunteer for sustained time periods, the provision for learners may suffer. There is also the implication that wider socio-economic factors have a huge impact on the ability to volunteer. On a policy level, social changes such as a more flexible, shorter working week, or a Universal Basic Income, a monthly payment to all adults which is not means-tested (BIEN, n.d.), may go some way to making volunteering more sustainable for those who are not retired.

Informal learning and integration

The discourse surrounding integration for migrants often uses the metaphor of the 'two-way street' to assert that 'integration is not assimilation' (HM Government, 2018: 10). However, when it comes to adult education, the expectation on migrants to learn English is often ostensibly one-way, as they are expected to learn English and about British culture. It has been noted by Heinemann (2017) that the creation of integration learning programmes in some European countries has contributed to reinforcing the dominance of colonialism and Euro-Centrism. However, this study did suggest that volunteer ESOL teachers do also learn informally from their students. Informal learning is something that is ubiquitous throughout life, but not something that people are always conscious of or have planned, as opposed to formal learning which is more structured and intentional (A. Rogers, 2014). Many volunteer teachers suggested that they experienced inter-cultural learning from meeting people from other cultures that they normally would not. This does show that it is possible for adult education to facilitate 'integration' which is not simply one-sided. However, ESOL teachers are a very small section of the population, so most of the expectation to learn and 'integrate' still remains on refugees. Further, this aspect of 'informal learning' is not frequently cited as a conscious outcome of adult education for people who are refugees and asylum seekers. This theme would be an interesting area to explore further in research, particularly how to involve wider sections of communities who are not asylum seekers, to help learning for integration become more two-way.

Further to this, volunteer teachers also developed their skills and experience, both as ESOL teachers and as a part of the organizations informally through the networks developed in the role. Bernadette, who was a volunteer at two organizations in England, remarked that 'In both the institutions I'm at now, essentially volunteers run the institution. With some administrative … and it makes things so much better. We know what we're doing, we know what we're trying to achieve.' Karen mentioned, 'I always ask the other volunteers if they can get me something good, or if they have some materials I can use and then we always try to like give each other materials […] that we can use in class, so it will like lessen the burden basically or the time preparation.' For Fran, feeling included in the running of the organization she had previously volunteered with in Scotland was an important part of the role for her: 'I was always part of the lunches, and got invited to the meetings and was part of the discussions and stuff and because it was the first time I was volunteering I didn't think about it so much so it was like "oh yeah of course" […] just given challenging tasks and responsibilities.' These opportunities for volunteer ESOL teachers to form networks and learn from one another and others in the organizations present themselves as important ways in which informal learning may occur.

Covid-19 and ESOL

It is important to note that this research took place in 2019, prior to the coronavirus pandemic. Since March 2020, English classes provided by NGOs across the UK have moved online. I have used a Zoom classroom to teach my students, providing some opportunities for some learners to access classes, but also resulting in some losses in terms of learning. Some participants have found it difficult to access classes because of lack of digital literacy or access to technology. Others have found regularly attending classes easier than before the pandemic, particularly with some women feeling more able to go to class from home, because of child-care or other care responsibilities. El-Metoui and Graham-Brown (2021: 17) reflect that 'In order for any remote and online ESOL offer to be truly successful, education institutions need to invest in resources, training and support for both staff and learners'. Of course, this will be even more challenging for charities supporting refugees, so will require additional government funding. The impacts of the pandemic on refugees and asylum seekers' access to learning in the UK as well as training in digital pedagogy in community ESOL will need further research. The issues highlighted in the original study, particularly the importance of stable funding, are still relevant in the post-Covid-19 time.

Conclusion

The lack of funding for ESOL in the UK, particularly England, has already led to numerous calls for change for more support for learning for refugees (e.g. Refugee Action, 2016, 2019). This study builds a bigger picture of how wider changes in policy and funding (or lack of them) impact communities of people who are seeking asylum in the UK, and it was evident that more secure funding, and support of more flexible non-formal community ESOL classes, are needed. The impacts of wider 'hostile environment' immigration policy, outside of ESOL, echoed through the experiences of ESOL learners and to the volunteer teachers. These also served to motivate the volunteering itself. It is possible that volunteering as an ESOL teacher can be a form of activism working towards social change. The fact that community ESOL classes encourage intercultural learning, and that volunteers learn from the refugees whom they teach implies that learning is an embedded part of this social action. The implementation of the 'hostile environment' therefore seems to have had the multiple impact of triggering both restrictions and resistance. Castles (2001) has asserted that social transformation is certainly not always positive change, and this is reflective of the tensions at play in how volunteering as a teacher might both react to and facilitate change. The act of volunteering for some volunteers was a defiance of the lack of funding for ESOL. Further, the act of learning English for people seeking asylum who would have been otherwise unable to access classes also resisted these policies. However, this study did suggest that this may not be sustainable in the long run, and that ESOL and wider adult education for anyone who needs it, regardless of migration status, should be available. Change is needed at a policy level, not just to provide more funding for adult education, but also in wider immigration policy, which is preventing sanctuary seekers from accessing learning opportunities which those in government themselves say they should do. The study also suggested that in order for people who are not yet retired to be able to volunteer sustainably in the long term as ESOL teachers, some kind of financial support is needed, such as a Basic Income. Sadly, the UK government's New Plan for Immigration (HM Government, 2021), and the

Nationality and Borders Bill (Home Office, 2021), discussed earlier, are a step in the wrong direction and will likely make it even more difficult for people seeking asylum to access adult education. But positives can be seen in the actions of volunteers and learners, who demonstrate how adult learning can resist the neglect of concrete provision for those who desire it to help them to build their lives in the UK.

References

Bales, K. (2013), Universal Credit: Not So Universal? Deconstructing the Impact of the Asylum Support System, *Journal of Social Welfare and Family Law*, 35 (4), 427–43. https://doi.org/10.1080/09649069.2013.851168.

Bennett, S. T. (2018), *Constructions of Migrant Integration in British Public Discourse: Becoming British*, London: Bloomsbury Academic, an imprint of Bloomsbury Publishing Plc.

BIEN (n.d.), *BIEN – Basic Income Earth Network*, Basic Income Earth Network. Retrieved December 2021, from https://basicincome.org/.

Braun, V. and Clarke, V. (2006), Using Thematic Analysis in Psychology, *Qualitative Research in Psychology*, 3 (2), 77–101. https://doi.org/10.1191/1478088706qp063oa.

Castles, S. (2001), Studying Social Transformation, *International Political Science Review*, 22 (1), 13–32. https://doi.org/10.1177/0192512101221002.

Cooke, M. and Peutrell, R. eds. (2019), *Brokering Britain, Educating Citizens: Exploring ESOL and Citizenship*, Bristol: Multilingual Matters.

Cortvriend, A. (2020), Coping with Vulnerability: The Limbo Created by the UK Asylum System, *International Journal for Crime, Justice and Social Democracy*, 9 (3), 61–74. https://doi.org/10.5204/ijcjsd.v9i3.1586.

Craggs, R. (2018), The 2018 Commonwealth Heads of Government Meeting, the Windrush Scandal and the Legacies of Empire, *The Round Table*, 107 (3), 361–2. https://doi.org/10.1080/00358533.2018.1476110.

Creswell, J. (2012), *Educational Research: Planning, Conducting, and Evaluating Quantitative and Qualitative Research*, 4th edition, London: Pearson.

Davies, T., Isakjee, A., Mayblin, L., and Turner, J. (2021), Channel Crossings: Offshoring Asylum and the Afterlife of Empire in the Dover Strait, *Ethnic and Racial Studies*, 44 (13), 2307–27. https://doi.org/10.1080/01419870.2021.1925320.

Dawson, R. (2017), A Snapshot of English Language Teaching in Seven Voluntary Sector Organisations in 2017, [Report]. *Merton Home Tutoring Services*. Available at: https://www.natecla.org.uk/uploads/media/208/16729.pdf.

De Genova, N. P. (2002), Migrant 'Illegality' and Deportability in Everyday Life. *Annual Review of Anthropology*, 31, 419–47.

Deci, E. L. and Ryan, R. M. (2008), Facilitating Optimal Motivation and Psychological Well-Being across Life's Domains. *Canadian Psychology/Psychologie Canadienne, 49* (1), 14–23. https://doi.org/10.1037/0708-5591.49.1.14.

El-Metoui, L. and Graham-Brown, N. (2021), Emerging from the Pandemic: Reflections for the ESOL Sector, *Language Issues: The ESOL Journal, 32* (1), 7–19.

Foster, D. and Bolton, P. (2018), Adult ESOL in England [Briefing], *House of Commons Library*. Available at: https://commonslibrary.parliament.uk/research-briefings/cbp-7905/#fullreport.

Halliday, J. and Brooks, L. (5 July 2019), Johnson Pledges to Make all Immigrants Learn English, *The Guardian*. Available at: https://www.theguardian.com/politics/2019/jul/05/johnson-pledges-to-make-all-immigrants-learn-english.

Heinemann, A. M. B. (2017), The Making of 'Good Citizens': German Courses for Migrants and Refugees, *Studies in the Education of Adults, 49* (2), 177–95. https://doi.org/10.1080/02660830.2018.1453115.

HM Government (2018), Integrated Communities Strategy Green Paper: Building Stronger, More United Communities [Policy green paper], *Ministry of Housing, Communities and Local Government*. Available at: https://assets.publishing.service.gov.uk/government/uploads/system/uploads/attachment_data/file/777160/Integrated_Communities_Strategy_Government_Response.pdf.

HM Government (2021), New Plan for Immigration: Policy Statement, OGL. Available at: https://assets.publishing.service.gov.uk/government/uploads/system/uploads/attachment_data/file/972517/CCS207_CCS0820091708-001_Sovereign_Borders_Web_Accessible.pdf.

Home Office (2021), Nationality and Borders Bill: Factsheet. Available at: https://www.gov.uk/government/publications/the-nationality-and-borders-bill-factsheet/nationality-and-borders-bill-factsheet.

Home Office (2022), Home Secretary's Speech on UK and Rwanda Migration and Economic Development Partnership. Available at: https://www.gov.uk/government/speeches/home-secretarys-speech-on-uk-and-rwanda-migration-and-economic-development-partnership.

Kirkup, J. and Winnett, R. (25 May 2012), Theresa May interview: 'We're Going to Give Illegal Migrants a Really Hostile Reception', *The Telegraph*. Available at: https://www.telegraph.co.uk/news/uknews/immigration/9291483/Theresa-May-interview-Were-going-to-give-illegal-migrants-a-really-hostile-reception.html.

Lewandowski, M. (2021), ESOL in the Times of Pandemic – getting the Full Picture, *Language Issues: The ESOL Journal, 32* (1), 29–33.

Refugee Action (2016), Let Refugees Learn: Challenges and Opportunities to Improve Language Provision to Refugees in England, *Refugee Action*. [Report].

Refugee Action (2019), Turning Words into Action: Why the Government Must Invest Now to Let Refugees Learn (p. 12), *Refugee Action*. Available at: https://www.refugee-action.org.uk/wp-content/uploads/2019/06/Turning-Words-into-Action.pdf.

Refugee Council (2021), Refugee Council Responds to the Home Office's 'New Plan for Immigration', *Refugee Council.* Available at: https://www.refugeecouncil.org.uk/latest/news/refugee-council-responds-to-the-home-offices-new-plan-for-immigration/.

Right to Remain (2021), Asylum Support: Financial Support and Accommodation, *Right to Remain.* Available at: https://righttoremain.org.uk/toolkit/asylum-support/.

Rogers, A. (2014), The Classroom and the Everyday: The Importance of Informal Learning for Formal Learning, *Investigar Em Educação, 2* (1). http://pages.ie.uminho.pt/inved/index.php/ie/article/view/3.

Rogers, H., Fox, S., and Herlihy, J. (2015), The Importance of Looking Credible: The Impact of the Behavioural Sequelae of Post-Traumatic Stress Disorder on the Credibility of Asylum Seekers, *Psychology, Crime and Law, 21* (2), 139–55. https://doi.org/10.1080/1068316X.2014.951643.

Rosenberg, S. (2007), *A Critical History of ESOL in the UK, 1870–2006*, Leicester: National Institute of Adult Continuing Education.

Scottish Government (2015), Welcoming Our Learners: Scotland's ESOL Strategy 2015–2020, [Report] Available at: https://dera.ioe.ac.uk/22892/2/ESOLStrategy2015to2020_tcm4-855848_Redacted.pdf.

Simpson, J. (2015), English Language Learning for Adult Migrants in Superdiverse Britain, in J. Simpson and A. Whiteside (eds.) *Adult Language Education and Migration: Challenging Agendas in Policy and Practice*, 1st edition, 200–13, London: Routledge.

Tuckett, A. (2015), Adult Education, Social Transformation and the Pursuit of Social Justice, *European Journal of Education, 50* (3). https://doi.org/10.1111/ejed.12135.

UNHCR (1) (2021), *What Is a Refugee?* UNHCR UK. Available at: https://www.unhcr.org/uk/what-is-a-refugee.html.

UNHCR (2) (n.d.), Asylum in the UK, UNHCR. Retrieved 31 August 2021, from https://www.unhcr.org/uk/asylum-in-the-uk.html.

UNHCR (3) (2022), UN Refugee Agency Opposes UK Plan to Export Asylum, UNHCR. Available at: https://www.unhcr.org/uk/news/press/2022/4/62585e814/un-refugee-agency-opposes-uk-plan-export-asylum.html.

UNHCR UK (2021), UNHCR Deeply Concerned at Discriminatory Two-tier UK Asylum Plans, Urges Rethink, UNHCR. Available at: https://www.unhcr.org/uk/news/press/2021/5/6097bce14/unhcr-deeply-concerned-at-discriminatory-two-tier-uk-asylum-plans-urges.html.

United Nations (1948), *Universal Declaration of Human Rights.* Available at: https://www.un.org/en/about-us/universal-declaration-of-human-rights.

Webber, F. (2019), On the Creation of the UK's 'hostile environment', *Race and Class, 60* (4), 76–87. https://doi.org/10.1177/0306396819825788.

5

A refugee third sector learning ecology for social change: 'covert activism'

Mary-Rose Puttick
Birmingham City University

Introduction

This chapter explores what adult learning for social change looks like in the refugee third sector in the UK, drawing from a two-year pedagogical ethnography that was part of an affective, participatory methodological approach for my doctoral research. One of the settings for my research was a small refugee organization in the West Midlands, UK. By foregrounding the voices and activities of three women at this setting, through what I have termed 'affective literacy events', I attempt to challenge hierarchical discourses of power from which girls and young women 'are commonly excluded' and to challenge 'issues of voice and representation in the literacies of activism' (Pahl and Rasool, 2020: 53).

Shirin, Entisar and Kejen's voices (all pseudonyms), interwoven with my teacher-researcher affective reflections, illuminate the ways in which diverse activist literacies organically emerged from both formal and informal learning activities within the organization. In this chapter, I argue that these are instances of activism that, for complicated reasons that I will explore throughout the chapter, would not be given special regard under 'normal' circumstances or accounts of activism. I propose that the examples drawn from the three women are also forms of social change that would likely be hidden from knowledge of adult learning in the UK. My research is framed within an approach to literacies informed by everyday social practices, that strives to unearth the powerful and politically rooted nature of what counts as literacy (Street, 1984), and that considers literacies as 'living', in which 'sites and spaces – places – can generate theory about literacy' (Rowsell and Pahl, 2020: 163).

In this chapter, I give an insight into the living literacies at a faith-based refugee charity (for which I use the name 'Trinity') in the West Midlands, England. By foregrounding the voices of Shirin, Entisar and Keje, I hope to bring to the fore the complexity in defining adult learning activities in the third sector, while proposing that this fluidity in terminology plays a useful part in processes of social change. I later use the affective literacy events to inform my conceptualizing of the refugee third sector as a learning ecology for social change, and with it propose some future thinking for research and practice.

The refugee third sector and its role in promoting and responding to social change

The UK's 'third sector' is an umbrella term that encapsulates an expanse of advocacy and activities, from those organized informally in communities by groups with a collective purpose to larger-scale national and international non-government organizations. Organizations within the sector vary according to their size, purpose and defining values or mission, with many organizations spanning multiple definitions and purposes, with external influences such as time-limited funding streams that are also often responsive to changing political events around the world. In capturing the diversity of adult learning activities in the third sector, and with it exploring what social change looks like, in this section I establish some of the literature in terms of the political context and the different types of organizations within the sector.

The term 'third sector' is used synonymously with the voluntary or non-profit sector and is considered to be located somewhere between the state (first sector) and the market (second sector) (Anheier, 2004). Politically, the third sector in the UK increased its public focus following the 2010 to 2015 Coalition government between the Conservatives and the Liberal Democrats: a formation accompanied by the Localism Act 2011, and former prime minister David Cameron's 'Big Society' initiative. The conception of both sought to 'devolve powers to communities and establish a greater role in public services for voluntary and community organisations' (Lowndes and Pratchett, 2012: 30) and was accompanied by a 'new language of social action' (McCabe, 2010: 2), with a particular emphasis on individuals giving their time and resources voluntarily (Civil Exchange, 2015). Soteri-Proctor et al. (2013) refer to the proliferation of grassroots activity in the third sector and, in identifying some defining components of the sector, draw attention to a combination of motivations, personalities, skills, space, information and resources working collectively towards a shared vision, with a focus on local activism, and a common interest in raising the profile of potentially isolated groups.

Griffiths et al. (2005) foreground the distinct role of refugee community organizations (RCOs) in comparison to other third sector organizations, with one such role comprising mediators of legislative communication such as the Equality Act 2010. Research has identified the 'inaccessible' nature of information for refugees navigating the immigration system (Phillimore, 2013), the 'information gaps' in access to and delivery of integration provision (Oduntan, 2018), and the ways in which such information gaps for refugees are bridged through people and places (Oduntan and Ruthven, 2019). RCOs play an important advocacy role that is closely linked to dispersal processes for those seeking asylum, providing accessible information related to housing support, welfare benefits and the asylum process (Mayblin and James, 2019). A report by two refugee organizations distinguishes three underpinning objectives of RCOs including, first, the ways in which RCOs address the needs of their community that are left unmet by public services. Added to this is the work that RCOs do to build bridges with others in order to secure wider social cohesion and the integration of their communities, and third, the ways in which they amplify the voices and concerns of those that use them in order to inform the process of social change (Hemon et al., 2011).

Paralleling the sector as a whole, RCOs vary in size and their political radar, ranging from large NGOs with a national voice such as the Refugee Council and Refugee Action, to those operating at a micro, local level, and those that cross over undefined spaces in-between. As well as their integral role in advocacy and communicative mediation, amongst others, many RCOs also provide adult learning provision, different in nature to government-funded adult learning provision, and often comprising a mixture of formal and informal activities. McCabe's (2010) work brings to the fore the 'below-the-radar' (BTR) sector, within which many smaller RCOs fit. McCabe (2010: 3) defines 'BTR' as 'a shorthand term for small voluntary organisations, community groups and semi-formal and informal activities'. As its name suggests, the BTR sector is in many respects a mysterious entity, and existing research in this area calls for a more detailed understanding of community-based information and insights into volunteering activities within the sector (McCabe, 2010; Ockenden and Hutin, 2008). This image of activities operating 'below-the-radar' chimes also with Falk and Harrison's (1998) recognition of the great deal of 'undercover' activity of community learning more generally, wherein the visibility of sociocultural, economic and environmental realms operates to different extents.

In capturing the nature of adult learning in the sector, it is useful to consider the ways in which activities can be simultaneously in/visible, with social change operating under political and/or wider public radars, perhaps with the importance of the work of activities, groups and organizations overlooked in societal discourses. Soteri-Proctor, in her micro-mapping street-level analysis of two English urban neighbourhoods, attempts to capture the expansive nature of learning activities within the third sector, referring to this picture of activity as '58 varieties of little Big Society' (2011: 10). Soteri-Proctor's research captures the diversity of below-the-radar groups that she was able to distinguish into six prominent categories, including: 'arts and music'; 'multicultural and multiple faith- and ethnic-identities and activities'; 'niche and specialist interest'; 'self-help/mutual-support'; 'single-identity cultural, faith and ethnic activities'; and 'social club-based activities' (2011: 10). While attempting to categorize such groups, Soteri-Proctor's (2011) research also illuminates the complexities in defining informal learning activities which operate in diverse and contemporaneous guises.

I propose that integral to informing knowledge of adult learning within the third sector it is important also to consider the disruptions and interruptions affected by locality and temporality that guide the continually changing nature of community learning. For example, my research occurred at a historical moment of immense political changes in European history, with the UK leaving the European Union in January 2020: a change accompanied by heightened animosity towards individuals from diverse migrant backgrounds. I argue that this hostility, and its accompanying fear, is ever more urgent to consider in light of the recently passed new UK immigration legislation, the Nationality and Borders Bill (2021–2). This new legislation threatens to effectively criminalize the seeking of asylum and destabilize notions of citizenship (UNHCR, 2021). Such political changes call for the need to foreground the integral work of those involved in the refugee third sector, as well as refugee organizations as a whole, operating within a precarious and volatile political climate.

The refugee third sector encapsulates a picture of collective activism: with activism taking place in often symbolic and covert forms, fulfilling an organizational role in negotiating and enabling access to resources in order to mobilize the agency of individuals and groups. This role is increasingly integral when considering that community knowledge is often regarded as having 'a lower ranking than other forms of knowledge' (Rasool, 2017: 314). As such, community activism can be viewed as productively challenging unjust societal narratives and acts of inequity. This collective aspect is also important, with some literature referring to contested definitions of 'activist' that can place too much importance on the individual at the expense of overlooking the collective nature of social movements (Rombalski, 2020). Of additional importance is Pahl and Rasool's conceptualization of community activism as a 'powerful tool for people made invisible by changes in our physical, social, and political landscapes to reclaim their own histories and achieve justice' (2020: 64). Taken together, community activism is thus demonstrated in the literature to be an active and enabling process that has the capacity to make important and interchangeable changes across a spectrum of the individual to the collective.

Making meaningful activist literacies

I start this section by raising some further important questions in terms of how community activism is defined and 'who gets to define it'. It therefore feels fitting to start this dialogue with the poignant words of Shahin Shah:

> Racism. That word. Real racism. It always rears its ugly head and those people who experience unkind and unforgiven words cannot forget them. The words are left unforgiven not because they are unforgiveable, but because forgiveness has never sought for either word or action. So the racism is left unforgiven.
>
> (Shah, 2018: 56)

As an educated white woman from an economically privileged country, carrying out research with women from refugee and newly arrived migration contexts, it is my deep-rooted belief that uncomfortable questions of racism, privilege and, with them, social inequalities need to remain at the forefront of any research and practice in the third sector. I propose that this needs to become a constant dialogue that is made visible and that strives to disrupt. In this chapter, this dialogue becomes a primary tool for informing understandings of the nature of activist literacies and pushes me to continuously question what this means in terms of adult learning for social change. This understanding is also aided by the experiences I gained from my doctoral research (Puttick, 2021a), in which I brought to the fore what my own living activism looked like. This included my diverse voluntary roles over the last five years in different third sector organizations, including two RCOs and a homeless charity, one of which was Trinity Centre, the setting focused on in this chapter, and for which I now continue to volunteer. My activism includes the time and resources I have contributed in different forms of literacy teaching, involvement in food and clothing dispersal for newly arrived families, and more recently welfare and asylum guide roles during the Covid-19 pandemic. A vital part of my learning from these experiences is that activism goes much deeper than these physical activities: for me it has become an embodied part of me that I will now make a lifelong commitment to. This is a commitment not only in terms of my time and energy, but a more deep-rooted commitment, particularly in the way it crosses over with my academic research role that demands of me to constantly interrogate my place in the wider social inequalities and discrimination that have prevailed throughout history. This is something that I argue needs to be repeated and revisited: 'fundamentally, my volunteering experiences have also challenged me to critically reflect on my position at a much deeper and political level: that is in terms of my place within Britain's history of colonisation' (Puttick, 2021b: 2).

Before transitioning into the examples of community activism brought to the fore by three women at the Trinity Centre, I keep in mind Pahl and Rasool's definition of literacies of activism that are 'collaborative, which produces accounts of literacy research that are rooted in questions of voice, power, and diversity and who gets to tell the story' (2020: 52). I frame each of the women's accounts around the notion of the 'literacy event', which in Heath's (1983) terms had a visible textual component as central, and which I expand to include more widely 'observable instantiations of practice' (Burnett et al., 2014: 2).

Although the accounts of Shirin, Entisar and Kejen's activities come to some extent from my voice, emanating from my ethnographic research journals, I do so from a place of deep respect for the women and my desire to learn from them, and from a larger piece of research underpinned by principles of co-production, dialogue and shared decision-making. In the three insights below, I also propose that 'voice' went beyond solely oral communication but importantly the notion of voice as embodied and entangled within relational cultural and historical aspects, and responsive to, and affected by, space and place. In this chapter, I therefore also bring to the fore affective dimensions intertwined within the literacy events. Through the voices and activities of the three women I attempt to give multifaceted insights in terms of the learning activities that took place within the setting that expanded out into the home and across digital spaces, and into what social action, and in the long-term social change, looked like in these three contexts. In order to establish the organizational context, I begin first with a picture of the expanse of advocacy and learning activities at Trinity.

Trinity Centre

Established in 1999, Trinity is an interesting example of a below-the-radar faith-based organization that has grown in size and now operates as one strand of a larger, more formalized, regional social care charity. Trinity maintains some characteristics of a BTR due to its reliance upon voluntary staff, the small number of paid roles reliant on fixed or short-term contracts, and its vulnerability in terms of survival, that is sensitive to uncertainties in the funding climate (Puttick, 2021a). The funding for Trinity is complex and intersects political (such as local council and larger government) as well as non-political, charitable funding streams. Trinity serves the wider local community, particularly supporting individuals with issues of addiction, as well as operating as an advocate for individuals going through the UK asylum process with a particular focus on individuals and families at risk of destitution. In terms of adult learning activities for individuals from refugee and asylum-seeking backgrounds, Trinity provides English for Speakers of Other Languages (ESOL) classes and International English Language Testing System (IELTS). Additional learning provision, often of a more informal, and sometimes shorter-term nature, includes family literacy, music classes and computer skills support. Advocacy support, such as baby packs, food and clothing provision, also at times crosses-over into the fluid nature of formal and informal learning provision.

Keje: Advocacy as affective and embodied

I met Keje when I first started volunteering at Trinity Centre in 2017. Keje, originally from Kurdistan, had arrived in the UK in 2013 and first accessed the Trinity Centre for ESOL classes. At this time, she was going through the asylum process and was unable to access ESOL provision at government-funded institutions due to funding regulations which restricted people seeking asylum accessing classes for their first six months of being in the UK. When enrolling for the ESOL class, Keje told me that she was also directed to additional support in the form of advice on the asylum process, as well as food boxes during a time in which she was struggling financially. Two years after her initial arrival, although she had by this time been rehoused further away, Keje continued to attend ESOL classes at Trinity and had also started voluntary employment at the centre, gaining experience in a variety of advocacy and administrative roles.

By the time I met Keje, her asylum case had been approved the year before and she was now working as a paid member of staff at the centre as an Advice Worker in both internal and outreach modes. This role involved her giving advice and assessing the immediate needs of refugees and those going through the asylum process across a diverse range such as housing, social and welfare support. Like two other paid staff at the centre who had also previously accessed learning or advocacy support at the centre, Keje's voice was distinct, coming from an inside place of shared experience with many of the clients who accessed the centre. Her work was reflective of that referred to in the literature as a 'community bricoleur': that is, individuals from specific cultural communities who do critical work coordinating, maintaining and building community sector provision, acting as mediator, intermediary or gatekeeper between the provision and the community (Hemon and Grove-White, 2011; Soteri-Proctor, 2011).

Keje had also attended training through the organization in community research methods and was a community researcher on two projects alongside researchers from a university in the West Midlands region of England: a project addressing health inequalities through language support, and another project exploring the lived experiences of individuals seeking asylum who had had their asylum claim refused. Whenever I saw Keje at the centre, she was always incredibly busy, yet remained calm and positive, with a long queue of people to see her on advice clinic days as well as her supporting individuals and families through a language perspective as an informal interpreter of both Kurdish Sorani and Arabic. Referring specifically to emergency conflict situations at refugee border camps, Todorova (2019: 157) asserts that through the mediation process the interpreter holds a special position; becoming an 'active participant' that can support empowerment by providing essential cultural knowledge and being a strong advocate for individuals, particularly in highly sensitive and affecting situations. I propose that the same process is applicable in the case of Trinity whereby Keje embodied advocacy in multiple forms at the border intersections of powerful political discourses of migrant policy, lived experiences and shared empathy.

During my ethnographic doctoral research at the centre, Keje supported me as an informal interpreter during my university's consent process as well as at different points throughout the two years in ethical decision-making processes. As well as supporting me in an informal interpreting capacity for my research, Keje played an important role in supporting Aza, one of the Kurdish mothers in my family literacy class who had lived in Birmingham only a short time and was going through the UK asylum process. As well as attending the class with her youngest child, Aza had a primary school-aged son of ten years old and she would often bring his homework into the class and become noticeably upset and frustrated that she was unable to understand all of the text and tasks. Although I could not understand the words that Keje used when she took time out of the advice clinic to call in and speak to Aza at the end of our class, I could sense the affective and soothing nature of her words and actions and the ease at which she put Aza who was navigating the multiple bureaucratic literacies of school, migration and welfare with little opportunity to have the literacies with which she had arrived to be acknowledged and valued. It was the valuing of what I term 'transitory literacies' that I strove to bring to the fore with the mothers in our co-produced pedagogies of family literacy (Puttick, 2021a) and with it an appreciation of Keje's, as well as the Trinity community as a whole's, place within that.

Shirin: Expanding repertoires and preserving cultural heritage

Shirin was in my family literacy class at Trinity when I took it over in September 2017 and she attended the class with her four-year-old daughter Aina. To set the context of the class, the family literacy class was not attached to any external funding streams at Trinity Centre and was solely voluntarily run. Shirin had been a student at Trinity since 2012 and attended the ESOL and family literacy class for different periods, in-between having two children, over the five years prior to my meeting her. Shirin would often refer to this temporality in self-dissenting terms: in terms of what she viewed as her lack of progression over the years in standardized ESOL terms, paralleling the powerful societal deficit discourses in relation to migrant parenting (e.g. Lareau, 1987; McCaleb, 1994) and deficit school-based literacy positionings according to social class (Auerbach, 1995; Street, 1997). Importantly, Crooks (2017: ii) refers to such deficit thinking as 'racialized and racializing', calling for acknowledgement of 'the significance of settler colonialism in shaping literacy practice'.

Rather than being English dominated, the Trinity mothers, their children and I had together cultivated an environment rooted in values of multilingualism and of literacy repertoires that comprised 'linguistic, semiotic and sociocultural resources' (Blackledge and Creese, 2017: 77) such as the use of visual and artefactual modes of learning, and communication modes through the body. Our shared literacy repertoire can thus be viewed as drawing on our transitory literacies, with teaching emanating outwards from the mothers, and a bespoke model of learning emerging from this negotiation.

In one class, I introduced the mothers to what became, at the mothers' instigation, a six-week poetry sharing. In the first session I shared with the mothers some poetry that had been written by a women's writing group, all of whom were attending ESOL classes, and were seeking asylum (Women Asylum Seekers Together, 2013). The poems were short and in accessible language (in this book written in English) and we were able to use the lines of the poems as prompts for discussion and to share some shared meanings and dialogues across the mothers' languages of Pashto, Dari, Kurdish Sorani, and Albanian.

Following this first session and the mothers' clear enthusiasm for the task, I asked them if they would like me to bring in some poetry from each of their languages and invited them to bring in any that they had too. The following week I took in a poem in the Pashto script that I had found in a collection of Afghan women's poetry to show Shirin. On seeing the poem, Shirin reacted with a mixture of what appeared to be both delight at the idea, accompanied with sadness as she told me she was unable to read the script. In response, I searched for the audio recordings of poetry I had found on the Internet from an Afghan women's writing group, yet discovered they were in Dari rather than Pashto. 'That's OK,' Shirin responded: 'I can speak Dari as well.' In this example, revisiting the notion of the literacy repertoire is important. Lorimer-Leonard (2017: 12) asserts that 'literacy is revalued because it moves' and posits the concept of 'literate valuation' as one way to conceptualize this process. Elaborating further, Lorimer-Leonard explains: 'multilingual migrants regularly experience the effects ... of economic or social forces that revalue their literate resources' (2017: 12). As Lorimer-Leonard (2017: 7) elaborates, the repertoire is a term that emphasizes what it '*has* rather than what it *lacks*'. The fluidity of the process of migration therefore can change the worth of literacies in societal structures, and flux can impact psychologically on language users and their feeling of freedom to use multiple languages at/with ease and across sites (Badwan, 2021). Shirin's words signify a shift from autonomous models in which literacy repertoires can be seen as a fixed, prescribed set of reading and writing skills to one in which she draws on her rich oral linguistic skills through her use of merging of three languages in the poetry task.

I played one of the poems and Shirin spoke enigmatically to Farzana, whose first language was Dari. Together, they gave us a translation of the poem by an anonymous Afghan woman who was speaking out about issues affecting women in Afghanistan. In a mixture of Pashto, Dari and English, Shirin and Farzana together shared with us the important tradition of oral storytelling and poetry among collective groups of women in Afghanistan and the 22-syllable secret poems speaking out about gender-based and political issues, that I later discovered are translated as 'landays', for which many Afghan women have died throughout history.

In the following class, Shirin arrived in an evidently excited mood and said that she had something to share with us all. She produced the Pashto poem from the previous week and said that her daughter had translated it into English, and she also had recorded her daughter on her phone saying the poem aloud so that we could listen to the Pashto words while we looked at the words in English. I felt deeply affected by this and asked more about her daughter. Shirin told me that Gulnoor was nine years old and that she had been learning Pashto at their local masjid, including in both oral and written forms for two years, and talked of how proud she was particularly that she was learning to read and write the Pashto script as she herself could not:

> I want to give my children, but especially my daughters, the opportunities that I did not have …. and to enable them to pass on my family's language to their children in the future.
>
> (Translated from Pashto, February 2019)

Gedalof's (e.g. 2009) and Erel's (e.g. 2011; 2013) work illuminates the silent or invisible cultural and caring work of mothers from migrant backgrounds, which, they claim, is in effect a process of modern-day labour exploitation and which contributes to essential citizenship work for the State. Erel refers to the necessary grounding of mothers' cultural and caring work in processes of 'agency, reflection and creativity' (2013: 975). Moreover, in Erel's (2013) research with Kurdish mothers in London, mothers are referred to as *performing* shared intergenerational belonging through the performative and pedagogic character of their work with their children. I propose that Shirin and her daughter's poetry event became a performative and pedagogic family literacy practice that was working towards intergenerational social change: Shirin had opened up opportunities for her daughter's literacy repertoire that would support the maintenance of cultural heritage as well as development of life skills, that would support her in such aspects as future employment.

Entisar: Instigating international dialogue

Entisar is a Sudanese doctor, specializing in women's health. When she joined the IELTS class at Trinity in 2019, she had refugee status. Like all of her peers, Entisar was attending the IELTS classes twice a week as a route to employment in the National Health Service (NHS). For this she was required to gain enough points on the IELTS examination in order for her to be able to then take the professional qualification through the British Medical Council. As Trinity was one of the only providers of free IELTS provision specifically for those from refugee backgrounds across the whole of the West Midlands, many of the students travelled a considerable distance to attend classes. During this period, many of the students spoke of the challenges faced by the test requirements and, as the IELTS teacher what I argue was a Western-centric privileging of the test format.

Entisar had shared with me how, during the year I taught the class, she and her children had had to move their living accommodation three times to different parts of the city. Her three children were spread across two different primary schools but to avoid disruption for them she spoke of spending considerable time and money on public transport every day to get them to school. Entisar never missed any of the IELTS classes and spoke of her determination to continue her GP career in the UK. She spoke regularly of her involvement in a US-based online platform whose manifesto seeks to support women around the world to motivate, speak out, guide and support other women, as well as to build a powerful network to make global changes in health.

During that year, I invited the IELTS students to contribute a piece of writing for a practice-based academic literacy journal I collaborate in, as a way of giving voice to their medical stories or, indeed, anything else they wanted to write about. Five of the students decided to participate and had their stories published. I respected how Entisar, through this process, chose to write about her role as an activist for women's health, something that had developed since moving to the UK when she became professionally displaced. Her article elaborated how she had become a regular blog writer on health-related issues such as reproductive health and breastfeeding. Reading her account was deeply affecting and really brought home the powerful nature of her writing and her passion for speaking out on an international platform for women's health. Of this process, Entisar shared:

> I have felt the freedom to discuss issues considered taboo, such as women's lives and rights after divorce. I have talked about health challenges that women face,

such as maternal mortality and reproductive health. I have touched on some political issues which have arisen in Africa recently. I believe it speeds up the space and pace towards global gender equality and is for women everywhere … it is a global social network where every woman's voice can rise up to transform her community and to change her life and other women's lives.

(Entisar in Puttick, 2019)

Research refers to refugee medical practitioners in the context of the NHS as a 'wasted', 'valuable' and 'critical' resource (Berlin et al., 1997; Stewart, 2002). Berlin et al.'s (1997) study brought to the fore several complex challenges refugees face in comparison to other overseas doctors such as: financial hardship, psychological distress due to the circumstances of their departure, experiences of loss and persecution, ambiguity regarding legal status and experiences of racism in the new environment. Such factors continue to be echoed in current research of refugee doctors in the NHS (e.g. Butler and Al Sharou, 2020; Willott and Stevenson, 2013). Despite not yet being able to gain professional recognition in the NHS, Entisar's actions embodied a valuable and critical resource: she was engaging in a self-organized activist movement that sat on the edge of her formalized IELTS education. This activist movement, I propose, was in many ways instigated by her existence in a liminal space between her professional recognition in Sudan and her lack of professional recognition in the UK. Entisar had, in this way, found an alternative outlet to speak out and reach out to a much wider audience for the purpose of social change, to instigate a dialogue with women all over the world in ways that were perhaps influenced also by the temporality and locality in which she now wrote from.

Conceptualizing the refugee third sector as a learning ecology for social change

Speaking to Rowsell and Pahl's (2020) proposition of theories of literacies as informed by place and across sites, the voices and activist literacies of Keje, Shirin and Entisar in different ways encapsulate the relational nature of the refugee third sector, the inseparability of its parts, and of learning that takes place beyond the physicality of the organization. I argue that Haugan's conceptualization of 'language ecology' adds pertinence to this understanding, encompassing psychological and sociological dimensions that are responsive to the language users and their social and natural environment: 'determined primarily by the people who learn it, use it, and transmit it to others' (2006: 57).

Pedagogically, Gutiérrez et al. (2011: 259) add to this conceptualization a focus on a multiliteracies approach in the learning ecology: multilingual practices 'mediated by meaningful relations, historicized and expansive notions of learning, distributed expertise, technologies, multiliteracies, and multilingualism', that value experimentation and multiagency across interconnecting strands of the learning environment. Adding to this, Rombalski (2020) calls for us to expand our notion of pedagogies beyond a focus on content and skills, towards one of interconnectedness, re-framed structures and collective work.

The insights of Keje, Shirin and Entisar brought to the fore activist literacies that were working towards multi-layered forms of social change in the home, the family, access and knowledge of gender-related healthcare, and of advocacy, mediation and empowerment operating at differing levels of society, much of which was previously invisible. Interwoven within their literacy activism was my own activism that was affected by my own multifaceted roles as volunteer, teacher, student, researcher and peer: always complicated by my place within deeply embedded historical and societal intersectional inequalities, in this case particularly racial and gender inequalities. I now recognize the privileged position my role in the university institution gives me in terms of the visibility of my activism: something that I seek to disrupt in my call for the amplifying of women's voices in asset-based community learning ecologies and the equal recognition of their problematically 'covert' activist literacies. The chapter brings to the fore the ways in which, often contradictory, notions of activism within the Academy become entangled with those of individual activism, as well as institutional third sector activism, and how the adult learning in this chapter cut across all facets: aspects in which I was also an adult learner and in which adult learning went beyond solely activities in the classroom.

Future thinking for social change

I concur with Rasool's highlighting of 'the importance of the capacity building of women through writing groups and community-based projects that support women's activism and that give them the confidence to speak out' and in the long term, that policy is informed by the recognition that communities 'are experts in their own lives' (2018: 8). Integrally, I propose that this capacity building should be underpinned by a dialogic and flexible environment in which the women lead what collective women's activism looks like in their context. In this chapter, social change was illuminated by the actions of Keje in her multiple practical roles and meaningful knowledge sharing and language support for Aza, by Shirin's instigation with the Pashto poem and hers and Farzana's historical knowledge sharing, and by Entisar's voice on an international platform that intersected with digital spaces, health, social and academic fields. I propose that refugee community organizations should be considered as multivoiced, living, learning ecologies and that future practice-research in the third sector should strive to illuminate these voices in diverse ways and mobilize the hopeful nature of this ecology for social change.

References

Anheier, H. (2004), Third Sector-Third Way: Comparative Perspectives and Policy Reflections, in Lewis, J. and Surender, R. (eds.), *Welfare State Change: Towards a Third Way*, Vol. 1, 111–34, New York: Oxford University Press.

Auerbach, E. (1995), Deconstructing the Discourse of Strengths in Family Literacy, *Journal of Reading Behaviour*, 27 (4), 643–61.

Berlin, A., Gill, P., and Eversley, J. (1997), Refugee Doctors in Britain: A Wasted Resource: Helping Them Would Help the Health Service, *British Medical Journal*, 315 (1), 264–5.

Badwan, K., 2021. *Language in a globalised world: Social justice perspectives on mobility and contact*. Springer Nature. Switzerland.

Blackledge, A., and Creese, A. (2017), Translanguaging in Mobility, in S. Canagarajah (ed.), *The Routledge Handbook of Migration and Language*, 31–46, London: Taylor and Francis.

Burnett, C., Davies, J., Merchant, G., and Rowsell, J. (2014), Changing Contexts for 21st Century Literacies, in C. Burnett, J. Davies, G. Merchant, and J. Rowsell (eds.), *New Literacies around the Globe: Policy and Pedagogy*, 1–13, New York and London: Routledge.

Butler, C. and Al Sharou, K., (2020), Voices of Refugee Doctors in the United Kingdom: An Exploration of Their Linguistic and Cultural Needs and Aspirations, in F.M. Federici and C. Declercq (eds.), *Intercultural Crisis Communication: Translation, Interpreting and Languages in Local Crises,*. Vol. 1, 173–90, London: Bloomsbury Academic.

Crooks, S. R. (2017), Family Literacy and Colonial Logics, PhD Thesis Toronto, Canada: University of Toronto.

Erel, U. (2011), Reframing Migrant Mothers as Citizens. *Citizenship Studies*, 15 (6–7), 695–709. DOI: 10.1080/13621025.2011.600076.

Erel, U. (2013), Kurdish Migrant Mothers in London Enacting Citizenship, *Citizenship Studies* 17 (8), 970–84. Available at: DOI: 10.1080/13621025.2013.851146.

Falk, I. and Harrison, L. (1998), Community Learning and Social Capital: 'Just Having a Little Chat', *Journal of Vocational Education and Training*, 50 (4), 609–27.

Gedalof, I. (2009), Birth, Belonging and Migrant Mothers: Narratives of Reproduction in Feminist Migration Studies, *Feminist Review*, 93 (1), 81–100.

Griffiths, D., Sigona, N., and Zetter, R. (2005), *Refugee Community Organisations and Dispersal*, Bristol: Policy Press.

Gutiérrez, K. D., Bien, A. C., Selland, M. K., and Pierce, D. M. (2011), Polylingual and Polycultural Learning Ecologies: Mediating Emergent Academic Literacies for Dual Language Learners, *Journal of Early Childhood Literacy*, 11 (2), 232–61.

Haugan, E. (2006), The Ecology of Language, in A. Fill and P. Muhlhausler (eds.), *Ecolinguistics Reader: Language, Ecology and Environment*, London: Continuum.

Heath, S. (1983), *Ways with Words: Language, Life and Work in Communities and Classrooms*, 57–66, Cambridge, UK: Cambridge University Press.

Hemon, K., Grove-White, R., and Anderson, L. (2011), *Migrant Communities and the 'Big Society' Report, March 2011*. [pdf], London: MRCF and MRN. Available at: https://migrantsorganise.org/wp-content/uploads/Migrant-Communities-and-the-Big-Society-report-MRCF-2011.pdf Accessed 27 August 2016.

Lareau, A. (1987), Social Class Differences in Family-School Relationships: The Importance of Cultural Capital, *Sociology of Education*, 60 (2), 73–85.

Lorimer-Leonard, R. (2017), *Writing on the Move: Migrant Women and the Value of Literacy*, Pittsburgh: University of Pittsburgh Press.

Lowndes, V. and Pratchett, L. (2012), Local Governance under the Coalition Government: Austerity, Localism and the 'Big Society', *Local Government Studies*, 38 (1), 21–40.

Mayblin, L. and James, P. (2019), Asylum and Refugee Support in the UK: Civil Society Filling the Gaps? *Journal of Ethnic and Migration Studies*, 45 (3), 375–94.

McCabe, A. (2010), *Below the Radar in a Big Society? Reflections on Community Engagement, Empowerment and Social Action in a Changing Policy Context*, [pdf] Birmingham: Third Sector Research Centre (Third Sector Research Centre Working Paper 51). Available at: https://www.birmingham.ac.uk/Documents/college-social-sciences/social-policy/tsrc/working-papers/briefing-paper-51.pdf Accessed 13 June 2018.

McCaleb, S. P. (1994), *Building a Community of Learners: A Collaboration among Teachers, Students, Families, and Community*, Mahwah, NJ: Erlbaum.

Ockenden, N. and Hutin, M. (2008), Volunteering to Lead: A Study of Leadership in Small, Volunteer-Led Groups. *Institute for Volunteering Research*. Available at: https://Volunteering-to-lead-study-of-leadership-volunteer-led-groups.pdf Accessed 20 May 2020.

Pahl, K. and Rasool, Z. (2020), Disrupting: The Literacies of Activism, in K. Pahl and J. Rowsell (eds.), *Living Literacies: Literacy for Social Change*, 49–66, Cambridge, Massachusetts: MIT Press.

Phillimore, J. (2013), Housing Home and Neighbourhood in the Era of Superdiversity, *Housing Studies*, 28 (5), 682–700.

Puttick, M-R. (2019), Creativity in Writing: Stories from the Medical Field, *RaPAL Journal*, 98 (1), 18–24.

Puttick, M-R. (2021a), Reimagining Family Literacy: Co-Creating Pedagogies with Migrating Mothers in Third Sector Spaces, PhD Thesis, Birmingham, UK: Birmingham City University.

Puttick, M-R. (2021b), Artefactual Co-Creations: Developing Practice-Based Research with Somali Women in a Third Sector Family Literacy Class, *Studies in the Education of Adults*, 53 (2), 165–83.

Oduntan, O. (2018), Navigating Social Systems: Information Behaviour in Refugee Integration, PhD Thesis, Glasgow: University of Strathclyde.

Oduntan, O. and Ruthven, I. (2019), People and Places: Bridging the Information Gaps in Refugee Integration, *Journal of the Association for Information Science and Technology*, 72 (1), 83–96.

Rasool, Z. (2017), Collaborative Working Practices: Imagining Better Research Partnerships, *Research for All*, 1 (2): 310–22. DOI: https://doi.org/10.18546/RFA.01.2.08

Rasool, Z. (2018), Faith, Culture and Identity: The Everyday Literacy Practices, in D. Bloome, M. L. Castanheira, C. Leung, and J. Rowsell (eds.), *Re-Theorizing Literacy Practices: Complex Social and Cultural Contexts*, 209–20, New York: Routledge.

Rombalski, A. (2020), I Believe That We Will Win! Learning from Youth Activist Pedagogies, *Curriculum Inquiry*, 50 (1), 28–53.

Rowsell, J. and Pahl, K. (2020), Applying a Living Literacies Approach, in K. Pahl and J. Rowsell (eds.), *Living Literacies: Literacy for Social Change*, 163–8, Cambridge, Massachusetts: MIT Press.

Shah, S. (2018), Silk and Steel, in E. Campbell and K. Pahl (eds.), (2018), *Re-Imagining Contested Communities: Connecting Rotherham Through Research*, Policy Press.

Soteri-Proctor, A. (2011), *Little Big Societies: Micro-Mapping of Organisations Operating below the Radar*, [pdf] Birmingham: Third Sector Research Centre (Third Sector Research Centre Working Paper 71). Available at: http://epapers.bham.ac.uk/1550/ Accessed 22 December 2017.

Soteri-Proctor, A., Phillimore, J., and McCabe, A. (2013), Grassroots Civil Society at the Crossroads: Staying on the Path to Independence or Turning onto the UK Government's Route to Localism? *Development in Practice*, 23 (8), 1022–33.

Stewart, E. (2002), Refugee Doctors in the UK, *British Medical Journal*, 325 (7373), 166–7.

Street, B. V. (1984), *Literacy in Theory and Practice*, Cambridge: Cambridge University Press.

Street, B. V. (1997), The Implications of the 'New Literacy Studies' for Literacy Education, *English in Education*, 31 (3), 45–59.

Todorova, M. (2019), Interpreting for Refugees: Empathy and Activism, in C. Declercq and F. M. Federici (eds.), *Intercultural Crisis Communication: Translation, Interpreting and Languages in Local Crises,* 153–71, London: Bloomsbury Publishing.

United Nations High Commission for Refugees (2021), UNHCR Observations on the New Plan for Immigration Policy Statement of the Government of the United Kingdom, Available at: https://www.unhcr.org/uk/publications/legal/60950ed64/unhcr-observations-on-the-new-plan-for-immigration-uk.html.

Willott, J., and Stevenson, J. (2013), Attitudes to Employment of Professionally Qualified Refugees in the United Kingdom, *International Migration* 51 (5), 120–32. ISSN 0020–7985. DOI: https://doi.org/10.1111/imig.12038

Women Asylum Seekers Together (2013), *Past, Present, Future: WAST Women Writing*, Manchester: Big Lottery Fund.

6

Discussion groups with older people: an interface of participatory ageing and social change

Kathleen Lane, University of East Anglia

This chapter describes discussion groups with older people who live in sheltered-housing, focusing on the participatory nature of the activity and elements of social change revealed among those who engage in it. Sheltered-housing for older people in the United Kingdom (UK), elsewhere often called assisted living, provides a supportive environment consisting of accommodation, typically flats or bungalows, and facilities including wardens and emergency safety alarms. Additional support and facilities can wary widely across individual sheltered-housing schemes, but nearly all schemes in the UK expect that residents can live independently. In the case discussed here, approximately seventy-five to eighty older adults ranging in age from seventy to over ninety years, the majority in their mid- to late eighties, live independently in a privately owned and managed sheltered-housing community in Norwich. Residents in this complex, whether self-funding or in receipt of social assistance, rent their accommodation.

In early 2010, I approached the manager of the sheltered-housing scheme to propose offering a discussion group once a month. I explained that my aim was to increase socialization and links among residents through conversations focused on a monthly topic which I would suggest. Permission was given, the manager recommending the on-site communal facility as the venue (a place familiar to residents, as it was used for diverse activities, including coffee mornings, singing groups and craft fairs). The discussion groups began in April 2010 and continued until March 2020 when they were suspended owing to the Covid-19 pandemic.

Discussion groups were held on a Saturday morning each month throughout the year, though seldom in December and very occasionally not in one of the summer months if I was away. Although I am a university-based researcher, it was not in this capacity that I volunteered to lead the discussion groups. I have long-standing professional and voluntary interest in older people's well-being and voice and had introduced a discussion group at a small sheltered-housing scheme in Cambridge, when I had lived there for two years. On returning to Norwich, I explored the possibility of introducing this activity in another sheltered-housing setting.

The discussion groups were open to all residents at the scheme. Both women and men attended, though women outnumbered men for reasons likely to include the much greater proportion of females living there, which in turn reflects the difference in longevity between males and females. I have not explored whether gendered differences in participating in a discussion group-type of activity also account for the greater number of women participants. My hoped-for aim in the discussion groups was that purposeful conversation would help to promote social engagement among attendees, foster participation within a safe, inclusive setting and provide a place where common ground could be discovered with the potential to generate new links among the participating residents.

Prior to the start of each session, I arranged a space within the large communal room suitable for conversation by pulling two long tables together at one end of the room and placing chairs around them. The discussion group was held for one hour from mid- to late Saturday mornings and residents tended to arrive between five and ten minutes before it started. I greeted residents as they arrived and offered each a cup of tea or coffee. Across the ten years of the discussion groups, average attendance ranged between eight and twelve; on several occasions, fourteen to sixteen residents attended. Maximum attendance was eighteen (one occasion), and minimum attendance was three (also on one occasion). Four to six residents came to nearly all of the discussion groups, while another six or seven usually came to several or to alternate sessions. Some residents attended sporadically; a very few came for a short period, anywhere between three and six sessions, then did not return. Owing to changes in health, often related to mobility or energy levels, some participants either decreased or stopped attending. Given the age group of those at the discussion groups, it should not be surprising that, over ten years, some residents moved from sheltered-housing into long-term care to meet their need for greater support and that other residents passed away.

At the initial discussion group, I began by introducing myself, welcoming the residents and setting out the general purpose of the activity: to discuss a topic on which individual views and opinions were expressed. The hope was to create a lively, respectful forum for exchanging and listening to others' views and where people might gain new insights or perspectives within an enjoyable social activity. Topics would cover a wide range of subject-matter, from the familiar to the less familiar and range across political, historical, cultural and every-day matters. I emphasized that the discussion group was not a reminiscence session, though people would very likely draw on their own experiences, which was welcome whether these were current or from the past.

At the initial session, I also suggested that ground rules be established for the discussion group. These were agreed to be: each person was entitled to their opinion; differences would be respected; everyone would maintain a safe, courteous space for expressing views, especially if these were minority views; and participants would try to avoid talking over or interrupting others who were speaking. Ground rules were repeated at the following two or three sessions and whenever a newcomer joined the discussion group. (Of these ground rules, the one which often needed a gentle reminder was the residents talking, often very animatedly, over one another. This reminder was voiced by myself but also by the residents themselves.)

Once the residents were seated, a typical session began with a greeting to everyone collectively and then my suggesting the topic. At the inaugural discussion, the topic was: What are the pros and cons of compulsory voting? Other topics across the ten years included:

- Truth seems to be getting a hammering in today's world. Is it particularly hard now or has it always been this way?
- What do you think about using technology such as robotics and sensors in the home?
- When you were young, what did you consider 'old-fashioned' in your parents or your grandparents?
- Do you have a favourite book that you would recommend to others – and why?
- It has just been reported that the chief executive of a national house-builder has received £75 million in pay: what are your views on corporate salaries?
- Is the law always just?
- What is the most interesting invention that you know of, whether invented in your lifetime or long ago, and why?

As reflected in the above examples, topics ranged widely and on occasion I chose a topic which deliberately invoked the past or a comparison with the past. No topic was received with negativity or silence. The group engaged with the topics, often very enthusiastically. Although no one was asked to disclose personal circumstances, the impression I gained from conversations across ten years was that attendees reflected a mixture of middle- and lower-middle class backgrounds, ethnicity was predominantly white British and attendees' educational history mostly that of school-leavers with a few obtaining professional qualifications (e.g. two nurses, one teacher).

Frequently a diversity of views was expressed but, even when clear differences of opinion were aired, none appeared to provoke hostility from others attending the group. In year five of the discussion groups, an exception occurred when a new resident who joined interrupted the flow of conversation and injected sharp or sarcastic retorts in a distinct contrast to the atmosphere previously established. The disruptive resident may not have been aware of the extent to which this behaviour appeared to unsettle many of the others. Without singling out the resident and demonstrating from my body language that I was speaking to the whole group, I repeated on two occasions our ground rules of respecting differences and maintaining pleasant conversation. The last session attended by the disruptive resident discussed the topic, 'do you have a favourite book that you would recommend to others – and why'. The resident engaged more enthusiastically than in any of the previous groups attended and exhibited none of the snappiness or interruptions from previous occasions. I do not know why this resident did not attend again. It may also be relevant to point out that I neither attached significance to a male exhibiting the disruptive behaviour nor was aware of discussions becoming dominated by the few male attendees. Gender dynamics, including leading the talk in groups, have been reported in some research on learning for older adults (de Medeiros et al., 2007), but this never appeared to have an impact in the discussion groups described here.

Another feature of the discussions is that veering off-topic happened on several occasions, which I did not discourage. What is interesting is that, once the discussion groups had become an embedded activity at the sheltered-housing scheme, one or two residents sometimes chivvied others good-naturedly to 'get back to the question' if they wandered off-topic. In general, veering into subjects unrelated to the original topic did not seem to bother people, suggesting they were treating the discussions not unlike the natural flow of every-day conversation.

A critical reflection on the discussion groups

Within a few months of introducing the discussion groups, I began to reflect on their apparent success, based on the positive reactions of those who attended and the enjoyment the residents seemed to derive from them. Similar to the participatory nature of the discussion group I had once facilitated in Cambridge, it was evident that while no *expertise* was expected or required in order for residents to participate, each person's *experience* was valued in a setting where trust was being built – reasons which may have underpinned why residents liked the activity. Further reflection on the Norwich-based discussion group made me become aware that my own reasons and aspirations for facilitating the discussion groups had evolved, based on what seemed to me to be their impact on the residents: they were not simply a purposeful conversation and enjoyable social activity. The intellectual stimulation of the discussion groups also served as a vehicle where common ground was being discovered among the residents, helping to increase inclusivity and the possibility of new links between them. By describing either old or recent events in their own life as they responded to the topic at hand, each person was opening a platform for others to tap into their related or contrasting experiences as they, in turn, offered their personal viewpoints. Simultaneously – though more importantly for myself, in light of my (unspoken) aspirations for the group – new connections were fostered and even forged between some participants. This was illustrated by the reaction of one woman who, after someone mentioned spending the early years of her married life in Canada, interjected, 'oh, I never knew that about you. I lived in Canada many years ago – we must talk about this later!'

Although I have never conducted formal research into the impact the discussion groups may have made on social connections or social change, I can report numerous occasions when connections surfaced between the residents as a result of the discussion group. An explicit example is the above connection made between two women during the discussion group when they learned they shared an experience of living in Canada. In addition, a poignant link seemed to be forged between two women when one, a resident relatively new to the sheltered-housing complex, mentioned that one of her uncles had been part of the D-Day landings in Normandy in June 1944 and the other, one of the oldest residents at the discussion group, responded that her husband had also served at D-Day.

Initial reflections – informal learning

On one occasion, as a lively discussion group on regional speech and local dialects came to an end, I told the residents how much I enjoyed the group because I always learned something from what was talked about at every session, using an example of a local figure of speech which I had not previously known.

Afterwards, this prompted me to reflect more carefully about the potential deeper impact of the discussion groups and to consider the extent to which *informal learning* was a feature of them. Might the residents also be engaging in a type of informal learning, consciously or sub-consciously? The answer seemed a definite yes based on comments and behaviours of the residents. These included a few residents staying on after a session to continue debating a point that had arisen in the discussion about mobile phones; another time, two men planned a route to walk along part of the river in the city, having learned from others in the group that the riverbank was much more accessible than they had realized; on another occasion, a resident thanked me as she left the venue for the 'really interesting discussion', adding: 'it gives us something to discuss later; we keep talking about it'.

Such evidence indicates that informal learning could arise from the discussions in non-instrumental, if imperceptible ways, and typically was generated by older people tapping into and sharing their own experiences in a social setting distinct from their usual activities. The learning did not necessarily involve myself as the facilitator, though perhaps I was an indirect catalyst for some of the connections made among the attendees. No claim is made that a discussion group is a unique site of informal learning for older people. New information and learning points obtained could also be acquired through other means and as a consequence of different types of meetings, settings or get-togethers. That does not, however, lessen the value of informal learning derived from the discussion groups.

Reflections from three residents – a suggestion of social change

My curiosity about the potential of informal learning impelled me to ask three residents who usually attended all the sessions if I might talk with them over a cup of tea about the discussion groups. This was not research, but an informal chat about the discussion groups as an activity – a 'sounding out', as I described it to them – which took place in 2015. I met the three residents, two female, one male, on a week-day afternoon in the flat of one of the women, deliberately arranging a time and venue separate from the discussion group itself to help encourage a sense of distance from the usual activity and perhaps promote reflection among the three. I thanked them for making themselves available and said I would like to ask questions on their general view of the discussion groups;

if they had a sense of what people might gain from attending them; and whether they were aware if anyone changed any aspect of their social patterns as a result of the discussion group. I emphasized that I did not want them to disclose anything confidential or private or anything which made them feel uncomfortable. Lastly, I told them that I was not seeking compliments and they were welcome to say if they felt something could be improved. I added that I would like to make a few handwritten notes for myself and that these would not be made public. In the next section, the residents are referred to as A, B and C (C is the male resident). Both A and C have since died.

Their general view about the discussion groups

In the opinion of the three residents, the discussion groups were a good thing. C called them a benefit and an enjoyment: a benefit to be doing something stimulating and different from other activities offered at this sheltered-housing scheme and enjoyment because it gives pleasure. The social participation at the discussion group was one of the highlights for B. She also remarked that it was interesting to see some people attend who very seldom took part in activities at the housing scheme. She theorized that such people were unlikely to have engaged in social activities earlier in their lives, so to break that pattern in later life is a major step for them. This comment seemed to trigger another thought in Resident C; he added that people who might seem 'insignificant' can turn out to be 'quite unexpected' as they contribute to the discussion and you learn a lot about how they have lived their lives. Resident A said that she looked forward to the discussion group each month, wondering, 'what will the topic be this time?'

If they had a sense of what people might gain from attending them

For both A and C, the discussion groups were an opportunity to mix with many others with different backgrounds and listen to their experience. They said it was interesting to hear their views, as a result of which 'you see them in a different light'. Because the discussion groups give you a chance to talk to them, if you bump into them elsewhere you always have something you can chat about because you know them in a way you had not before. I wondered if they would call that a kind of informal learning? All three agreed, A adding that any good conversation 'lets you learn something', while C mentioned that the discussion which ended with people talking about using mobile phones had helped him greatly, as he felt 'very ignorant' about technology. C added a further perspective on what he thought was gained from the discussion groups: he said that 'a lot of people here seldom get out' or socialize, so for them to attend the discussion group could be an important part of their week. He felt this was particularly true for those who, for whatever reason, had little contact with family or friends. B said she found the discussion groups more stimulating than most other activities at the housing scheme, which is why she always came. She added that having a place where one could express and hear views was a good thing because it was such an unusual activity for people at her time of life. Resident A added that she liked the way that, as facilitator, I had 'control of the conversation'. When asked what she meant, A told me that 'you instil a kind of discipline that helps the conversation to flow, that keeps things going smoothly'.

Whether they were aware if anyone who attended changed any aspect of their social patterns as a result of the discussion group

B claimed that one lady who had been the shy-and-retiring type was opening up as a result of the discussion group and was now mixing a bit more with others in the housing scheme. Resident A described being approached at a coffee morning by two ladies who did not attend the group but who had learned from someone who had been there that A's parents had been in the theatre. The two women had greeted her with, 'gosh, you've had an exciting life; come and talk to us about it'. B seemed to corroborate what one attendee once told me – that 'we keep talking about' the topic after the discussion group has ended. B mentioned she had overheard a conversation in the communal lounge in which one member of the group was talking to others about a topic recently discussed among the group. As a result, B stated, two new people joined the group. C said that the discussion group reminded him that 'still waters run deep', which sometimes meant he did not 'see people for who they were'. Based on his experience of the discussion groups, he claimed he now tried to 'bring people out of themselves' through conversation and encourage them to give their views.

I thanked the three residents for the informal 'sounding out', which I told them helped my understanding of the wider impact of the discussion groups. Over the next few weeks, I considered their remarks and observations, which seemed to attest that interactions at the discussions enhanced social connectedness among the older attendees, the impact of which occasionally spilled over to affect at least a few residents in the sheltered-housing scheme who had not attended previously. According to the three individuals who spoke with me, informal learning was occurring at the discussions, though they had not given it such a label. For them, the discussion groups were a distinctly different and welcome type of activity and an opportunity for enjoyable intellectual stimulation through which social connections were made or re-enforced. Their own examples also suggested that elements of social change had been observed, notably in the case of the person whom resident B described as shy and retiring but who now, B argued, was starting to socialize in a few ways as a result of the discussion groups.

Analysis and discussion

My own self-reflection, combined with what I learned in the 'sounding-out' conversation with three residents, led me to think critically about the impact of discussion groups on participatory ageing and social change. I feel that the experience provides a beneficial contribution to the field, given the distinctive nature of discussion groups in the setting described here.

Purposeful conversation in sheltered-housing for older people, distinct from everyday conversation, provided a stimulus to both interacting and communicating, opportunities that can tend to decrease as many older people age. Purposeful conversation offered in the discussion groups may also have re-introduced, even in small ways, aspects of social engagement that occur less frequently in later life. Talking with others on a focused topic was an exceptional opportunity for the older people who engaged with the discussion groups, according to what I was told by participants, and appeared to be a distinctly new experience for some, perhaps as much intellectually as socially. Participating in the group did not require expertise; rather, it encouraged each individual to express their views and perspectives, which could draw on experiences from their own past and the current day. It also encouraged active participation, as familiarity, respect and trust became established among those taking part in the monthly discussions. The atmosphere within the group seemed to generate feelings of being connected to a community, though not an exclusive community as some residents joined at different times across the ten-year span of the discussion groups. It is not known to what extent the discussion group may have also addressed feelings of social isolation. While anecdotal evidence suggests that several people gained or increased their social capital from participating, it is probably true that each person absorbed different meanings and associations from the activity.

The intellectual stimulation provided by discussing a range of different topics was enhanced by the inclusive atmosphere which I tried to encourage and maintain. As facilitator, I was careful not only to welcome and value the presence of the residents but also to help them to feel safe and comfortable, whether or not they contributed to a discussion or whatever opinion they held. I tried consciously to accomplish this by ensuring my manner remained open and that I modelled respect and impartiality, with an appropriate leavening of good humour. The residents with whom I held the informal conversation told me (unsolicited) that my 'leadership' made the sessions flow and go smoothly. It is only with the hindsight afforded by the pandemic, along with much self-reflection, that I have come to realize that my behaviour contributed to establishing some of the base for the discussion groups to become a site of positive socialization, participation and informal learning, points which are enlarged upon below.

It was reported above that on one occasion only three residents attended. This took place in the winter on a particularly cold Saturday, which deterred several residents from coming out to attend, according to the three women who had turned up. Rather than the usual discussion group, however, the three preferred to sit and chat over their cup of coffee. It seemed very appropriate to do this and, in terms of the discussion groups as a whole, indicates the importance of flexibility and adaptability in the facilitator.

Residents' participation began to include a new dynamic around the fifth year of the discussion groups: one resident asked another what he thought about the topic then added, in a friendly tone, that he had been unusually quiet and she was sure everyone would be interested in his views. The male resident, a regular attendee, did not seem to mind being singled out and expressed his opinions. This gentle chivvying of one resident by another differed from previous resident-to-resident interactions, none of which had been as direct as on this occasion. Over subsequent years, this happened again occasionally but only between regular attendees. This might seem a small change to the dynamics but I welcomed it because it suggested that some residents were shaping their own participation and felt confident and comfortable doing so.

A noteworthy limitation to the participatory nature of the discussion groups was – at first – surprising to me. On two or three occasions during the ten years of the discussion groups, I invited the residents to choose a topic for the following month. My motivation was to foster inclusion and increase participatory opportunities within the group. The residents seemed reluctant to do this and declined the opportunity. Some residents said they felt choosing the topic was 'your role'. I raised the issue of the reluctance of anyone to suggest a topic in my informal conversation with the three residents. They expressed their mutual opinion very strongly that 'it would be wrong' for a resident to choose a topic or, 'even worse', to chair a session. Resident A stated that 'people wouldn't like questions that others chose', to which both B and C agreed. C added that the topics would 'not be interesting' and that they wouldn't have the same way of 'encouraging people to speak'. The only exception to the residents declining to suggest a topic occurred at the end of a November session, when a woman proposed that at the following discussion group we talk about poems, carols and readings about Christmas. The timing might account for this one-off occurrence: the discussion group very seldom met in December, owing to it being a very busy season, but on this occasion the group was meeting early in the month. Possibly this gave an idea to a resident to propose a Christmas-related theme for that discussion group. Nevertheless, this was a unique exception for all discussion groups. It might imply that, as a site of informal learning, a tacit perception seems to have been held by the residents that the discussion group's facilitator was also the leader and that separation of roles should be observed.

Informal learning was acknowledged in different ways by many participants, though no participant used that term. Instead, many residents said to one another as well as to me that they 'learned something new' about cultural, historical or household matters from the discussion topic or that they 'found out' something about another resident which formerly had been unknown, all of which they seemed to value, not least for creating new social links which extended beyond the discussion-group setting.

Adult learning often springs from the need to adapt to meet natural social change. All residents shared the common experience of moving from their previous home into the sheltered-housing community, designed specifically as a place for older people. It would not be expected that all residents would know each other when they moved into the scheme, but they all shared the nature of this social change. The discussion group became a vehicle to help effect further social change as it offered, in addition to the activity itself, the chance to broaden their networks (Lindsay-Smith et al., 2018).

Nothing could guarantee that social connections resulting from the discussion group would trigger social change, but there was some evidence that this happened to a certain degree. What seemed to emerge was that the discussion groups demonstrated an increase in individual residents' agency in their everyday lives. Concrete examples include the 'we keep talking about' the discussion topic with residents not present at the group, two of whom then decided to join the discussion group; the decision to move forward gingerly from a 'shy' lifestyle towards attempting a few new social interactions; and the impact of the discussion group on another's perception that 'still waters run deep' and to reach out to other residents in the community. Taken collectively, these suggest a notable impact. They illustrate social change in action, the discussions providing a platform and apparatus for individuals to feel more agency in their lives and to feel connected to the community around them.

Conversation and social interaction are a key combination for supporting older people's engagement. This has been indicated in research reporting on befriending (Cattan et al., 2011), social activities (Age UK, 2021) and maintaining communication and connection with people living with dementia (Birt et al., 2020). The structure, design and purpose of the discussion groups described here differ very distinctly from befriending and social connection activities; both, however, attest to the positive significance of combining meaningful conversation with social engagement, as borne out in the discussion groups.

The context of purposeful conversation and social connection for older people aged in their eighties and nineties bears not only on informal learning but also on physical, mental and emotional well-being. To that end, it deserves mentioning that 'meaningful social interaction and engagement' play a significant role in healthy ageing, with some arguing that these may provide a 'buffer from the negative changes associated with ageing' (Shune and Duff, 2012: 823). Furthermore, I would argue that the increased participation in everyday life offered by the discussion groups here may echo aspects of the well-being cycle described by Walker (2009: 87), which begins with increased participation, leading to increased abilities and opportunities and then, in turn, to higher levels of personal well-being and social networking. A significant benefit of the discussion groups is not only the social connections they provide, an outcome which research has long emphasized as key to older people's health and well-being (Van Orden et al., 2020). It is also that the discussion groups offer a diversity of social interactions to those who are neither family nor necessarily close friends. Social diversity of this kind has been linked with positive outcomes for older people (Fingerman et al., 2020), which may suggest another benefit of the discussion groups.

Finally, a typical consequence of ageing is decreased social contact and research indicates that social relationships are associated with better cognitive functions. Although the 'exact nature of this association remains unclear' (Kelly et al., 2017), research elsewhere confirms that 'feeling socially connected to people' has health benefits (Holt-Lunstad et al., 2018) and is a protective factor for morbidity (Holt-Lunstad, 2021). A separate enquiry might explore the health-related aspects of an activity such as the discussion groups and the specific nature of any benefits that may accrue from them.

Discussion groups for older residents in sheltered-housing have been shown to generate discussion not only for its own sake but also to encourage informal learning relevant to the participants, as the discussion reflects and responds to their own experiences. Evidence from the discussions indicates that this type of informal learning arises in non-instrumental, sometimes imperceptible ways, and typically is generated by older people tapping into and sharing their own experiences in a social setting distinct from their usual activities. The discussion groups also have the potential to increase social capital and forms of personal empowerment. The overall consequence of the residents' interactions is enhanced social connectedness, a positive impact on participants' well-being and social change as evidenced by many examples of individual and collective agency among the residents.

References

Age UK (2021), Join Social Groups for Older People. Available at: https://www.ageuk.org.uk/get-involved/social-groups/ Accessed 7 November 2021.

Birt, L., Griffiths, R., Charlesworth, G., Higgs, P., Orrell, M., Leung, P., and Poland, F. (2020), Maintaining Social Connections in Dementia: A Qualitative Synthesis, *Qualitative Health Research*, 30 (1), 23-42. DOI: 10.1177/1049732319874782.

Cattan, M., Kime, N., and Bagnall, A. (2011), The Use of Telephone Befriending in Low Level Support for Socially Isolated Older People–An Evaluation, *Health & Social Care in the Community*, 19 (2), 198-206. DOI: 10.1111/j.1365-2524.2010.00967.x.

de Medeiros, K., Harris-Trovata, D., Bradley, E., Gaines, J., and Parrish, J. (2007), Older Adults: Does Gender Play a Role? *Educational Gerontology*, 33 (2), 111-25. DOI: 10.1080/03601270600850644.

Fingerman, K. L., Huo, M., Charles, S. T., and Umberson, D. J. (2020), Variety Is the Spice of Late Life: Social Integration and Daily Activity, *The Journals of Gerontology: Series B, Psychol Sci Soc Sci*, 75 (2), February 2020, 377-88. DOI: 10.1093/geronb/gbz007.

Holt-Lunstad, J. (2021), The Major Health Implications of Social Connection, *Current Directions in Psychological Science*, 30 (3), 251-9. DOI: 10.1177/0963721421999630.

Holt-Lunstad, J., Robles, T., and Sbarra, D. (2018), Advancing Social Connection as a Public Health Priority in the United States, *American Psychologist*, Sep 72 (6), 517-30. DOI: 10.10378/amp0000103.

Kelly, M. E., Duff, H., Kelly, S., McHugh Power, J. E., Brennan, S., Lawlor, B. A., and Loughrey, D. G. (2017), The Impact of Social Activities, Social Networks, Social Support and Social Relationships on the Cognitive Functioning of Healthy Older Adults: A Systematic Review, *Systematic Reviews*, 6, 259. DOI 10.1186/s13643-017-0632-2.

Lindsay-Smith, G., O'Sullivan, G., Eime, R., Harvey, J., and van Uffelen, J.G.Z. (2018), A Mixed Methods Case Study Exploring the Impact of Membership of a Multi-Activity, Multicentre Community Group on Social Wellbeing of Older Adults, *BMC Geriatrics*, 18, 226. DOI: 10.1186/s12877-018-0913-1.

Shune, S. and Duff, M. (2012), Verbal Play as an Interactional Discourse Resource in Early Stage Alzheimer's Disease, *Aphasiology*, 26 (6), 811–25.

Van Orden, K. A., Bower, E., Lutz, J., Silva, C., Gallegos, A. M., Podgorski, C. A., Santos, E. J., and Conwell, Y. (2020), Strategies to Promote Social Connections among Older Adults during 'Social Distancing' Restrictions, *American Journal of Geriatric Psychiatry*, 29, 816–27. DOI: 10.1016/j.jagp.2020.05.004

Walker, A. (2009), Commentary: The Emergence and Application of Active Aging in Europe, *Journal of Aging & Social Policy*, 21 (1), 75–93. DOI: doi.org/10.1080/08959420802529986.

Tales of adult learning, relationships and social change within the National Citizen Service

Natasha Rennolds, University of East Anglia

Introduction

The octopus is a fascinating creature and is illustrative of the tale I wish to tell with regard to adult learning and social change. Godfrey-Smith (2016) presents a fascinating account of octopuses and challenges the anthropocentric belief that humans are the pinnacle of evolution. As he writes, 'The Octopus is not Ishmael from Moby Dick, who escaped alone to tell the tale, but a distant relative who came down another line, and who has, consequently a different tale to tell' (Godfrey-Smith, 2016: 13). This chapter will attempt to tell a tale that has come down this 'other line'; a tale of learning and social change that follows the unintended, unplanned and transformational in the midst of contexts that do not necessarily plan to foster this kind of learning.

My first day of PhD ethnographic fieldwork was full of trepidation and excitement, backed with a touch of cynicism. I joined a cohort of sixty-eight sixteen-year-olds and their eleven members of staff as they embarked on their National Citizen Service (NCS) programme. I was enthused about the possibilities that lay before me while slightly disillusioned with the legislative and political context of NCS as the youth provision for social change. Could the realities of the programme convince me that social change is possible within a learning programme charged with nurturing a neoliberal ideology at its core?

These observations and experiences inform my doctoral thesis which explores the learning environment and learning relationships for both young people and adults as they move through a curriculum designed to promote citizenship. The programme was a fertile site to consider how learning emerges and facilitates social change, and the ethnographic methodology allowed me to encounter various situations, paying attention to the vibrancy and agency of the human and more-than-human in fostering learning and transformation as part of the programme. Drawing on the influence of posthumanism, in this chapter I will explore areas that I have not been able to fully explore as part of my PhD, namely the programme as a whole for learning, and the 'doing' of the minor gestures that make a difference and come to matter in opening up future potentialities of social justice and change. I will be exploring NCS as a case study from the overarching governance through to the everyday activity and interactions when engaged in the programme, to consider the stories that emerge – learning that is planned and unplanned, and the implications for social change.

Research context

I became involved with NCS tangentially during the programme's first year of delivery in 2011. I was a member of the steering group for the local delivery partnership in my county area, and I was asked to deliver the training for their first group of staff. Following a successful first summer, the regional contract holder asked me to deliver to a wider audience and for the last decade, I have been delivering training to a number of NCS local providers. It was through this connection that I approached an organization, we shall call 'Community Inc' in this chapter, to be my research partner. They agreed and I will always be grateful to Community Inc, its staff and the young people attending for welcoming and accepting me into their programme. The cohort I joined was the fifth programme out of eleven for Community Inc. We were eighty adults and young people plus a cast of other instructors, managers and support staff dropping in and out of the programme at different times. During this time, I lived in the local area which is an ex-mining town in the North of England. The data I collected included interviews, photographs, audio and video recordings, personal reflections, ongoing notes in my 'little books' (as one young person referenced them), national and local paperwork, references to website pages and a lot of 'wonder'.

This background helps set the context but it also highlights that I am, was and have for a long time been in and among the research context that I am researching. My story to tell is in and among their story, we have tales that are entangled. Within this my stance is influenced by the Baradian ideas of objectivity; that is, I do not seek to bracket my experience; instead, I aim to be accountable within and as part of being and becoming in the world (Barad, 2003, 2007).

Posthumanism and social change

While this chapter does not afford the space to cover posthumanism in depth, I will briefly highlight important concepts that influence my thinking about learning and social change as it applies to my fieldwork in the NCS programme. Posthumanism is not one approach and encompasses many different lines of thought and philosophical underpinnings (St. Pierre, 2020; Ulmer, 2017). Without a singular definition (MacLure, 2017), it offers growing and multiple paths of thought and action in research (Ulmer, 2017). The essence of posthumanism is to displace the prominence of the 'human' in how we understand and live, and indeed, to think about how the 'more than' human world is enmeshed with and constitutes the human, to recognize both ontologically and epistemologically that humans are in and part of the world; as Ulmer writes, 'Humans are characters in a cast of many' (2017: 833).

Feminism and postcolonial theory remind us that traditional research has not only centred the human, it has been predicated on a very particular human, often affording power and privileges (Braidotti, 2016) to that constituency of white, heterosexual, European (wealthy) males. This hegemonic perspective fails to acknowledge the embodied and felt experience or knowledge of others (Ahmed, 1998; Million, 2009) including the more than human – the animal and the material. This perspective would account for the interdependencies of the world we live in, in all its materiality where matter (also) comes to matter in its intra-action with discursive and cultural practices (Barad, 2003). Seen through a programme such as NCS with its different contexts and practices, this offers alternative potential lines of enquiry about learning and its movement relevant for social change.

The diversity of thought within the umbrella of 'posthumanism' sometimes leads to confusions/different interpretations, not least because it is often characterized as a negative approach – almost dystopian in its recognition of the damage humans have enacted on the planet, and raising concerns that the democratization of human and non-human elements may further harm the interests of the most dispossessed humans. However, I view posthumanism as a position of hope in that it is relational (Barad, 2007), multiplistic (Barad, 2019; Strom, Mills, Abrams and Dacey, 2018) and affirmative (St. Pierre, 2013). Therefore, we come to know the world through being in the world; there is not a binary separation, our encounters with other bodies make the world intelligible (Barad, 2007). These entanglements are assemblages that are in continuous movement and they emerge together as 'sympoietic arrangements' (Haraway, 2017: M25). Sympoiesis meaning bodies evolving together, and within this constant negotiation of interactions, pathways for learning and relearning open within the relationship(s) (Le Guin, 2017) which has/have the potential for transformational thinking (Ulmer, 2017).

The claim for transformational thinking is predicated on the ethico-onto-epistem-ological premise of posthumanism; as we intra-act and evolve as part of the becoming of the world, each encounter offers a space for change (Barad, 2007), not open-ended but with a number of possibilities. The entanglement of encounters matters in its intra-action, as these are the moments of affect, and as individuals we can, too, affect the movement towards different futures. This places a responsibility not as being a responsible citizen in the neoliberal perspective but as a response-able (Barad, 2007) agent in which there is opportunity to consider the imbalances of positioning and the impact these have on power dynamics (Millora, Maimunah and Still, 2020), and to re-imagine a belonging based on reciprocity, relationality and responsibility in a 'shared world' (Braidotti, 2016: 25; Harris and Wasilewski, 2004).

The tales of learning and social change: The national programme

The National Citizen Service (NCS) is a government-supported programme established by the then coalition government in 2010. NCS was put onto a statutory footing following the introduction of the NCS Bill in December 2016. According to the 'Seasonal Staff Guide' (fieldwork document), NCS reached over 300,000 young people between 2010 and 2018, with all programmes overseen by the NCS Trust which was given Royal Charter status in April 2017. The NCS Trust (the trust) retains a staff base that sets the operational requirements of the programme and monitors the delivery contracts. Delivery is further overseen by regional partners who subcontract the work to local community organizations, e.g. existing youth work providers, schools, sports clubs.

NCS is aimed at fifteen- to seventeen-year-olds, with the majority of young people accessing the programme in the summer after Year 11 has finished; therefore, the majority of young people participating are sixteen years old. As stated in the Charter, the function of the programme is:

> to provide or arrange for the provision of programmes for young people in England with the purpose of
>
> i. enabling participants from different backgrounds to work together in local communities to participate in projects to benefit society, and

ii. enhancing communication, leadership and team-working skills of participants.

The Charter details that the scheme should be promoted to children, young people, parents, schools, local authorities and other educational providers and public bodies. Other documentation further expands on the function of the programme – for example, the three stated aims on the current public website are:

> '**Social Cohesion** – Cultivating stronger, more integrated communities by fostering understanding between young people and their neighbours from different backgrounds …
> **Social Mobility** – Building essential skills for work and life, making sure young people can get ahead and are prepared for whatever the future holds – think of it as investing in our country's future talent …
> **Social Engagement** – Engaging young people in social action in their community as well as the democratic process, creating more understanding of their responsibilities as a citizen and their potential to affect change.'
> (wearencs.com, 2021)

The underlying principles of the programme are arranged as five core components for delivery organizations and staff and include words such as 'agency', 'responsibility', 'civic engagement' and 'diverse personal networks' (data taken from Community Inc Seasonal Staff Guide). These are implemented by the 'Enabling Conditions' which 'underpin quality and impactful delivery, detailing how programme set-up, staff training, etc. create programme environments that support young people's development' (fieldwork document).

The structural framework of NCS is foundational to the delivery of the programme; action flows from the various governing documentation and guidelines. Posthumanism is critiqued for its lack of recognition of wider structural contexts (Rekret, 2018); however, by examining the ideological and political underpinnings as they manifest in the 'doing', there is a recognition of the material bodies/artefacts, such as charters and staff guidelines, and their own vitality/agency. This is not a discursive analysis but a consideration as to how the text as part of a cultural and political assemblage is enacted by bodies that affect the learning about social change for the programme participants. The governing documents are active and compelling in that the words set a framework which defines future actions (d'Agnese, 2020); it compels ways of doing within a particular perception of being. The documents privilege certain knowledges and ways of learning at the expense of others. Learning on the programme is framed within the neoliberal idea of character and society (d'Agnese, 2020; Mills, 2021), and analysing the documents allows us to see where future action and control is directed (Taylor and Fairchild, 2020).

As a way of exploring this, we can follow the movement of the charter from governance to practice. As a political and statutory document, the Charter affects the programme deliverables by way of prescribed expectations as to what activities are to be included and how this should be delivered (see below for more detail). A key activity is the social action project in which young people are expected to volunteer on projects within their local communities so that they understand their 'responsibilities' as a citizen and that they have 'agency' to make social change. The premise is that they should choose what they want to work on. The practice of this is problematic; it is difficult to have genuine participation when you have hundreds of young people participating in one local area over the summer period. Logistical issues include the number of projects available in the area, the safeguarding of all involved and realistic expectations as to what can be achieved in the one or two weeks allocated. Therefore, often projects are pre-planned with community partners to ensure programme requirements of hours participated and a completed project are met. This leaves little choice or agency in the social action projects the young people embark on and restricts the actions they may want to engage in and learn about. This lessens opportunities for real community engagement, which takes time and skill if it is to be meaningful, and the learning that comes with this. This was not just apparent on the programme I joined but has been evidenced elsewhere (Mills and Waite, 2017).

With practical challenges of running a programme alongside the focus on individual responsibility within the delivery framework, the NCS programme has been critiqued as embodying a neoliberal view on social change (de St Croix, 2017). The outcome being compliance as opposed to justice or participatory learning as citizenship (Mills and Waite, 2017) as evidenced by many social action projects. Judith Butler (2015) cautions against a notion of responsibility with an onus on individual capacity, as social isolation, not social cohesion, is a possible outcome predicated on individuals becoming further disconnected from others as they attempt to maximize their employment potential and alleviate the precarity of living. Research with a similar age group in a different context has demonstrated that self-motivation for participants tends towards personal, rather than altruistic, reasons (Brooks, 2007) which troubles the social change narrative further.

Within the delivery framework of NCS, consideration of the wider social change is absent, as is the opportunity to think critically about society and what young people may want their futures to look like (Nieto, 2018). It is a potential of change based on the notion of individual worth or human capital which fails to take desired cultural and material factors into account for either achieving individual success or social change (Friedman and Laurison, 2020). Therefore, notions of citizenship are linked to learning to enact a neoliberal, individual citizen rather than a citizenship that is cultivated for the wider, interdependent collective.

However, instead of framing this as an either/or situation, posthumanism invites us to think about what else may be happening, framed as a 'both/and' lens for looking at a problem. The implementation and subsequent critique of NCS may suggest that social change is binary, it is either possible or not; however, examining other aspects of the programme helps us understand other tales being told around learning and social change.

Our next tale – the doing

The next tale moves from the strategic direction towards the line of doing, exploring what transpires within the activities as they happen. As a formally designed programme delivered over three or four weeks, each week has a different focus, located in different environmental settings. I joined a cohort of sixty-eight young people and eleven staff on a typical four-week (Monday–Friday) programme which looked like the following:

Week 1: Residential at an outdoor centre located away from the home area. Activities include typical outdoor education activities dependent on the centre; all are designed to build character, e.g. perseverance and self-efficacy (NCS Summer Evaluation, 2019) and teams. Each team consists of ten to fifteen young people and two members of staff.

Week 2: Residential living in a local university hall of residence in the home area. Activities delivered as workshops or lectures include social issues such as first aid, mental health and substance misuse. When not in formal activities, the young people engaged in activities to help with independence, sociality and individual resilience including cooking, budgeting and living with others in shared flats.

Week 3: Work days – 9am–4pm based in a college- or school-type setting. The activities are to plan and prepare for the week of Social Action.

Week 4: Work hours – Thirty hours for the week completed according to the nature of activities undertaken. The week is spent doing the Social Action

Project in their individual teams for the partner charity/business. Activities are dependent on the nature of the partnership but can include sponsored activities, quiz nights, garden renovations, distributing second-hand school uniforms, raising awareness of an issue.

Post-programme: The final event as a whole cohort involves a 'graduation celebration' where all their achievements are enjoyed, and certification is given. The certificate demonstrates completion of the programme which can be used on individual CVs.

With its mix of formal adult-led activities, non-formal learning opportunities and the informal learning in everyday practice, NCS illustrates the complexity of defining learning parameters. This is not unusual, as it has been noted that the blurring of the distinction is increasingly common in the space of character education (Mills, 2021) which potentially problematizes the value and attribution given to the learning achieved (Rogers, 2014). Therefore, assessing what you have learned is challenging, particularly if wishing for others to understand and recognize the change.

One method and a thread through the programme is the concept of reflection as a way of learning. The staff were encouraged to engage the young people in informal reflection after each activity with a formal, daily timetabled reflection session on the residentials. The 2019 NCS Summer Evaluation states that the formal sessions 'intend to improve self-expression, emotional regulation and a sense of well-being' (2021: 32). Again, this pertains to learning as individuals rather than learning through reflection for collective change or transformation with matters of justice and power.

However, the range and difference in activities suggests that quantifying their learning within a purely neoliberal framework does not do justice to the experiences of the young adults involved. They are expected to learn anything from rock-climbing to mental health awareness to budgeting to dealing with a difficult team member, alongside making a change within their communities. The programme is about 'doing', it is 'active' in its activity and this involves contact with other bodies, both human and non-human. The fluidity and movement are affective; they do things not just physically but emotionally and cognitively and in this movement, new perhaps unanticipated and unplanned learnings emerge.

> The actual walk started at the top of the mountain. It was wet as usual and the walk up was not long but it felt like hard work. I am so unfit. At the top we went into a dip and there was a large, foreboding rusty iron door, it looked scary ..... They went through a very small tunnel, they had to crawl through to get to the next cavern. .... In each cavern they talked about something moral,

philosophical, ethical or all three ..... The discussion focused on the value of life and how we value each other, and what if someone errs or commits a crime.

(My own reflection, Week 1, Day 4)

This example is in reference to an activity called the 'Walk of Life'. The walk begins in a small room made to look cosy with a striped rug on the floor and pictures of words like 'joyful' and 'powerful' on the wall. After twenty minutes in the relative comfort of the room, we were taken outside in the rain and walked up to the top of the hill where we were confronted by the rusty door set within an overgrown and wild piece of land. On entering the door, we were greeted with a small, confined space only big enough for three people at a time and to move ahead you had to get on your hands and knees and crawl through a dark tunnel of about ten metres; this was so dark you could not see the person in front of you. Each tunnel opened up into a cavern just big enough for half the group of five to seven young people at a time in which any noise echoed and bounced around us. At various intervals we stopped to discuss questions posed to us. The questions were not questions in which there was a right or wrong, in fact they were the type of questions familiar to youth work, questions to open up dialogue, that require careful negotiation while listening to others. As Stacey (participant) remarked to me during lunch:

> I like that everyone's opinion was just like normal and everyone just talked to everyone about their opinion even though they were different, it wasn't like arguing, you know like the tone of arguing, it was like 'no', not like 'no, it's this', it's alright ... like listening to other people's opinion, I became open to possibilities.
>
> (Interview audio, Week 1, Day 4)

Stacey's comment acknowledges reciprocity of dialogue but does not capture the full picture of events. In addition to discussion, the activity was physical; it involved effort, not only crawling along the dirty floor but other smaller physical movements such as reaching out to others by way of grabbing a hand to help you up, the scraping of knees on the floor, maintaining a touch awareness of the foot in front of you and the high fives and hugs at the end of the walk. If I could play the audio recording, you would hear sounds of high-pitched shrieks, of someone close to tears, nervous laughter in conjunction with voices of encouragement and care, specific instructions as how to move forward, e.g. 'duck your head', 'it's OK, you can stand now', 'just look ahead to the light'. The sounds of the group helping each other in the challenging moments are interspersed with moments of respectful silence while hearing the voices of others. While Stacey remarks that she has become 'open to possibilities' because of hearing different perspectives and not 'arguing', I would suggest that it is in the micro moments of reciprocal care that this message is reinforced. It is not just the spoken dialogue but the material dialogue of care for each other in challenging circumstances. Recognizing the dynamic entanglement of the activity, the human and more than human (Pink, 2015) acknowledges that as a whole group they are not only gaining knowledge about others but they are 'knowing-with' others (Taylor and Fairchild, 2020: 523) through the sharing of the embodied experiences.

I understand this sharing of learning and knowing together to be important in thinking about social change. It is in the future that potentials of collective change are evidenced, while it is in the now that we may come to understand what it can be – if we seek to understand the experiences of others (human or more than human), we are learning about what it may be like to live a different life from our own. In exercising 'empathy and solidarity', we can seek not only social change but social justice (Grant and Gibson, 2010).

It may seem like an overstatement to assert that one learning event can facilitate social justice. However, there is a temporal and spatial aspect to this learning which means it is not necessarily just one learning event. It is an emotional and cognitive experience, a lived memory, that has the potential to be re-lived at different times and in different spaces, and with each re-living, it is a reminder of kindness, other ways of being and perhaps of overcoming difficulties together. There is a connectedness to this learning which blurs temporal and spatial boundaries attributed through everyday/common sense understandings. In order for citizenship teaching to do more than repeat existing hegemonic practices, 'young people must be affected' (Garratt and Piper, 2012: 75) and the affective experience opens up potential to move the learning from situated learning to future making.

However, while these types of experiences may be useful building blocks in learning for social change, future achievement requires more than just shared experiences; concrete support and facilitation are required. Staff need to be able to facilitate and nurture critical learning of political and social discourse, and as this next section illustrates, this is not straightforward within the NCS delivery.

Whose tale is this? – young adults as team leaders

This book is about adult learning, and it may seem that by using NCS as a case study this chapter focuses on the stories of young people (who are not yet of legal age). In response, I suggest that NCS encounters problematize the boundaried thinking of who is teaching and who is learning.

In terms of government and statutory service provision in the UK, young adults are generally classified as sixteen- to twenty-five years old, and as we have seen NCS is both time-limited and aimed at fifteen- to seventeen-year-olds for delivery. These factors can blur the distinction between adult and young person on NCS, and a casual observer may be hard-pressed to discern a staff member from a participant. Due to the nature of the programme, many local providers tend to have a very small core staff base, typically three to five full-time staff employed on a year-round basis. However, with delivery of the programme reaching from 60 to over 700 young people for each provider, the numbers of staff considerably swell for the summer delivery period. This results in some providers recruiting more than fifty sessional staff for just a few weeks each year. The implications of this work pattern are that the providers rely heavily on university students and/or staff who are able to work flexibly for a short period of time. This means it is difficult to build organizational knowledge and learning – organizational memory – from previous years, as staff move on. Teams are always in flux, having to start afresh in terms of collective knowledge and practice.

Within each cohort of staff, the lack of experience and knowledge is compounded by numbers of staff who can be both young and/or delivering to young people possibly for the first time, particularly as NCS encourages former participants to return as staff once they reach eighteen years of age. For example, within the cohort I joined, the oldest member of staff was thirty-four years old, there was a seven-year age gap between this member of staff and the Cohort Leader who was twenty-seven years old, followed by the rest of the staff who were all twenty-three years and under. I should probably note that at the time of my fieldwork, I was forty-seven years old, contributing to a massive age difference not just in terms of years lived but years worked – I had started working with young people before all but two of the members of staff had been born. Of the staff team, five were previous NCS participants (although not necessarily in their first year as staff) and for four of the team, it was their first time working with young people. This opens up the questions about learning – who is doing the learning and who is doing the teaching, what may they be learning or teaching?

While the statutory starting point of NCS places formal expectations on the learning in terms of timetabled activities, the inexperience or limited experience for many of the staff meant that many of them were learning in the practice of the role, learning 'on the job'. The learning in the doing was not just confined to understanding how to work with young people but also required learning some of the functional skills alongside the young people, e.g.

> and then in this third week, erm I probably learnt more as I haven't really done a kind of, any sort of social action. I've obviously done powerpoints and presentations and I've kind of like developed my own work but I haven't really worked within a large group and then presented it to someone … …, you don't like create something and then, erm, go out and get money, you kind of go in, and go in to a school and do your like coaching hours or, erm, or you go in and work in like an applied hospital setting or, so it's quite different in terms of.
>
> (Adele, twenty-two years, interview audio, Day 5, week 3)

Adele demonstrates the complexity of experience for the staff, as not only were they responsible for learning events but they were engaged in doing their own learning in the process. This was particularly relevant in the second week which was based around learning skills for independence, and many of the staff expressed their concerns to me about helping the young people to cook meals, professing lack of confidence in their own skills and knowledge. This was ironic as I never cook in my own home and despite all my years of other experience, I was learning with them too. Callum (eighteen years old, first-time staff member) said to me as he handed me a cup of tea, 'I hope that's alright, I don't often make cups of tea, I don't really know how to do it' (audio recording, week 2, day 4).

The basic life skills learning went alongside learning in the more relational and emotional aspects of the role. The second week was a challenging week for everyone, me included, but for Callum it had been particularly difficult. He reflected in an interview with me, when talking about the challenges he had had with the young people:

> More like attitude, like attitude's worse, has been worse this week than last week, … Put your phone away, 'no, I'm texting', like that kinda attitude or …, or do this. 'No', it's just like little stuff like that, the littlest, the **more little** that it is the more annoying it is. 'cos you know you shouldn't be on your phone, so when I come tell you to turn your, put your phone away … like you should know that was coming anyway. And they're saying 'no, like why do I have to put my phone away?' It's like disrespectful. You should just put your phone away straightaway or don't even go on it at all.
>
> (Interview audio, Week 2, Day 5)

The whole cohort finished the first week happy and in good spirits. It may have been prescient to assume that this success would continue into week two.

However, as Callum's reflection depicts, this was not the case, and new areas of conflict arose which caused issues for staff-participant relationships. I am struck how his words open up a line of enquiry as to the vital materiality (Taylor and Fairchild, 2020) of the mobile phones in the learning dynamic for both staff and participants. The mobile phone had become a point of contention. Callum saw the behaviour with phones as 'disrespectful', because he felt the participants should not be on their phones during sessions. He had made an assumption that the 'good behaviour' of the first week would continue, without understanding that a change in environment may have implications. There had been little possibility of the phones acting as a space of struggle in the first week because we were staying in a signal-free part of the country. The compulsion to reach for a phone was not as strong, as participants could not interact with what a phone offered. However, the second week with its onus on listening activities and an abundance of Wi-Fi meant that we all experienced the pull of the phone in a more intense and typical way. This brought new challenges and learning, for Callum and others, in managing both the activities and the young people.

While the youngest and most inexperienced, Callum was not alone in the amount of learning he was doing. I held interviews weekly where possible with as many of the staff as possible, and without fail they would talk about how much they were having to understand and learn in the doing of the programme. The staff were teaching and learning at the same time, whether the event was directive or unintentional (Rogers, 2014). What does it mean to acknowledge that the young adults on the programme were all learning in different ways within the variety of activities? My sense of wonder here opens other lines of enquiry, and foremost is how this influences what the cohort can learn and understand about social change. In the next section, I offer my own perspective from my time as a young youth worker, and as someone entangled in this field of work for many years.

My tale – my entanglement with learning and social change

I have been engaged in working with young people for over twenty-five years and often the programmes I have worked on have been titled or have had objectives/outcomes/aims, etc. that refer vaguely to social change. The inference has been that changing the behaviour of the targeted individual or cohort will allow social change. As a young woman from a working-class background, in delivering these programmes I never stopped to think about what this might really mean. What social change was I supposed to be achieving, who was setting the criteria for social change, how did this help the young people? I never stopped to question the wider political, institutional and social structures within which the programmes were set, although there was a recognition of the unfair barriers and obstacles put in front of us. I didn't know that I could perhaps question this. Was I responsible or a unwitting object of the production and reproduction of powerful hegemonies (Page, 2018)?

I use my own example, not to say that this is the experience of everyone, but instead to problematize the reliance on temporary and inexperienced staff within the NCS framework for delivering social change. Learning is not always intentional, new kinds of learning happen without recourse to the planned context and by drawing attention to this premise, social change as transformation becomes a potentiality.

My aim was always to build and maintain supportive relationships with whoever I was working with to give them the foundation that may enable them to flourish in the future. Was I wrong that this was my focus? I don't think so but I, now, understand that my thinking reflected what values of learning and social change were available to me both as an individual and within a societal context. What I observed in my work was young people being 'othered' by adults in their lives; their experiences were not heard or recognized, and they had very little agency in important decisions in their lives. Now taking the ethico-onto-epistem-ological positioning of posthumanism, recognizing that it is in the entanglements of the now that agency is affective, I can identify that they did not have agency in the traditional sense of power, but they were able to subvert and exert affect within their encounters, for example by refusing to speak to adults, leaving rooms without asking, throwing or kicking material objects, etc. They were affecting the change they could control, a provocation to others to respond and deal with the effects. With mutual care and reciprocity, we were able to work together to affect a different path, the change they needed to potentially flourish. The potential of change was in the relationship. However, this learning took time and is still happening; broadening and challenging frames of experience is an iterative process and necessitates being open to uncomfortableness as you learn, as well as acknowledging that collective frames of reference and learning emerge over time. Were there parallels on the NCS programme?

The influence of posthumanism invites questions as to the centrality of humans, particularly humans with privilege, not just in research but as part of everyday living. Encounters with others and making sense of these encounters as part of 'becoming' with the world means we can see learning in new ways, beyond what is sanctioned by organizational demands. This learning is not static, prescriptive or functional but dynamic, fluid and open-ended. These encounters can be planned learning events such as the 'Walk of Life' which facilitate an engaging with others in a meaningful, compassionate and empathetic way that opens up relationships with others.

However, returning to Callum and the interview in which he reflected on his struggles, it is apparent that these connections do not have to be planned. When I asked how he resolved the challenges he had had, he told me:

> Talk to 'em, because they know I'm young anyway so that only like 2 years above them, I think they feel they can talk to me, they can feel like, they know I can relate to them like maybe more than other staff 'cos I'm so young … …..**little chats** like that.
>
> (Interview, Week 2, Day 5)

What intrigues me here is the 'little chats'. NCS, like many youth programmes, offers many opportunities for seemingly innocuous chats, and these chats are part of getting to know each other and building relationships with others. This was echoed by Mae, another new staff member who was only 18, although she did have experience of doing NCS as a participant. I asked her what advice she might give other new staff:

> Try to get on their level, understand what they might be going through, I think, considering, like even with the training, I think we're all aware of the kind of issues that young people might face when they come on programme and erm, I kinda kept that in mind, like this young person might not have a good home life or just try to be friendly with everyone, make sure you be confident, if you're not confident they're not gonna be confident and just be so like clear when you presenting to them, well yeah apart from that.
>
> (Interview, Week 3, Day 5)

In the first sentence, Mae talks about empathy and solidarity as necessary to support the young people, which for me illustrates something I experienced time and time again in my work and that is, it is not necessarily the activity that is important for learning but the 'doing' of the activity that makes a difference. This may seem analogous to learning through communities of practice (Lave and Wenger, 1991) but the experiences of both staff and participants illuminate that the embodied, material and emotional connections are vital for learning and transformational change. This perspective may sound simple but is often neglected in more traditional approaches to research on education and character education, which tend to focus more on the tangible, measurable and accountable matters on programmes.

Posthumanism centres perspectives that look beyond individual or collective humans, at the elements that work between and among them too. This priority of focusing elsewhere, where 'other than' human-centred learning emerges, then opens up new avenues of exploration. As the octopus in the opening quotation illustrates, there are different stories to tell. These are not either/or stories but 'both/and' stories – they do not ignore humans or human intent and action, but also look beyond. Wondering about the 'doing' of learning opened up phenomenon of the 'brilliance/shimmer' of what was happening beyond the mundane programmatic elements and the impact this has – the hand held out for someone, the insubstantial chat about the everyday, the cup of tea for someone, not getting the phone out, trying to get on the 'level' with each other, delivering a presentation together, and listening. There was reciprocity and care in the small actions; they were making embodied and emotional connections both with each other and with the world around them. When you have made connections once, you can make connections again. When you have learned how to have empathy and solidarity, then you can do this again and a collective change becomes possible. Both the staff and the participants were engaged in the learning of/within these encounters, building relationships that make a difference to the world around them, and all that was entangled.

Our tales conclude

NCS proposes a vision of social change, we are told what it is without question, much like the institution of school (Ball and Collet-Sabé, 2021), but that does not mean this is the only vision. The criticisms of NCS as a programme – its reach, its cost and its neoliberal underpinnings – are rightly highlighted in any examination of the programme. However, as I have explored here, and with reference to the octopus, there are other stories to tell, a multiplicity of stories. The actual practice of NCS involves young adults learning together, whether as staff or as participants, and in doing so, their immersion in the programme enables transformation. It is the 'doing' with and alongside each other – elements that exceed organizational aims or intentions, elements that are unplanned by any one agent but which happen in the thick of the assemblage, that offers learning opportunities and the building of relationships. These in turn widen perspectives and knowledge, and create new worlds.

To finish, I want to acknowledge and thank the staff and young people for their generosity of spirit in welcoming me, alongside the core and temporary staff of all the providers I work with and have worked with over the years. The people I meet are generally open, willing to learn and kind to each other; it is a pleasure to work with so many people who do want to make a difference to society in whatever way they can. Therefore, critiquing the programme premise may be valid but what I have learned is the warmth of so many people cannot be criticized. While this may seem conflictive or contradictory, we live in a world that is not binary, it is messy, complicated and indeterminate, so why would the tales of learning for social change be anything else?

References

Ahmed, S. (1998), *Differences That Matter: Feminist Theory and Postmodernism*, Cambridge, UK: Cambridge University Press.

Ball, S., and Collet-Sabé, J. (2021), Against School: An Epistemological Critique, *Discourse: Studies in the Cultural Politics of Education*, 1–15. DOI: 10.1080/01596306.2021.1947780.

Barad, K. (2003), Posthumanist Performativity: Toward an Understanding of How Matter Comes to Matter, *Signs*, 28 (3), 801–31.

Barad, K. (2007), *Meeting the Universe Halfway: Quantum Physics and the Entanglement of Matter and Meaning*, Durham, NC: Duke University Press.

Barad, K. (2019), After the End of the World: Entangled Nuclear Colonialisms, Matters of Force, and the Material Force of Justice, *Theory and Event*, 22 (3), 524–50.

Braidotti, R. (2016), Posthuman Critical Theory, in D. Banerji, and M. Paranjape (eds.), *Critical Posthumanism and Planetary Futures*, 13–32, New Delhi: Springer (India) Private Limited.

Brooks, R. (2007), Young People's Extra-Curricular Activities: Critical Social Engagement – Or "Something for the CV"? *Journal of Social Policy*, 36 (3), 417–34.

Butler, J. (2015), *Notes toward a Performative Theory of Assembly*, Cambridge, MA: Harvard University Press.

d'Agnese, V. (2020), Contrasting the Neoliberal Educational Agenda: Wonder Reconsidered, in *Wonder, Education, and Human Flourishing*, Amsterdam: VU University Press.

Department for Digital, Culture, Media and Sport (2021), *National Citizen Service 2019 Summer Evaluation – Main Report*, UK Government.

de St Croix, T. (2017), Time to Say Goodbye to the National Citizen Service? *Youth and Policy*, n/a (n/a).

Friedman, S., and Laurison, D. (2020), *The Class Ceiling: Why It Pays to Be Privileged*, Oxford: University Press.

Garratt, D., and Piper, H. (2012), Citizenship Education and Philosophical Enquiry: Putting Thinking Back into Practice, *Education, Citizenship and Social Justice*, 7 (1), 71–84.

Godfrey-Smith, P. (2016), *Other Minds: The Octopus, the Sea, and the Deep Origins of Consciousness*, New York: Farrar, Straus and Giroux.

Grant, C. A., and Gibson, M. L. (2010), 'These Are Revolutionary Times': Human Rights, Social Justice, and Popular Protest, in T. K. Chapman and N. Hobbel (eds.), *Social Justice Pedagogy across the Curriculum*, 25–51, Abingdon: Routledge.

Haraway, D. (2017), Symbiogenesis, Sympoiesis, and Art Science Activisms for Staying with the Trouble, in A. Tsing, H. Swanson, E. Gan, and N. Bubandt (eds.), *Arts of Living on a Damaged Planet: Ghosts and Monsters of the Anthropocene*, M25–M50, Minneapolis: University of Minnesota Press.

Harris, L. D., and Wasilewski, J. (2004), Indigeneity, an Alternative Worldview: Four R's (Relationship, Responsibility, Reciprocity, Redistribution) vs. two P's (Power and Profit). Sharing the Journey towards Conscious Evolution, *Systems Research and Behavioral Science*, 21 (5), 489–503.

Lave, J., and Wenger, E. (1991), *Situated Learning: Legitimate Peripheral Participation*, Cambridge, UK: Cambridge University Press.

Le Guin, U. K. (2017), Deep in Admiration, in A. Tsing, H. Swanson, E. Gan, and N. Bubandt (eds.), *Arts of Living on a Damaged Planet: Ghosts and Monsters of the Anthropocene*, M15–M22, Minneapolis: University of Minnesota Press.

MacLure, M. (2017), Qualitative Methodology and the New Materialisms: 'A Little of Dionysus's Blood?', in N. K. Denzin and M. D. Giardina (eds.), *Qualitative Inquiry in Neoliberal Times. The International Congress of Qualitative Inquiry*, 48–58, New York: Routledge.

Million, D. (2009), Felt Theory: An Indigenous Feminist Approach to Affect and History *Wicazo Sa Review*, 24 (2), 53–76.

Millora, C., Maimunah, S., and Still, E. (2020), Reflecting on the Ethics of PhD Research in the Global South: Reciprocity, Reflexivity and Situatedness, *Acta Academica*, 52 (1), 10–30.

Mills, S. (2021), *Mapping the Moral Geographies of Education: Character, Citizenship and Values*, 1st edition, Abingdon, UK: Routledge.

Mills, S., and Waite, C. (2017), Brands of Youth Citizenship and the Politics of Scale: National Citizen Service in the United Kingdom, *Political Geography*, 56, 66–76.

NCS website. Available at: https://wearencs.com/our-objectives-and-impact Accessed 11 September 2021.

Nieto, D. (2018), Citizenship Education Discourses in Latin America: Multilateral Institutions and the Decolonial Challenge, *Compare: A Journal of Comparative and International Education*, 48 (3), 432–50.

Page, T. (2018), Teaching and Learning with Matter, *Arts*, 7 (82), 1–12.

Pink, S. (2015), *Doing Sensory Ethnography*, London: SAGE Publications Ltd.

Rekret, P. (2018), The Head, the Hand, and Matter: New Materialism and the Politics of Knowledge, *Theory, Culture and Society*, 35 (7–8), 49–72.

Rogers, A. (2014), *The Base of the Iceberg: Informal Learning and Its Impact on Formal and Non-formal Learning*, Berlin, Germany: Barbara Budrich Publishers.

St. Pierre, E. A. (2013), The Appearance of Data, *Cultural Studies ↔ Critical Methodologies*, 13 (4), 223–7.

St. Pierre, E. A. (2020), Why Post Qualitative Inquiry? *Qualitative Inquiry*, 27 (2), 162–6.

Strom, K., Mills, T., Abrams, L., and Dacey, C. (2018), Thinking with Posthuman Perspectives in Self-Study Research, *Studying Teacher Education*, 14 (2), 141–55.

Taylor, C. A., and Fairchild, N. (2020), Towards a Posthumanist Institutional Ethnography: Viscous Matterings and Gendered Bodies, *Ethnography and Education*, 15 (4), 509–27.

UK Government (2017), Available at: https://assets.publishing.service.gov.uk/government/uploads/system/uploads/attachment_data/file/649129/National_Citizen_Service_Royal_Charter__26_April_2017_.pdf Accessed 29 September 2021.

Ulmer, J. B. (2017), Posthumanism as Research Methodology: Inquiry in the Anthropocene, *International Journal of Qualitative Studies in Education (QSE)*, 30 (9), 832–48.

8

The achievements of informal adult reading group talk through vernacular expression: challenging the dominant discourses of literary study

John Gordon, School of Education and Lifelong Learning,
University of East Anglia

When reading is framed as literary study in formal education, especially in the secondary phase (ages eleven to eighteen), it has an influence on how individuals view themselves as readers (Clark, Osborne and Akerman, 2008). This can have enduring effects on the reading habits and self-esteem of individuals into adulthood, becoming an issue of social justice when it begins to affect how we think about what reading is for, what sort of reading we value and who can engage in what types of reading and when. This chapter examines how adults participating in book groups talk about what they read, and identifies how the focus, structures and discourse of their conversations differ significantly from how students talk about texts with their teachers in formal education. This approach complements research by Duncan (2012) which made the case for reading circles as contexts for developing adult literacy, and which 'epitomize reading as being at once individual and communal' (165). Reviewing Duncan's book, Satchwell (2015) noted that the concepts of literacy and literature 'often seem to inhabit different areas in both academia and life'. This chapter connects the two concepts by taking a lifelong learning perspective on shared reading, proposing that changes to pedagogies could make school reading experiences more inclusive than established practices allow, and more likely to establish orientations to reading – including leisure reading as an autodidactic pursuit – that can support adult literacy development in later life. My research investigating the achievements of adults taking part in informal reading circle conversations about literature suggests that a shift from education policy's focus on cultural capital (Bourdieu, 1986) as content knowledge (Shulman, 1992: 'the theories, principles and concepts of that particular discipline') in curricular designs would be beneficial. In formal reading education, where authors and texts are prescribed and attributed value by official curricula, this means acknowledgement that there are many different ways to read and discuss books with insight, hence this chapter's focus on how readers talk about books together. Duncan's research elicited the interests and motivations of members of the reading circle she convened, exploring the benefits of group reading in adult literacy pedagogy. The approaches recommended here derive from comparative micro-level analyses of conversations in reading circles and in formal education, conducted using methods influenced by conversation analysis (Gordon, 2020a). They describe what we might learn for policy and pedagogy by paying close attention to how adult learners talk about literature. They have potential to inform pedagogies that are more sensitive to varied cultural, gendered and class-oriented reading practices and which place greater emphasis on promoting and consolidating the pleasures of reading narratives and reading together for their own sake. They invite teaching based on more nuanced understanding of how readers respond to texts in group settings, and how they involve one another in comment and reflection. By accommodating different modes of enjoying narrative and talking about books, pedagogy can engage more people in the pleasures of reading from a young age, with potential to mitigate current gaps in reading engagement and attainment. Currently schooling compounds rather than diminishes those gaps, alienating many nascent readers.

Literary study in schools can have a lasting impact on our relationships with reading through life (Gordon, 2020b). The way we view literary reading therefore has potential to extend or limit our reading for leisure, and our self-perception of ourselves as readers, in contexts of formal education and employment. How we read, what we read and the value we attribute to each relate to culture and identity, both vital in processes of social transformation (Castle, 2001: 30). The concept of literary reading relates to broader conceptions of reading and reading development, overlapping with their categorization of reading skills according to relative sophistication. Literary reading is usually aligned with supposedly higher-level skills, for example, involving interpreting texts 'between' and 'beyond' the lines that comprise them (Guppy and Hughes, 1998), where readers bring to their interpretation of texts the skill of inference and consideration of the contexts in which they were created. The alignment of literary reading with these skills is demonstrated in assessment criteria for examinations in GCSE

English Literature (Department for Education, 2013), applying to courses in schools and further education. These courses assume the existence of something called 'literature', a body of texts somehow different from the myriad texts we encounter across media (online, on television), in our daily environments (traffic signs, advertisements) and in print generally (magazines, textbooks, 'airport novels'). Course specifications delineate 'literature' by specifying groups of texts – canons – which represent and embody 'literary value', itself a contested term (Eagleton, 2008). One widely accepted dimension of literary value is the artistry of a given text, the sense that it is a product of an author's craft. This lends literary reading a specific and defining trait: sensitivity to texts as items of aesthetic beauty (Rosenblatt, 1978), and capacity to appreciate and articulate the effects of those texts on readers. This form of reading may also entail evaluation, judging the aesthetic qualities and achievements of one text relative to others of the same genre or similar provenance. Evaluation in turn allows readers, or critics, to place texts in hierarchies of artistic merit, identifying them as more or less literary, and determining which texts are elevated to the category of 'literature' and included in recognized canons. These conventions constitute a disciplinary pedagogic device of literary study, the rules of which shape pedagogical communication and act 'selectively on meaning potential … [and on] the potential discourse available to be pedagogised' (Bernstein, 1996: 41). They are a code 'regulating what comes out of it', shaping what we accept as literary reading in conversation.

Our sense of what constitutes literary reading is dependent on our cultural values, and relates to what we recognize as skilled reading, whether in the institutionalized practices of reading literature in formal education or in reading for pleasure. Where literary reading entails evaluation of aesthetic merit, and where our understanding of the 'literariness' of texts requires some degree of hierarchizing them, we must step back from the concept of 'literature' and recognize that wherever it is invoked, it relates to cultural values and assumptions that should not and cannot be regarded as universal or fixed. The current movement to decolonize curricula across disciplines indicates this position is widely held. The contemporary survey *Lit in Colour* (Elliott et al., 2021) explores diversity in the canon of English Literature, though the fact that themes of colonization, gender politics and identities have long been a focus of literary studies in higher education also signals that the qualities of text valued in any given period will continually shift, as different groups and different agendas influence literary discourse over time. Literary discourse changes, as does the consensus about what 'doing' literary discourse looks like

(Eaglestone, 2002). Reading may become 'literary reading' when it happens in a seminar of a university course in English Literature, where students and tutors adopt a specialist vocabulary to talk about the focal canon and the texts which comprise it, already designated 'literature'.

How do we determine 'literary reading' in reading practices outside formal education, where institutional markers do not designate the quality of 'literariness' activities so confidently? In recent debates around school curricula for England and Wales, government ministers (Gove, 2010), think tanks (Simons and Porter, 2015) and OFSTED (2021) have framed the study of English Literature relative to cultural literacy (Hirsch, Trefil and Kett, 1988) and cultural capital (Bourdieu, 1986), while the discipline has become content-oriented in the context of the 'knowledge-rich curriculum' of 'important facts and truths, delivered through a well-sequenced, knowledge-rich curriculum' (Gibb, 2021). The arrangements shape an experience of literature that is very different from informal reading for pleasure outside school, and which differs from the experiences of reading literature framed in first-language literary studies in other countries. While government ministers have presented the movement towards the knowledge curriculum as a policy response to gaps in educational attainment and as a means to achieve social justice (Gibb, 2015), this institutional and official version of literary reading offers little or no place for students' voice or expressions of literary achievement in vernacular speech. It is, essentially, a 'top down' model of literary knowledge and discourse, realized through a narrowly prescribed canon of study texts. Though there have been recent and welcome attempts to widen the canon (e.g. the adoption of texts recommended by the Lit in Colour initiative as examination texts by Pearson), the dominant mode of assessment remains one of individual formal examination, without coursework or oral assessment, sustaining pedagogies that privilege memorization.

Relationships between adult reading habits and school experiences of literary reading

The survey data and the two transcripts of book group conversations presented in this chapter were generated during research for a project called *Literature's Lasting Impression*, funded by the British Academy across 2016 and 2017. The research explored adults' recollections of literary reading in formal education, and literary reading in three phases of formal education (primary, secondary and higher), and in book groups.

The survey suggested connections between the literary study experience of current GCSE students and adults who grew up, studied literature and took examinations in schools in the mid- to late twentieth century. Though the regulatory frameworks for literary study in schools have changed, and ideological influences shaping its conception have varied, voices from the different generations reported similar experiences and similar concerns about the effects of some conventions of literary reading in schools and their reading habits into adulthood. The perspective of adults reflecting on reading some decades after their own schooling provided insights to the relationship between their experiences of reading in school, their self-perception as readers and the implications for social justice relative to adult literacy.

To investigate literary reading in practice, I joined eight different reading communities, two of each type, and observed their discussions about literature while also making audio recordings of their conversations. Table 8.1 shows the number and distribution of my observations according to each setting.

Table 8.1 Literary study talk in 'Literature's Lasting Impression'

Setting		Age range	Sessions observed	Focal text(s)
Reading group	A	Mixed	1	*Life after Life*, Kate Atkinson
	B	Mixed	2	*Daddy Long-legs*, Jean Webster
Primary school	A	10–11	4	*The Boy in the Striped Pyjamas*, John Boyne
	B	10–11	3	*The Windsinger*, William Nicholson
Secondary school	A	14–15	6	*The Strange Case of Dr Jekyll and Mr Hyde*, Robert Louis Stevenson
	B	11–12	4	*The Boy in the Striped Pyjamas*, John Boyne/*Coraline*, Neil Gaiman
Higher education – university	A	Undergraduate year 2 (mixed)	3	*Tom Jones*, Henry Fielding
	B	Undergraduate year 2 (mixed)	2	*Pond*, Claire Louise Bennett

I analysed transcripts representing each type of reading group using an adapted form of conversation analysis. The micro and emic perspective afforded by my adaptation of conversation analysis allowed me to identify distinctive features of each conversation, of their structure, the orientation of speakers to each other, their use of paralinguistic features of communication and how they used and represented texts in the progress of conversations. The complete analysis is represented in *Researching Interpretive Talk around Literary Narrative Texts: Shared Novel Reading* (Gordon, 2020). In transcripts representing secondary school discussions of literature, for example, teachers embedded quotation in their speech with far greater frequency than speakers in any other format, including one teacher who embedded at least one quotation of the study text in a third of all her turns in conversation. In transcripts representing higher education seminars, the practice of making links between numerous texts (intertexting) was more common than in lesson data from each school phase of literary study or in reading groups, consistent with progression outlined in frameworks for higher education (e.g. UKHEQC). This discussion shares some of the findings related to book group conversations, represented in plain text transcripts, with a greater emphasis on the implications of the research findings for social justice. Though transcripts from formal education are not presented here, this discussion is informed by them and the different features of collective reading they revealed.

The project survey of 165 adult participants represented school experiences dating back to the 1940s, and generally interviewees described positive experiences of reading in primary and secondary schools. Participants in the survey included adults engaged through face-to-face public events in Norwich, at Norwich Forum (a public forum in the city centre, also home to the city's Millennium Library) and through community groups (e.g. related to Norwich City Football Club), and via an online version. Where adults reported enjoyment of reading in school, they often associated it with the novels selected for study by their teachers, but less frequently with how those texts were taught. Their views about the teaching of literature suggested complex effects and impacts of literary reading in schools. At times, participants made direct links between the obligations of preparing for examinations and the experience of reading literature in school, suggesting the design of assessments impels particular ways of engaging with and speaking about literature. Though the survey participants were educated in each decade since the 1940s (represented in broadly equal numbers), their experiences suggested that the damaging correlation of examination and reading was experienced by at least some of them in each decade. Some of the following remarks about negative experiences of reading in school were shared by participants who also reported long fallow periods when they read little for pleasure. They attributed these periods to negative experiences of reading literature in school, with linked impacts on their self-perception as readers.

This participant, remembering reading Conrad's *The Nigger of the Narcissus*, identifies a particular quality of literary reading, one of looking beneath the surface:

> This was the first time we read as critique/understanding of a novel. The teacher challenged our responses and although I cannot recall much about the story, I recall being asked what it meant. Previous to that, it had always been just a story. As a class we were taking our first post-secondary exams. In the late 50s schools were just introducing opportunities for Secondary Modern school pupils to take a leaving exam. Previous to that you left school at 15 for work with no qualifications.

Another participant identifies a similar orientation to reading, though she conveys some ambivalence about such activity:

> My introduction to reading for an exam was perplexing. I had always read though at home: *Ivanhoe, Jane Eyre, Wuthering Heights*. Joseph Conrad was a difficult read. However, being introduced to previously unencountered writers – while not totally enjoyable – did make you think. Negative experiences of understanding can have the effect of looking harder. I have fond memories of that final year at school before going to Secretarial College.

In each of these examples, literary reading in school is about approaching novels as more than 'just a story'. Some level of difficulty, even discomfort, is inherent in literary reading. Other participants elaborated this experience in a focus group interview conducted in a community group, an exchange of peers who had known each other since school:

> Derek: The way we were taught at the grammar school, the classical books, they kind of jarred you off, because I kind of started to watch a bit … every time I get the opportunity now, I watch a Shakespeare play they show on TV sometimes, and I enjoy them. Whereas, my experience from school jarred me off Shakespeare, if you know what I mean.
> Ted: It was difficult to follow the writing, yes.
> Derek: Because we were expected, as Ted says, to … clause analysis and all this sort of thing. You were kind of missing the point of the story almost, weren't you?

Our contemporary frameworks shaping teaching and learning around literature, now very similar to those in use until O-levels were abolished in the late 1980s, continue to inhibit students' enjoyment of stories for their own sake, as this GCSE student indicates:

> The problem is we have to do these books for our final exam. There are no books that we can read purely for the enjoyment of it as a class, to like sort of discuss and find out more about, because I'm sure there are plenty of books out there that not many people understand but that have a really good storyline. But we can't do that because of exams.
>
> Like *Dr Jekyll and Mr Hyde* is like ... it's a lot about analysing key quotes about themes and stuff whereas other books might not necessarily be about themes, they might be about something else and it's like trying to balance what we need to learn and what we want to read.

Across the survey and focus group interviews, participants made clear that engagement with literature in school had a value for them, but also that literary reading framed by curricula and teaching conventions can deter students from reading for pleasure, in whatever decade it occurs. One older speaker made a similar distinction between reading for examination and the powerful experience of reading for the sake of the story:

> I do recall it vividly, because it was the first book I'd really been introduced to. My parents were working people. I certainly wasn't encouraged much to read at home. I was out kicking a ball about like most kids did, I suppose, but that did open my eyes from that point. I think it must have been the first year of grammar school, *Lorna Doone*. After that, the thing I probably found with grammar school was that it was an exam factory. I suppose the best way to describe it is that the intention was to get you through your O levels.

The accounts demonstrate the importance that readers of all ages place on enjoying narratives for their own sake. They suggest that approaches to literary study in formal education should allow more space for this pleasure in story, and the possibility that with some alteration the pedagogy of reading could be more effective in establishing patterns of reading literature for pleasure into adulthood:

> Ted: It could almost be a memory test couldn't it, examination?
> Derek: Yes. It's got to be something that fulfils you and drives you forward and gives you a thirst for ... but that didn't do that for me. Once you got into work you had other issues to take up your mind and reading went by the by. As I say, as I got more into middle age, I joined a book club and I went to university actually, after I finished work, and that expanded my mind a lot

more. So, I just feel sorry that for about 25 years of my life, from the years of 16 to mid-30s, I didn't read virtually at all.
Ted: But, it's nice that you could always catch up. You're not ... there were missed years ...
Derek: Yes, I do feel like I'm catching up.

The rest of this chapter presents data drawn from observation of informal book group conversations around literature, undertaken in the same research project. The conversations demonstrate participants' enjoyment of reading literature, of reading together, and of sharing their experiences of reading. The way members of these groups discuss literature is also important. They do not adopt the core conventions of literary study in formal education, for instance the regular quotation of text by teachers and students, yet they realize comparable achievements of reflection, analysis and insight, which emerge gradually from their shared experiences of story (see Gordon, 2020a for analysis of conversations in schools, universities and book groups, using conversation analysis).

The conversational resources these book group members use to build their interpretations of literature differ from those used in the discourse of school literary study. They tell stories of different types to express and connect their responses, and cite other stories to interpret the focal texts in their conversations. Their ways of discussing literature constitute adult reading practices of inherent value. Their conversations also suggest ways of reading that can inform formal pedagogies, if we choose to identify and value the features of discourse they use.

Methods for recognizing the literary reading achievements of book groups

The data presented in this chapter represent the conversations of two informal reading groups, whose members join voluntarily in discussions which occurred outside the frame of formal literary study. As I considered my experience of listening to their conversations and the data that arose from their talk in the form of transcripts, I became interested in their communal reading practices, their reading achievements and the reading positions participants adopted in these conversations.

When readers meet to discuss texts together, they express opinions about the stories or poems they read, agree or argue with one another and – in some instances – prompt or organize the contributions of others in the conversation. Teachers, for example, have a responsibility to shape and guide discussion of texts in their classes, but members of some informal reading groups may also adopt similar directing roles, 'acting like a teacher' in a 'storyline of instruction' (Harré and van Langenhove, 1999: 17). In these activities, readers adopt positions relative to the texts under discussion and relative to the views shared by others, or they have positions designated for them. Where members of reading communities choose to guide or organize others, they influence (or attempt to influence) the reading positions of others. This may have some resonance with what Duncan (2012) called participant-led differentiation.

The institutionalized practice of reading in literary studies encourages and seeks to develop reading positions that orient to texts as aesthetic objects. It provides a specialist disciplinary discourse for teachers and students of the subject to articulate their own reading positions within the subject-defining frame of aesthetic orientation. Often, reading in the discipline of literary study involves readers expressing their own reading positions relative to the views of literary critics and authors, especially at advanced levels of study, most overtly at the stage of writing assignments where students must cite or quote the perspectives offered by these figures of authority in the discipline. Lessons or seminars are often a rehearsal for this genre of writing, an apprenticeship in the discourse of literary studies. In summary, the practice of literary reading in formal education usually entails some or all of these traits: adoption of an aesthetic reading orientation to texts, frequent quotation of focal texts, use of a specialist vocabulary to describe features of texts and the author's craft (*simile*, *assonance*, *narrative voice*, etc.), and invocation of other canonical texts or literary-critical works (a form of intertexting).

My analysis of the book group conversations adopts and adapts *positioning theory*, a perspective initially established in the social sciences to explore how people position one another in speech and rhetoric (Kayi-Adar, 2018; Raggatt, 2015), focussed on their rights and duties during conversation, and on changes in their repertoire of communication strategies for responding to or involving others (Harré and Moghaddam, 2015: 7). The potential of positioning theory to explore the distribution and exercise of power during conversations is demonstrated in its application in studies of identity (Hermans, 2001), gendered subjectivities (Holloway, 1984) and religious discourse (Tan and Moghaddam, 1999). Harré and van Langenhove (1999) investigate aspects of classroom teaching, including verbal reprimands and congratulations, recognizing that school students can choose to reject or resist the positions teachers delegate to them. Positioning theory has also been adopted by the discourse of literary criticism (Kayi-Adar, 2013; Maynard, 2009; Stockwell, 2013), recognizing that literary forms such as the novel invite readers to adopt various positions to the events, characters or ideas they present. Gordon (2019; 2020b) synthesized the applications of positioning theory in education research and literary studies research to investigate the adoption and delegation of reading positions in talk around texts, identifying four broad reading positions prompted by teachers. The way in which teachers use and embed quotations from study texts in their own speech is central to their positioning of students. Sometimes teachers quote the reported speech of characters in novels directly, dramatizing their voices. This action seeks students' *immersion* in the world of the story, positioning them relative to characters, places or events in the text's diegetic world. At other times, teachers invite students to *step back* from the world of the story by isolating quotations for comment and analysis, marking them overtly ('Let's consider this quotation here') and with resources of speech that orient readers' attention to specific words or phrases (*deictic* resources), for example through repetition used to foreground quotations for attention. Sometimes this positioning overlaps with invitations for students to *appreciate aesthetic qualities* of the text, where teachers may exploit stress and intonation to highlight features such as assonance, or to suggest how a passage of text builds suspense. Occasionally teachers select and present quotations in their speech for students to adopt an *interpretive* position, for example reflecting on the juxtaposition of two quoted details. The positioning affordances of spoken quotation in literary pedagogy are summarized in Table 8.2.

In book group discussions, participants may express, build and designate reading positions using resources that differ from those used in formal literary studies, though they may also arrive at precise and sophisticated insight. In this study they used direct quotations with less frequency, instead sharing anecdotes

Table 8.2 Positioning affordances of spoken quotation, and their effects on readers

Spoken quotation – positioning affordance	Effect on readers
Diegetic	Immerses readers in the world the novel represents, for example by dramatizing a character's voice in reported speech.
Analytic	Isolates spoken quotations for analysis, inviting readers to step back from them and to consider them as special and discrete objects worthy of attention.
Aesthetic	Emphasizes or enacts aesthetic qualities of the text for the appreciation of other participants in the conversation, for example through stress and increasing pace to enact speed or momentum.
Interpretive	Directs attention to possible readings of the text, often by juxtaposing quotations in an utterance.

of different types or paraphrasing episodes of the novels for discussion. They also referred to popular culture texts more extensively, in ways which elucidated their interpretation of the focal texts in their conversations differently from those found in classroom data (for full discussion of these differences, see Gordon, 2020a). The concept of *small stories* (Bamberg and Georgakopolou, 2008: 5) provides a way of describing the actions in talk taken by book group members to position others, referring to 'tellings' of ongoing, future, hypothetical and shared events. Thinking of conversational speech as a flow and mix of different *small stories* is a form of narrative theory, usually applied to everyday speech. Gordon (2020b) used the concept to describe the different narrative actions performed by book group members, either when they spoke about the narrative of the novel under discussion, or when they introduced to their conversations various anecdotes about their reading activity, stories of their daily lives or allusions to other stories in any media. The small stories they shared that paraphrase episodes from novels are *text-generated* small stories. When speakers share these and connect them with other textual details, they become *recasting* small stories. Book group members also offered anecdotes about the circumstances in which they read and how they read, focussed on the novel under discussion and in more general terms. These are *reading* small stories, stories about the act of reading. It was also common for speakers to introduce anecdotes about their daily lives and experiences, for example where an episode in a novel resonated for them: *personal* small stories. As well as building discussion of novels around these four types of small story, book group members often referred to other stories in popular culture. Theories of text and reading describe this phenomenon as intertextual (Allen, 2000; Kristeva, 1980), indicating that the interpretations readers generate of one focal text depend on the links they ascribe to other texts. The shared process of reading in book groups can be considered intertextual where speakers in the conversation cite, quote or paraphrase intertexts (Lemke, 1992), whether they are other novels, films, songs or television programmes, in fact any other text in any form or genre.

Positioning readers and reading in book group conversation: Using small stories to analyse Jean Webster's *Daddy-Long-Legs*

This conversation shows members of a different book group developing a cumulative analysis of the novel *Daddy-Long-Legs* (Webster, 1912). Four female members of the group, meeting in the village home of one, share small stories of different types, each contributing to their developing analysis of the novel. The form of *Daddy-Long-Legs* is epistolary, with drawings. It comprises monthly letters by a teenage orphan, known as Judy, to her mysterious benefactor 'Mr John Smith'. She describes and sometimes provides illustrations of her life at college. In the book group conversation about the novel, Angela begins the exchange:

1	Angela	I thought the accounts of the rooms they shared and the boarding school japes were quite fun.
2	Pat	And they're very descriptive as well. When she [Judy] went to the farm and the surroundings, the landscape – I thought that was really nice, that she enjoyed it and it was something that she looked forward to for a start, but then didn't want to go in the end, but it was just the descriptions of what it was like around the farm and how cosy it obviously felt to her. It was a home, not an orphanage or a school, it was somewhere she could actually relate to that she thought – this would be nice as mine, as my home.
3	Val	I thought it was very clever the way that the letters were just one person and there was never any reply. I thought that was incredibly clever to go right the way through the whole book like that without having any input from the other party.
4	Mary	Yes, you were having to fill in a lot for yourself, weren't you? – the assumptions of what had happened, and of course there never were any replies, that was the whole point. The sheer tenacity with which she kept up that correspondence was again very indicative of her character.
5	Val	The fact that she got those flowers and the gift when she was ill in hospital, it was almost like a highlight. There's something coming in the other direction for once. Then of course it all settled down because there wasn't anything else.
6	Angela	Yeah, reading it on the Kindle, you could see there were quite a few highlighted bits that people had made notes on, which is where I prefer a book where you can stick those in really.

Their conversation achieves many of the interactions between reader and text that we would expect to find in institutionalized literary study, accomplished through the sharing of small stories and demonstrated in members' shifting positions to the text and each other. Angela's statement (turn 1) articulates her evaluative reading position in response to the text-given small stories of 'accounts' of school life. Pat indirectly reports a small story narrative derived from the novel. Pat's position relative to this small story is at once participatory (she dramatizes Judy's quoted voice), embodying the protagonist and thus the world of the story, and one of aesthetic appreciation (of descriptive prose, turn 2). Her pleasure and empathy combine. At turn 3, Val positions group attention on the 'letters' (the form taken by the 'accounts'), and adopts a more overtly literary-analytic position to the text in evaluating its 'cleverness' as a manipulation of the epistolary form. Mary's interest in the gaps in the text (turn 4) – which readers must fill to make sense of the narrative – combines an interest in the novel's form with a perspective on characterization, responding to the text-given stories of *Daddy-Long-Legs*, but also to the small stories it *does not* narrate, the latent stories of events that fall between letters and which go undescribed. Val recasts a text-given small story to elaborate (turn 5) – the fact of 'something coming in the other direction for once' – to signal disruption of the novel's normative form of epistolary imbalance: this is a *recasting small story*. The variety of small story forms entering book group discussions is also demonstrated in how Angela takes up Val's assertion that the 'flowers' episode is a highlight (turn 6). Angela understands it as meaning the action of readers to annotate texts with highlighting pens or using corresponding functions in mobile reading devices. This is a *reading small story*, at first about Angela's personal experience but then generalized to position herself as one reader in a collective abstraction of 'readers' whose earlier annotations are available to her in the Kindle book.

In much of this book group discussion and reading, *recasting small stories* are an important feature in that they embody or articulate participants' positions relative to the texts under discussion. They offer a resource for expressing sophisticated individual responses to texts, and for positioning or developing the reading of other members. Their functions differ from those of the *text-given small stories* they recast. Further on in the conversation partially represented in the transcript above, Pat recasts a narrative presented as one letter in *Daddy-Long-Legs*. Pat's recast version elides its details with information drawn from another letter in the book, with the effect of highlighting for other members the heightened emotion of the protagonist June that Pat identified in the *text-given story* of the focal letter. This constitutes subtle framing of the source text in the context of the book group's social interaction, a gentle and level peer-to-peer pedagogy that concurrently articulates Pat's own literary reading and positions the focal text so that other members may appreciate the same features of the text. Together the group achieve subtle readings, an analysis of the text as literature, in a manner quite different from what we find in formal literary studies in secondary and higher education.

Book group literary reading by intertext proxies: Categorizing Kate Atkinson's *Life after Life*

In this second example of book group discussion, which a different book group conducted over a restaurant meal, participants developed a nuanced and cumulative analysis of Kate Atkinson's novel *Life after Life* (2013). The book has a complex form relating to its representation of narrative time, also reflected in its 2022 BBC television adaptation. As the novel's title suggests, it presents alternate pathways of one person's life across the early twentieth century and Second World War. The relationships between timelines and episodes in the book are therefore potentially challenging to represent clearly in talk. Nevertheless, this group's conversation demonstrates a range of analytic achievements akin to high-level literary study. The group participants also co-construct an affiliative environment for their consideration of the novel, using a variety of conversational resources to position the challenging text as an object of shared reflection. These include various invocations of the text, usually through indirect means which differ from a tendency found in school and university discussions, especially in teachers' talk, to invocation through direct quotation. The group members use repetition, small details drawn from texts used to represent larger units (e.g. episodes and themes) and other texts as proxies for elaborating their discussion of the text, illustrated in this extract where they speculate on how the novel could be adapted to other media:

1	Phil	I can kind of imagine it being one of these box -
2	Andrea	(*aside*) well, one of my-
3	Phil	-sets, where different events ... different comp- series come in different epi- different episodes coming out.
4	David	It would be very difficult to film.
5	Eric	oh yeah,
6	Barbara	I mean that I can't see that it could.
7	Eric	Oh yeah, impossible, impossible, in one film it wouldn't work, it wouldn't work in one film.
8	Barbara	You couldn't do it, no.
9	Eric	but in a sense-
10	Phil	no, but in a series-
11	Andrea	you could do it in a series-
12	Phil	it would work-
13	Andrea	yeah, you could do it in a series.
14	Barbara	Well, The Time Traveller's Wife ...

15	Andrea	I never saw it, no.
16	Barbara	That wasn't as-
17	Andrea	no, that wasn't such a good film.
18	David	Especially if all the actors are mumbling as well.
19	All	(*laughter*)
20	Phil	Yeah, there's a lot of time-travelling series on Netflix, isn't there?
21	Andrea	But is it time travel?
22	Phil	-don't know.
23	David	Well, it's not really time travel-
24	Barbara	no, it's not time travel-
25	David	is it?
26	Phil	No, it's a diff- it's a-
27	Andrea	no, I'm not saying it is.
28	Phil	different form of it–
29	Andrea	yes-
30	Phil	isn't it?
31	David	'cause it's only one person doing the-
32	Eric	but it's just a series of what-ifs -
33	Phil	and the dog, and the dog, you know-
34	David	yeah.
35	Andrea	It's a what-if book.
36	Eric	(*laughs*)
37	David	A what-if book, yeah.
38	Phil	Yeah, but it's got the same theme, because it's looking at different, different – alternate universes, really.

The group participants arrive at consensus that this is a 'what if' book, and have worked through a process of categorization, essentially an exploration of genre. This is enabled by and follows from Phil's proposal (turn 1) that it could be a 'box set' narrative (meaning those available on demand through TV streaming services, or on disc formats such as DVD or Blu-ray), and David's point that 'it would be very difficult to film' (all of this pre-dating the BBC adaptation). David's remark initiates some further interrogation of the novel's form, relative to these genres, as the group seek to identify a suitable form for adaptation (a series) and then identify a parallel, *The Time Traveller's Wife*. Across turns 20 to 30 the participants are animated in their discussion of the extent to which *Life after Life* is about time travel, an issue which has been triggered by the introduction of *The Time Traveller's Wife*. This invocation of another text provides a proxy by which the participants articulate incrementally more precise statements about the themes of the text and its genre, so that by turn 38 Phil ties theme and genre together in his definition of the what-if form: 'it's the same theme because it's looking at different alternate universes really.'

The way in which members of this book group use repetition to develop their analysis is hinted at in this extract in Phil's reference to 'the dog, y'know' (line 33). The comment may seem inconsequential in this context, but it is significant when examined according to the full book group meeting on this occasion. His comment about the dog does not generate requests for clarification in the exchange above, a consequence of the participants' invocations of this detail earlier in the conversation. In conversation analytic terms, the repeated 'dog' invocation demonstrates indexicality. It is a shared reference point for participants, an index around which they tether their discussion. It is therefore not only an object of analysis, it is also a resource for cohesion in conversation. In this context, the 'dog' index introduced at this point in the conversation carries with it all the associations of each prior invocation of the phrase in the conversation (not included in the transcript above) when Barbara said:

> But then, later on, with the dog on the wall, she seems to have to go through three lives before she survives the Blitz, because-

When Phil economically introduces 'the dog, y'know' at turn 43, he invokes not only the novel but also the connection Barbara draws between that detail and the protagonist's 'three lives'. By juxtaposing the 'three lives' with 'the dog on the wall' detail, Barbara's remark tacitly identifies the 'dog' detail, which is repeated in different timelines of the protagonist, as an index in the novel. When Phil comments on the dog here his input is probably more than a casual aside: it is entirely relevant to categorization of the book as a 'what if' story and consistent with the overt attention of the speakers to 'alternate universes' represented in the novel.

Conclusion

The two transcripts of book group conversation presented here show adult readers collaborating in generating sophisticated readings of novels. They demonstrate achievements of analysis and reflection that we associate with literary studies in formal education, though they use few of the resources of speech (such as frequently embedding textual quotation in their own utterances) and little of the specialist vocabulary we find in institutionalized literary study. Small stories appear to be a powerful tool for articulating thoughts and responses to the works of fiction considered by each group, especially when they combine in interplay of their text-given, recasting, personal and reading forms. In the second transcript, we see an iterative process of analysis and argumentation that exploits repetition (Tannen, 1989) and intertextual invocation. It is a recursive process with a rhythm that differs from the linearity of conversations in formal objective-led teaching, though it nevertheless achieves analytic readings with its different resources.

The reflections of adults on their reading experiences at school, presented in my overview of the survey and interview data, suggested that formal pedagogies of literary study should allow more space for enjoyment of story, in the form of narrative fiction, for its own sake. The perspective was echoed by contemporary students participating in the main study. The transcript data presented here show how stories can be both an object of attention, for enjoyment and critique, and a part of a vernacular method of literary analysis. For now, however, the analytic achievements of these vernacular storying methods of literary reading are not widely recognized or identified in education research which informs mainstream education policy for literacy, reading or literary study pedagogies. As long as they are not seen or valued, the achievements of some adult reading practices around literature will be underappreciated. Worse, the ways in which students continue to experience literature in school may deter them from reading literature for pleasure once the obligation to read for examinations has passed, to the potential detriment of their lifelong leisure, learning and opportunities. The possibility of lifelong learning through the autodidactic offer of literary fiction and collaborative education of group reading will be lost to many. A situation where 'the organization of education often produces cleavage and insulation between subjects and levels' (Bernstein, 1996: 173) persists, as aptitudes and interests we all possess relating to reading and talking about fiction together are not accorded status or function – and therefore not systematically developed – in the institutional structures for reading literature. Our access to the words and thoughts of others may be diminished, and with it our scope to participate in explorations of the different ways the world might be. The consequences for social transformation are subtle but profound, touching on literacy, access, cultural value, voice and participation.

References

Allen, G. (2000), *Intertextuality*, London: Routledge.
Atkinson, K. (2013), *Life after Life*, London: Doubleday.

Bamberg, M., and Georgakopoulou, A. (2008), Small Stories as a New Perspective in Narrative and Identity Analysis, *Text & Talk*, 28 (3), 377–96.
Bernstein, B. (1996), *Pedagogy, Symbolic Control and Identity*, London: Taylor and Francis.
Bourdieu, P. (1986), The Forms of Capital, in J. G. Richardson (ed.), *Handbook of Theory and Research for the Sociology of Education*, 241–56, New York: Greenwood Press.
Castles, S. (2001), Studying Social Transformation, *International Political Science Review*, 22 (1), 13–32.
Clark, C., Osborne, S., and Akerman, R. (2008), *Young People's Self-Perceptions as Readers: An Investigation Including Family, Peer and School Influences*, London: National Literacy Trust.
Department for Education (2013), *English Literature: GCSE Subject Content and Assessment Objectives (DFE-00231–2013)*, London: Department for Education.
Duncan, S. (2012), *Reading Circles, Novels and Adult Reading Development*, London/New York: Continuum/Bloomsbury Academic.
Eaglestone, R. (2002), *Doing English*, London: Routledge.
Eagleton, T. (2008), *Literary Theory*, 3rd edition, Minnesota: University of Minnesota Press.
Elliott, V., Nelson-Addy, L., Chantiluke, R., and Courtney, C. (2021), *Lit in Colour: Diversity in Literature in English Schools*, London: Runnymede Trust/Penguin Books.
Gibb, N. (2015), How E. D. Hirsch Came to Shape UK Government Policy, in J. Simons, and N. Porter (eds.), *Knowledge and the Curriculum*, 12–20, London: Policy Exchange.
Gibb, N. (2021), The Importance of a Knowledge-Rich Curriculum. Available at: https://www.gov.uk/government/speeches/the-importance-of-a-knowledge-rich-curriculum.
Gordon, J. (2019), The Turn of the Page: Spoken Quotation in Shared Reading, *Classroom Discourse*, 11 (4), 366–87.
Gordon, J. (2020a), *Researching Interpretive Talk around Literary Narrative Texts: Shared Novel Reading*, New York: Routledge.
Gordon, J. (2020b), Literature's Lasting Impression, in *The Bloomsbury Handbook of Reading Perspectives and Practices*, London: Bloomsbury.
Gove, M. (2010), All Pupils Will Learn Our Island Story. Available at: http://conservative-speeches.sayit.mysociety.org/speech/60144 Accessed 17 July 2017.
Guppy, P., and Hughes, M. (1998), *Development of Independent Reading: Reading Support Explained*, New York: McGraw-Hill Education.
Harré, R., and van Langenhove, L. (1999), *Positioning Theory*, Oxford: Blackwell Publishers.
Harré, R., and Moghaddam, F. (2015), Positioning Theory and Social Representations, in G. Sammut, E. Andreouli, G. Gaskell, and J. Valsiner (eds.), *The Cambridge Handbook of Social Representations*, 224–33, Cambridge: Cambridge University Press.

Hermans, H. (2001), The Dialogical Self: Toward a Theory of Personal and Cultural Positioning, *Culture & Psychology*, 7 (3), 243–81.

Hirsch, E. D. (1967), *Validity in Interpretation*, New Haven, CT: Yale University Press.

Hirsch, E. D., Trefil, J., and Kett, J. F. (1988), *Cultural Literacy: What Every American Needs to Know*, New York: Vintage Books.

Holloway, W. (1984), Difference and the Production of Subjectivity, in J. Henriques, W. Holloway, C. Urwin, C. Venn, and V. Walkerdine (eds.), *Changing the Subject: Psychology, Social Regulation and Subjectivity*, 227–63, London: Methuen.

Kayi-Aydar, H. (2013), No, Rolanda, Completely wrong!' Positioning, Classroom Participation and ESL Learning, *Classroom Discourse*, 4 (2), 130–50.

Kayı-Aydar, H. (2018), Positioning Theory and Discourse Analysis, in *Positioning Theory in Applied Linguistics*, 27–40, Cham: Palgrave Macmillan.

Kristeva, J. (1980), *Desire in Language: A Semiotic Approach to Literature and Art, European Perspectives*, Oxford: Blackwell.

Lemke, J. L. (1992), Intertextuality and Educational Research, *Linguistics and Education*, 4, 257–67.

Maynard, J. (2009), *Literary Intention, Literary Interpretations, and Readers*, Ontario: Broadview Press.

Raggatt, P. (2015), Positioning: Dialogical Voice in Mind and Culture, *Theory & Psychology*, 25 (6), 775–97.

Rosenblatt, L. (1978), *The Reader, the Text, the Poem*, Carbondale: Southern Illinois University Press.

Satchwell, C. (2015), Book Review: Reading Circles, Novels and Adult Reading Development, *British Journal of Educational Studies*, 63 (1), 117–19.

Shulman, L. (1992), Ways of Seeing, Ways of Knowing, Ways of Teaching, Ways of Learning about Teaching, *Journal of Curriculum Studies*, 28, 393–96.

Simons, J. and Porter, N. (2015), *Knowledge and the Curriculum: A Collection of Essays to Accompany E. D. Hirsch's Lecture at Policy Exchange*, London: Policy Exchange.

Stockwell, P. (2013), The Positioned Reader, *Language and Literature*, 22 (3): 263–77.

Tan, S., and F. M. Moghaddam. (1999), 'Positioning in Intergroup Relations', in R. Harré and L. van Langenhove (eds.), *Positioning Theory*, 178–94, Oxford: Blackwell.

Tannen, D. (1989), *Talking Voices. Repetition, Dialogue, and Imagery in Conversational Discourse*, Cambridge: Cambridge University Press.

Webster, J. (1912), *Daddy-Long-Legs*. London Hodder and Stoughton.

Learning through the Covid-19 pandemic: how the pandemic has affected the ways in which adults experience learning in the UK

Karen Fairfax-Cholmeley and Clare Meade

Introduction

The Covid-19 pandemic has brought abrupt social change for everyone in the UK. It has transformed how we behave at work, at home and in society. It has challenged our attitudes, customs and traditions. As we come out of the pandemic, we need to forge and adapt to a 'new normal' as yet unclear but likely to encompass more but different social change in which we experience different degrees of agency. In this context we are focusing on adult learning as a response to, and a way of dealing with, the social change that the pandemic has brought.

In this chapter we explore, through a case study approach, the experiences of adult learning providers and adult learners during the pandemic. We look at how learning providers have adapted, at how, what and with whom learners are learning, and at the role of adult learning in supporting learners through the social changes wrought by the pandemic. We draw on the experiences of a range of learning providers and adult learners who took part in formal and informal learning before and during the pandemic. The learning providers in the study were chosen as they represent a cross-section of provision; from a large county-wide statutory service working with over 300 learners, to very small voluntary organizations often working with very specific communities and small numbers of learners. The projects were known to the researchers and cover rural and urban areas and different communities of interest and needs. The majority of these learners experience social inequalities: insecure work, English as an additional language, religious and cultural issues, issues of confidence and well-being. Many of them have been disproportionately affected by the pandemic.

Context of adult learning and the pandemic

Before the start of the pandemic, the conclusion of the Centenary Commission on Adult Education (2019) was that adult learning should be seen as an essential element of any response to the challenges society faces. It advocated the 'permanent national necessity' of adult education to deal with democratic, societal and industrial challenges. A report from the European Association for the Education of Adults (EAEA, 2020) argues for the importance of educational areas such as health education, well-being and civic education as vital to rebuilding communities and economies as they are important to individuals. UNESCO (2020a and b) argues for promoting stronger adult and community learning policies and practices to tackle pressing economic, social and environmental challenges.

Lopes and McKay (2020) make the connection between adult learning and curbing a pandemic through changed behaviours. They see adult learning as an essential tool for providing literacy, numeracy and digital inclusion leading to political, communicational and social action (EAEA, 2020).

A British Academy report in 2021 identifies nine areas of long-term societal impact thrown up by the pandemic, including: the increasing importance of local communities; renewed awareness of education and skills; worsened health outcomes and growing health inequalities; low and unstable levels of trust; rising unemployment and changing labour market. The report points to the 'pre-existing social deprivations and economic inequalities' which gave space for Covid-19 to thrive. It argues that the pandemic will not be controlled merely by the provision of stronger safety nets for those who suffer most from these inequalities. It is vital that at this moment of societal change, any response needs to look at things differently. It argues that adult learning will need to adapt, to find new ways to meet the needs of learners and to look at where and how learning takes place.

Stanistreet (2020) argues for the need for education which is proactive rather than reactive in times of change:

> the purpose of education cannot be reduced to the creation of productive economic units. Its purpose is, rather, to foster the development of a better

society – a learning society in which people are empowered to change the future instead of being prepared for a future they did not choose and cannot control.

Challenges of responding to the pandemic

The rapid spread of online information sharing and conspiracy theories added to the complexity for governments and health professionals in providing information and for individuals in processing the information they received. The World Health Organisation warned in February 2020 that 'misinformation related to COVID-19 constitutes an "infodemic"' (Arts and Humanities Research Council, 2020). To decipher this plethora of information about the pandemic requires not only literacy skills but also skills of logic, comprehension and reasoned argument. Lopes and McKay argue that adult learning should be an essential element in national emergency strategies to help people understand, interpret and make informed health-related decisions (Lopes and McKay, 2020).

The formal education system has struggled to remain open through the pandemic in many countries, and learning spaces have been redefined. Some homes have been transformed into places for online schooling. Some communities have become disseminators of health information, opening the door for creative non-formal and informal learning opportunities. In Swansea (Wales), the City Council published a parental guide to support the well-being and learning of children during the Covid-19 outbreak (UNESCO, 2020b), while a college in Lancashire (England) has made a 'COVID-19 build back better "pledge" to commit adult learning funding to retraining and upskilling to provide pathways into employment and apprenticeship' (Hopwood Hall College, 2020/21). However, with restrictions on movement and face-to-face gatherings, it is digital learning that has exploded.

The British Academy report (2021: 7) points out the opportunities and challenges inherent in this development: 'The lockdown has created an opportunity to embrace digital technology in enhancing the way we do things but it has also highlighted the disparities in digital access and heightened the need to ensure no groups are left behind by the rapid changes in the way people live, work and learn.' The Learning and Work Institute Adult Participation in Learning Survey (Aldridge, Jones and Southgate, 2020) found that the pandemic is widening social inequalities in particular for young people, women and people with no qualifications and those lacking effective essential skills, including online skills.

In his editorial to a special issue of *Adult Education Quarterly*, Boeren (2020) argues that 'during this trying time, adult education can be a force for connecting people, who, after months of social isolation and physical distancing, recognize more than ever the value of supportive networks and solidarity among members of society'.

The pandemic has put great pressure on education providers. At different times, governments have closed down schools and learning centres, funding has been affected and students have stayed away for safety reasons. Government guidelines tended to focus on formal education, leaving providers of non-formal and informal learning to find their own solutions to Covid-19-compliant delivery. Conversely, there have been huge possibilities for moving away from traditional methods of teaching and learning and to rethink delivery models to take account of the needs and changes to people's lives owing to the pandemic. The biggest change has been the rapid development of virtual learning opportunities which carries with it the need for capacity building, especially for teachers, investment in digital access and the development of adult learning programmes and approaches (Gartenschlaeger, 2020). At the start of the first lockdown, adult learning providers had to stop all face-to-face teaching provision and, where possible, provide online learning instead.

Data published by the Office of Communications (Ofcom) in April 2020 suggests that the UK lockdowns have narrowed the country's digital divide of UK homes without internet access. More people went online for the first time for shopping, banking and to keep in contact with others. However, the report stated that those still offline felt even more disempowered during lockdown as so many everyday tasks moved online during the pandemic. Adults not online reported finding the internet too complicated (46 per cent), uninteresting for them (42 per cent) or they lacked equipment (37 per cent).

Methodology

We have drawn on data from a range and spread of adult learning providers in England:

- Case Study 1: a Local Authority Adult and Community Learning Service
- Case Study 2: a charity working with mainly Pakistani Muslim heritage learners
- Case Study 3: a Community College

- Case Study 4: a Community Interest Company (CIC) working with ex-offenders
- Case Study 5: a Community Interest Company (CIC) providing informal adult learning groups

The case studies have been anonymized; they are not representative of all providers but give a snapshot of how the pandemic has affected learning providers, provision and learner experiences. The projects were identified through the authors' existing knowledge of their work with adult learning across a range of communities of interest, needs and settings. The research, which was unfunded, took place through 2020–1; projects were identified and initial contact made to establish interest in taking part. Managers, staff, current and former learners were interviewed online, by telephone or completed questionnaires. They provided information about how learning had been affected by the social changes brought about by the pandemic and what outcomes they felt had been achieved during this period; managers provided background information and some case studies.

Key themes from the case studies

A number of key themes emerged from our case studies. These included the way in which adult learning providers adapted rapidly to the changing situation; increased opportunities for digital learning and training for staff; more flexibility to adapt provision in response to the needs of learners; the importance of face-to-face learning; increased opportunities for learning and the importance of learning for health and well-being.

Rapid response to providing learning through new methods

One of the key aspects that came through all of the case studies was that after the initial shock of the first lockdown learning providers responded rapidly to the changing situation.

Case Study 1 is a Local Authority Adult Community Learning Service which works with a range of subcontractors to provide learning across the area. Its services encourage disadvantaged adults and communities to enjoy learning and to prepare for employment, self-employment or further training. Courses include English and maths, employment skills and confidence building, while learners with English as a Second or Other Language are supported by the local Further Education College. The Adult Community Learning Services's service manager commented:

> This period has been very challenging, with a need for swift changes and responses, including upskilling staff in use of technology; staff, sub-contractors and learners have all responded to these challenges. We have had to adapt provision to make it COVID safe, including reducing class sizes, providing more online learning opportunities and support.

> During the first lockdown in March 2020, programmes and delivery had to be changed. Functional Skills classes continued: around 50% continued online, 25% were supported with workbooks and exercises sent by post, 25% found it hard to participate at all (or very rarely) due to balancing home life, own anxieties, home schooling or competing for internet access/devices.

In the case of this service provider, the pandemic had a significant impact on family learning and parenting programmes in partnership with schools. Space within schools was reduced as they had to adapt to support Covid-19 safety and social distancing which left little room to accommodate parents working alongside their children. The Learning Service had to look for alternative approaches including a class during half-term, online workshops via Zoom or Google and after-school family activities. Some classes focusing on confidence, mental health and employability moved to one-to-one via video conferencing, using whatever tools the learners had at their disposal, including FaceTime, Zoom, WhatsApp and SMS messenger.

When restrictions were lifted in autumn 2020, classes used a blend of face-to-face and online content. Courses which were seen as essential to providing learners with skills for work, for example Functional Skills as well as digital provision, were prioritized, due to an anticipated rise in unemployment. However, with the second lockdown in November 2020, all face-to-face classes stopped and delivery returned to being 100 per cent online.

Case Study 2 is a registered charity which works with Black and minority ethnic adults, young people and children of mainly Pakistani Muslim heritage from the local community in a town in central England. The adult provision focuses on women, providing informal learning opportunities through weekly women's groups lasting for two hours where women can improve their confidence, well-being and English language while mixing with a wider circle of women to feel less isolated. Some are new immigrants with little English, while others have been in the UK for many years. About forty women attend every week.

The project manager describes life as 'a hard struggle' since the start of the pandemic.

> We pride ourselves on running an open-door policy, always here for the community; they can drop in whenever they need us. This all stopped with lockdown in March. We had to shut all our face-to-face provision and close access to our building. For the women that was weekly English as a Second or Other Language (ESOL) classes and two drop-ins where we had workshops planned on power dynamics in relationships and staying safe.

The charity applied for extra information technology (IT) equipment, including for families and trained staff, and moved sessions onto Zoom. However, most learners found this difficult. Some did not have the right IT equipment; others lacked confidence in using computers. The numbers of women taking part fell dramatically at first, although the sessions became more popular as staff used learners' first language to ensure understanding of the pandemic. Time was spent going through the Covid-19 regulations and dealing with individual and group concerns about the virus. This gave opportunities for learners to explore their individual and community responses to the pandemic.

Under ordinary circumstances, one of the main functions of the sessions is to reduce isolation and give the women a safe space to share issues in their lives. However, this was largely lost during lockdown. Staff tried to provide opportunities to address this lack of social contact. One example was a Zoom Eid party which gave the women a chance to celebrate together. The women planned a menu and then all cooked a dish. The project worker collected all of the different dishes and delivered one of each dish to each of the participants' homes. Then everyone ate the meal together while on Zoom. They all said how they enjoyed sharing the meal together with tasty food and it was good fun and they felt closer together again. During summer months the learners were able to meet outside in the park. These sessions were very popular and better attended than the traditional drop-ins.

Project staff have tried to keep in contact with learners but know that many will have been overwhelmed by family issues during the pandemic and it will take time to build back motivation to attend sessions again. However, for some women, the pandemic has given them the chance to learn new IT skills in particular which increase their confidence, and for some the sheer survival of the infection has changed their outlook on life and learning. Twenty months after the start of the first UK lockdown in March 2020, more women are attending weekly sessions regularly with greater commitment to learn, particularly in areas such as general health and healthy lifestyles. Staff feel this is in direct response to the pandemic and the effect this has had on the lives of learners and their families.

Increased opportunities for digital learning and training for staff

Our research showed that at the start of the first lockdown in March 2020, where possible the majority of adult learning moved online. This was more problematic for some of the smaller organizations and community groups in terms of equipment and staff training and for some learners where the social aspects of learning were very important. How individual learners reacted to this change depended on a variety of factors, including pre-existing confidence and experience of using ICT, access to equipment, additional support to improve ICT skills coupled with motivation to improve ICT skills.

One learner from Case Study 2 commented:

> I didn't have my own computer at home and didn't know much about computers but the Centre lent me an iPad. The outreach worker showed me how to use it and then my son taught me how to shop online and I learnt how to do Zoom and use WhatsApp. I joined in the weekly ladies group session using Zoom. It was better than nothing but I missed meeting friends face-to-face and we didn't have workshops or interesting activities like crafts. I feel much more confident online now. I'm joining an English course using WhatsApp at college. But I still like face-to-face best.

Our research found anecdotally that in some households with a shortage of equipment, it was the women who had less access to information technology as often it was the men working from home and children with school work who were given priority in the household. This is borne out by views that women are more likely to bear the greater burden of the pandemic: they will be most heavily affected where they face 'intersecting systems of oppression', including ethnicity, race, sexual orientation, gender, age, economic class, dependent status and/or ability (Malisch et al., 2020).

Case Study 3 is a Community College in a large town in central England providing English, maths, information technology and continuous professional development courses for adults, most of whom are not native English speakers. Prior to the pandemic, learners studying for English and maths qualifications at level one and two worked in groups of eighteen to twenty. With the March lockdown, all learning had to move online. This was a completely new experience for staff and learners. The college installed Google Classroom as the learning platform. Initially participation fell from 280 to about 80 learners but slowly picked up again as staff stayed in contact with learners and supported them to access the new technology.

The adult learning manager explained:

> There were two main barriers to students joining the classes – none of us had used Google Classroom before and for some learners this was just too much. They didn't understand how to access it and some didn't have the necessary technology at home. Many learners do not have a good learning environment at home – no privacy, competition with other family members to use the technology and there was no flexibility in session times. They were at one fixed time every day and this did not necessarily fit with learners' other work and life commitments.

Greater flexibility to be able to adapt provision in response to the needs of learners

Many providers showed adaptability and innovation in their response, moving flexibly to meet the needs of learners. With the suspension of externally moderated qualifications, new avenues opened for curriculum development. Case Study 3's adult learning manager commented:

> The curriculum was definitely richer as we had more freedom to develop different ideas. We did virtual trips round local museums and spent two weeks on Black Lives Matter. It felt like a brief moment when we could actually teach, unrestrained by having to follow a curriculum and collect evidence all the time. It removed pressure from teachers.

The curriculum was adapted in response to the learners' immediate concerns, needs and interests in relation to the pandemic. Learners were generally positive about the experiences and, above all, developed their digital skills. However, staff also noticed how learners' listening skills improved, commenting that learners had to listen so intently online as they could not rely on anyone else to help them keep up.

Providers acknowledged that they needed to provide additional pastoral support for learners, with some becoming safeguarding concerns, particularly heightened when lockdown restrictions were in place. It was also clear that with the social distancing required by the resumption of face-to-face learning, some learners felt hesitant to engage in social interaction, so group bonding was slower which inhibited the learning experience. One learner commented that 'the pandemic has meant it's harder to meet people'. Another said: 'I feel I have gained more support and confidence, but working from home and online was very different and I felt the loss of an atmosphere of learning.'

Face-to-face learning as a critical key element to learners' experience

While providers and learners adapted and adjusted to online learning, the importance of face-to-face learning was also evident in giving a richer and more meaningful experience for learners.

Case Study 4, a community interest company in a large coastal town, working with ex-offenders and those at risk of offending, aims to reduce reoffending by providing a supported and realistic work environment. This provision is open to prison leavers and those at risk of committing crime. They provide daily volunteer work placements in a fully equipped workshop set up to work in wood, metal and other artistic techniques, including painting, screen-printing, photography, lino-printing and digital design. They also run an accredited qualification in business and enterprise.

The project manager identified that most participants see themselves as isolated and lonely, living predominantly in probation, rehabilitation or homeless hostel accommodation. As they have no or little family contact, the project is their community and support system. The manager commented:

> After initially closing the workshop in March 2020, staff tried to keep in touch with people through WhatsApp chats and phone calls, but it was clear this was not enough. Participants needed face-to-face contact and engagement in practical, creative work. The project reopened in June 2020 with additional hygiene and fewer participants to enable social distancing.
>
> We have had to balance the physical health of our participants with their mental health and decided in the long term, staying open is beneficial and essential to stop them descending into depression, anxiety, boredom and possible return to criminal behaviour. It is hard to imagine that most of our service-users have no-one to turn to in times of need, having lost touch with family, friends and community through repeated criminal behaviour, addiction or lengthy spells in prison. We also must balance their need to attend with our need to keep safe too.

The pandemic and lockdowns affected the participants greatly. Mental health issues have increased with two major breakdowns and a suicide among participants. Participants talk of really missing face-to-face contact with anyone. They already felt isolated and marginalized, and this was exacerbated by the pandemic. With poor or no IT equipment, they could not keep in touch. As the project manager pointed out: 'If you do not operate in the techno world, you do not exist. The project is a lifeline. It gives people a reason to get up in the morning.'

The project is also taking on new premises, so that two teams of people can work at the same time and retain social distancing. Meanwhile they had to further reduce the number of participants coming into the workshop as infections rose. The manager pointed out that one learner's comments reflect how the majority of learners have felt: 'I would definitely choose to go back to face-to-face learning to gain more from the environment and from other learners asking questions. I feel learning opportunities are more limited now. Learning has given me more confidence and hoping it will help with jobs.'

Increased opportunities for learning

For some learners, the pandemic gave them a spur to try out new and different learning experiences. One learner from Case Study 5, who joined family learning, parenting, craft and photography classes over recent years, gave her reason for taking up learning again as 'low confidence levels affecting all areas of my life, including parenting and work'. An important part for her in learning was to mix with other parents. By the time of the pandemic, she felt the learning had lifted her from an all-time low to a period of growing confidence both with work and in her own abilities. The pandemic felt like it could undo all this. Although her work stopped during the first lockdown, she signed up to an online professional development course in photography and trained herself using online resources in new photography skills which were needed for the changes in her work situation, taking photographs for online house viewings due to Covid-19 restrictions.

She accepted that the pandemic has given her opportunities to expand her skills professionally and she has made new online friends although she misses real contact. She also feels she now has a better understanding of contingency planning and a desire to plan for the future.

> It [the pandemic] has made me focus on what I can change and what I can plan for. To encourage us all to focus on what we can do and enjoy doing, not what we can do very little about. My learning has changed – the learning I did back

in 2017 to 2019 helped to improve my confidence enough to get more regular work. The learning I'm doing now or when I can get back to it should help me to develop a more flexible business and plan for the future.

Other learners too felt that the pandemic had changed their outlook to learning and life. Some felt increased agency. They spoke of increased ability to adapt to new situations, feeling more comfortable in life and to take on new opportunities, including job opportunities, changed attitudes, flexibility: One learner from Case Study 1 commented: 'I realise that I put limits on myself and now I feel freer inside. Although the outside limits us.... It gave us a break to look consciously at how we can deal better according to the changes and care more about what we are missing'.

Some individuals, suspended from work on furlough, had more time to study. A learner with Case Study 1 shared:

> Having always struggled with maths, I decided to finally bite the bullet and do Maths Functional Skills through adult community learning. Jan my tutor was fantastic and always took the time to explain things clearly and in a way that was easy to understand. Since completing my qualification, new doors have opened for me and I am now applying to university which is something I have always wanted to do but didn't think would be possible. I have a new-found confidence in my ability and that is thanks to my tutor. I recommend anyone considering the course to just go for it. You won't regret it.

This learner also said that because of the support of the tutor she felt more confident to explore other online learning opportunities and resources when classes were not available. One or two of the learners from Case Study 5, who were confident with using the internet, said that they tried out some online learning and felt they had benefitted with some new ideas which they could share with others when they were able to meet up.

Learning for health and well-being

An important aspect of learning for many learners was information about the pandemic, government regulations and how to protect themselves and their families. This was often outside the anticipated curriculum for the sessions but reflected the needs of the learners and the state of the pandemic.

> Without these sessions the women would have been lost. They did not understand the dangers or the restrictions being put in place by the government. When the

vaccine programme started we spent a lot of time reassuring people that the vaccine was halal for Muslims and they should have it.

(Project manager Case Study 2)

Learners from the informal learning groups in particular valued being part of a community, whether face-to-face or online and felt this contributed to their well-being and self-confidence. Some learners did not feel that online learning met their wider learning needs. One student, although having access to a computer at home and support from centre staff, did not feel motivated to continue attending sessions or improve her skills, although she did occasionally use Zoom to attend the community group sessions. She gave her main reason for attendance prior to the pandemic as social interaction and peer support which helped her maintain her well-being. She felt this was lost with online sessions. Her family placed limitations on her movements outside the home but agreed to her attendance at sessions at the project centre.

Case Study 5 is a small Community Interest Company in one of the most deprived areas in a seaside town in England. The project is community-run and provides a range of informal learning opportunities for adults. Many of the participants have disabilities, underlying health problems, mental health issues or suffer from anxiety and isolation. The community groups were initially established around 2008, starting with very small numbers; by the time of the pandemic, they had grown into self-sustaining groups providing social and emotional support plus friendship, reducing isolation and providing opportunities to learn new skills.

Between lockdowns, the community craft group managed to open again adopting social distancing and limiting numbers. This gave something of a feeling of normality to individuals who belonged to vulnerable groups and who, outside the group, were remaining isolated because of the risk of infection. Staff commented on the importance of attending sessions for participants' well-being.

> Seeing a group sitting around the table (keeping their distance) but talking, laughing, sharing and learning made me feel so good. The pandemic for older people has been devastating, led to depression, you can see it. People are not bothering to get their hair done, put on new clothes to go out. Meeting at the centre has given a purpose and a sense of community.

One participant commented: 'This has been a lifesaver for me.'

Conclusion

The research has shown a mixed picture of response to and experience of learning through the pandemic. What is clear is that the pandemic has certainly driven forward digital learning at a rapid pace and providers have responded innovatively, developing digital opportunities. However, for many learners face-to-face learning is a critical element, which cannot be fully replaced through online platforms. Our case studies show the value that many learners put on face-to-face learning for providing quality experiences, a sense of community and well-being.

The digital divide has increased for those with little or no access to technology and low levels of English and/or literacy skills. Learning for this group has been very limited, and the situation increased a sense of isolation and exclusion. Conversely, online learning has allowed for some learners to stay engaged through periods of ill health and increased childcare.

Adult learning is a vital resource in managing and driving social change. Clearly, adult learning changed dramatically in response to the pandemic. Our research shows that providers have tried to adapt to the changing social and economic situation to enable adults to continue to access learning through adapting learning environments to make them Covid-19-safe, reducing numbers attending and providing a wide range of online learning opportunities. All providers acknowledge that online learning has been a positive experience for some learners, but for others it has created a barrier to learning, thereby increasing the digital divide. Several of the learners reported that they felt that during the pandemic they had made most progress in their confidence and skills in using information technology. For some it was that they had improved their literacy and English language skills, and in particular spoken communication mainly through speaking online. Study skills improved with some learners saying they felt better at self-study and independent working.

The case studies show the importance for many learners of a community of learning and the need for face-to-face support from staff and peers to maximize the learning experience. In some instances, a freeing up of the curriculum during lockdown allowed for new and wider learning experiences. Staff development was essential for tutors as they had to develop new online delivery methods, and for some this was a real opportunity to use these new skills and delivery methods to change existing practice and enhance provision (Case Study 1).

For some people, the pandemic has accelerated their ability to manage their lives online, many learning to use digital platforms such as Zoom and FaceTime for the first time. For others, often the most vulnerable, the pandemic has created greater isolation and distancing from friends, family, peers and other support. Many people reported that they felt in 'limbo' not really able to make any changes to their lives at this time – a feeling of waiting for the next thing to happen to them, rather than feeling a greater sense of agency.

The pandemic has changed the structure of community groups in particular, forcing providers to look at new ways of reaching and keeping in touch with learners. This has resulted in some new learners being suited to online learning, for example people who are housebound through illness or childcare needs or have no transport to groups. Some learners have dropped out, particularly those who cannot cope with digital learning; do not have access to information technology at home or who need the social interaction of face-to-face provision. Grassroots providers came to the fore as centres of informal learning providing information and support for the most marginalized learners, helping them to cope with the emergency. Being part of adult learning, and able to share with others in the face of social change, was an important shared experience and helped build resilience and creativity. The BAICE (British Association for International and Comparative Education) UK Case Study (Newell-Jones et al., 2021) backed up this finding, highlighting the speed with which providers adapted the curriculum to address the immediate challenges in learners' lives resulting from the pandemic.

Providers responded by offering more support, but the initial barriers to making the step towards learning appear to be greater. Some people are filling this gap by turning to other support networks such as religious groups, social media groups and free online courses. Although some of the Black and minority ethnic community learners received information through their mosque networks, they still needed the support provided through their adult learning groups to interpret and put into practice the initial information they were given. Well-established groups tended to keep going, while it was difficult to launch new groups without face-to-face contact.

The negative impact of the pandemic on well-being and mental health has been significant for many people. Without the companionship often found in face-to-face small adult learning groups, feelings of isolation, uncertainty and exclusion have grown, and, for many, face-to-face learning remains essential. This is borne out by the findings of the BAICE UK Case Study: 'The pandemic has highlighted the role of ALE [Adult Learning and Education] as a frontline community service, strengthening the sense of community and providing valuable links between service providers and some of the most marginalised in the community' (Newell-Jones et al., 2021: 16).

As the UK comes out of the pandemic, there are opportunities for informal adult learning to respond to the challenges thrown up by the social changes in life and work. These may be led by or be a reaction to increased use of digital methods of delivering. Not all digital delivery will be discarded post-pandemic. One provider acknowledges that post-lockdown they would resume meeting face-to-face but retain a Zoom link for those who were unable to attend in person.

A senior manager commented: 'So far as social change is concerned, it feels like the pace of development, the direction of travel has probably squeezed five years of progress into one year – particularly with regards to technology, whether it is online shopping, accessing services, booking appointments for healthcare, learning and working online, conducting online meetings.' The Community Interest Company (CIC) working with ex-offenders and those in danger of re-offending is taking the opportunity to extend its offer by developing a new face-to-face programme of creative activities for businesses and charities to support their post-pandemic organizational cohesion. This will provide a stable funding stream and more opportunities for the CIC participants to develop independent life skills through involvement in the planning and delivery.

The pandemic has thrown a spotlight on the need for individuals to have a breadth of skills and resilience to deal with: social change; changing work practices; dealing with anxiety and mental health challenges; health literacy for staying safe from disease. Roy (2020: 3) describes pandemics as 'a portal, a gateway between one world and the next', and goes on to say that we can choose if we take our old lifestyle, values and prejudices with us or decide to imagine another world and fight for it. The Covid-19 pandemic has highlighted how health, education, social and economic inequalities are disadvantaging the most vulnerable people and limiting their agency in the social changes arising from the pandemic. Governments need to acknowledge and develop the role of adult learning in levelling up society and equipping everyone with the skills and knowledge for future national/international health, climate or other emergencies.

The government Department of Education White Paper (2021) does identify reforming adult education and skills policy as a priority. It announces a £2.5 billion National Skills Fund and the Lifelong Loan Entitlement, but there are few details. It acknowledges that the UK needs to address the complexity of skills which are needed to keep up with technological change and the changes wrought by the pandemic and economic and market shifts. However, as Sibieta, Tahir and Waltmann (2021) point out, overall spending across adult education, apprenticeships and work-based learning fell by 35 per cent, or by £1.9 billion in real terms, between 2009–10 and 2019–20, so there is much ground to be made up. In addition, the White Paper makes no mention of the wider benefits of learning or of the need for a broader set of skills to cope with and take advantage of post-pandemic social change or to prepare for more emergencies. A new funding structure for adult learning needs to take notice of learning from the grassroots upwards. Our research has shown the importance of small grassroots organizations in enabling the most vulnerable learners to interpret crisis situations and to build skills of resilience leading to greater agency.

A model for the future of adult learning which responds to what we have discovered through our research about learning and future needs can be found in the concept of 'Learning to become' framed in UNESCO's Futures of Education initiative (UNESCO, 2020c). It views knowledge and learning as the core of transformations in human minds and societies. In this way, no one need be left behind and society will be better able to cope socially, environmentally and economically with future uncertainties and opportunities.

References

Aldridge, F., Jones, E., and Southgate, D. (2020), *Learning through Lockdown: Findings from the 2020 Adult Participation in Learning Survey, Learning and Work Institute*. Available at: [online] https://learningandwork.org.uk/resources/research-and-reports/learning-through-lockdown/ Accessed 26 April 2022.

Arts and Humanities Research Council (AHRC) (2020), The Infodemic Project [online] Available at: https://infodemic.eu/ Accessed 26 April 2022.

Boeren, E., Roumell, E. A., and Roessger, K. M. (2020), COVID-19 and the Future of Adult Education: An Editorial, *Adult Quarterly Review*, 70 (3), 201–4. [PDF] Available at: https://journals.sagepub.com/toc/aeq/70/3 Accessed 26 April 2022.

British Academy (2021), Shaping the COVID Decade: Addressing the Long-term Societal Impacts of COVID-19, *British Academy London* [PDF]. Available at: https://www.thebritishacademy.ac.uk/publications/shaping-the-covid-decade-addressing-the-long-term-societal-impacts-of-covid-19/ Accessed 26 April 2022.

Centenary Commission on Adult Education (2019), 'A Permanent National Necessity': Adult Education and Lifelong Learning for 21st Century Britain, *Nottingham: University of Nottingham School of Education*. Available at: [online] https://rdmc.nottingham.ac.uk/handle/internal/7890 Accessed 26 April 2022.

Department for Education (2021), Skills for Jobs: Lifelong Learning for Opportunity and Growth. Available at: [online] https://www.gov.uk/government/publications/skills-for-jobs-lifelong-learning-for-opportunity-and-growth Accessed 26 April 2022.

European Association for the Education of Adults (2020), Resilience of Individuals, Communities and Economies: We need more Adult Learning and Education in and after the Coronavirus Pandemic, *European Association for the Education of Adults*. Brussels. [PDF] Available at: https://eaea.org/wp-content/uploads/2020/04/EAEA-statement-on-COVID-19-and-ALE.pdf Accessed 26 April 2022.

Gartenschlaeger, U. (2020), The New Dynamic of Adult Learning and Education in the Corona Pandemic, *DVV International*, October 2020. [online] Available at: https://www.dvv-international.de/en/our-work/blog/detail/the-new-dynamics-of-adult-learning-and-education-in-the-corona-pandemic Accessed 26 April 2022.

Hopwood Hall College (2020/21), Covid-19 Build Back Better Pledge. [PDF] Available at: 202098_155022.pdf (rochdaleonline.co.uk) Accessed 26 April 2022.

Lopes, H., and McKay, V. (2020), Adult Learning and Education as a Tool to Contain Pandemics: The COVID-19 Experience, *International Review of Education*, 66, 575–602. [PDF] Available at: https://doi.org/10.1007/s11159-020-09843-0 Accessed 26 April 2022.

Nalita, J., and Thériault, V. (2020), Adult Education in Times of the COVID-19 Pandemic: Inequalities, Changes, and Resilience, *Studies in the Education of Adults*, 52 (2), 129–33. [online] Available at: https://www.tandfonline.com/doi/full/10.1080/02660830.2020.1811474 Accessed 26 April 2022.

Newell-Jones, K., Cheffy, I., Fuller, S., Furlong, T., and Millora, C. (2021), Impact of COVID-19 on Adult Learning and Education (ALE): A UK Case Study. Available at: https://balid.org.uk/wp-content/uploads/2021/12/UK-case-study-ACL-Islington-04.08.21-for-sharing.pdf Accessed 26 April 2022.

Malisch, J. L., et al. (2020), Opinion: In the Wake of COVID-19, Academia Needs New Solutions to Ensure Gender Equity, *Proceedings of the National Academy of Sciences of the United States of America*, 117 (27), 15378–81. [online] Available at: https://doi.org/10.1073/pnas.2010636117 Accessed 26 April 2022.

Ofcom (2020), Digital Divide Narrowed by Pandemic, but around 1.5m Homes Remain Offline. [online] Available at: https://www.ofcom.org.uk/about-ofcom/latest/media/media-releases/2021/digital-divide-narrowed-but-around-1.5m-homes-offline Accessed 26 April 2022.

Roy, A. (2020), The Pandemic Is a Portal, Disarming Times, *The Journal of Pax Christi Australia*, 45, 2. [PDF] Available at: https://www.paxchristi.org.au/wp-content/uploads/2020/07/Disarming-Times-Vol-45-No-2-1.pdf Accessed 26 April 2022.

Sibieta, L., Tahir, I., and Waltmann, B. (2021), Big Changes Ahead for Adult Education Funding? Definitely Maybe. Briefing note [online] Available at: https://ifs.org.uk/publications/15405 Accessed 26 April 2022.

Stanistreet, P. (2020), Resources of Hope: Towards a Revaluing of Education, *International Review of Education*, 66, 1–7. [PDF] Available at: https://doi.org/10.1007/s11159-020-09827-0 Accessed 26 April 2022.

Tett, L., and Hamilton, M. eds. (2019), *Resisting Neoliberalism in Education: Local, National and Transnational Perspectives*, Bristol, UK: Policy Press.

Tett, L. (2020), A Response to Vol. 11, supplementary issue, 2020, *Concept Journal*, 11 (2), 1–3. [PDF] Available at: http://concept.lib.ed.ac.uk/article/view/4459/6043 Accessed 26 April 2022.

Tuckett, A. (2017), The Rise and Fall of Life-Wide Learning for Adults in England, *International Journal of Lifelong Education*, 36, 230–49.

UNESCO (2020a), Adult Learning and Education and COVID -19, Sector issue note 2. 6 October 2020 [online] Available at: https://unesdoc.unesco.org/ark:/48223/pf0000374636 Accessed 26 April 2020.

UNESCO (2020b), How Cities Are Utilizing the Power of Non-Formal and Informal Learning to Respond to the COVID-19 Crisis, Sector issue note 6. 2 August 2020 [online] Available at: https://unesdoc.unesco.org/ark:/48223/pf0000374148 Accessed 26 April 2022.

UNESCO (2020c), Futures of Education Learning to Become. [online] Available at: https://unescochair-ghe.org/2020/02/13/unescos-futures-of-education-initiative/ Accessed 26 April 2022.

Williams, R. (1989), *Resources of Hope*, London, UK: Verso.

10

Learning to live sustainably? A case study of a community gardening scheme in Norwich

Mahesh Pant

Introduction

This chapter explores the role of non-formal and informal learning in promoting sustainable living. In the materialist world we live in, how can we reduce our wasteful consumption habits and promote sustainable living? How can we maintain harmony between people and the environment? These are big questions. The relationship between learning and living sustainably is a complex one. In this chapter, I explore the connection between learning and practice: what is learnt, how the skills and knowledge gained are put into practice or retained for future use. I start by looking at some key debates on sustainable consumption, exploring the importance of connectedness between humans and the environment. I will then review the literature on adult learning focusing on non-formal and informal learning.

The primary data for this chapter is drawn from a case study of a community gardening scheme in Norwich called Grow Our Own (GO^2) under the umbrella of a charity called Sustainable Living Initiative (SLI). I set up the GO^2 community gardening scheme in 2004 as a pilot initiative and led the organization until 2020. The scheme is still ongoing, involving more communities and individuals interested in learning how to grow their own food organically, cook using seasonal produce and to share resources and experiences.

From the very beginning of the scheme, an annual report has been published summarizing the main activities undertaken during the year, the number of people joining the scheme and detailing members' comments about the scheme and suggestions for improvements. These reports are available on SLI website: www.grow-our-own.co.uk. In addition to the personal comments made by SLI members, an evaluation of the project was carried out in 2017. Although this data was collected for the purpose of project evaluation, I am using it to explore the links between adult learning and sustainable development. Members, whose comments were used in this chapter, were contacted for their approval.

Finally, I will discuss the potential and limitations of adult learning in a small-scale community action project in promoting sustainable living.

Sustainable living

Our physical existence and well-being depend on the consumption of goods. However, it is hard to establish how much we really need (not how much we want) to live well and be happy. According to Max-Neef (Max-Neef et al., 1991: 16–17), fundamental human needs are finite and constant, only the 'satisfiers' (i.e. the means to fulfil our needs) are infinite and change over time and culture. For example, 'subsistence' is one of the fundamental human needs and food and shelter are satisfiers. Even then, the unanswered question is: What type of food and shelter do we **need** for subsistence as opposed to what type of food and shelter we **want**?

Jackson (2005: 29) analyses consumer behaviour in detail and explains the 'functional and symbolic role of material goods' which suggests that not all the material goods that we possess have relevance to our well-being. He argues that 'it is possible to live better by consuming less and at the same time reduce our impact on the environment' (Jackson, 2005: 25). What is required is 'concerted social efforts to realise' such potential (2005). Likewise, Ozturk and Shah (2005: 1) argue that 'one planet living' while maintaining our quality of life is possible. How to translate such possibilities into reality remains a challenge.

The imbalance between our desire to consume material resources and our planet's capacity to sustain this consumption has long been questioned. 'If everyone in the world lived as we do in Europe we would need three planets to support us' (Ozturk and Shah, 2005: 3). A similar view was voiced by Gandhi nearly 100 years ago. The publication of *Limits to Growth* (Meadows et al., 1972) and its subsequent updates confirmed with evidence that unlimited economic growth is unsustainable:

> Limits to growth include both the material and energy that are extracted from the Earth, and the capacity of the planet to absorb the pollutants that are

generated as those materials and energy are used ... There are limits, however, to the rates at which sources can produce these materials and energy without harm to people, the economy, or the earth's processes of regeneration and regulation. (https://donellameadows.org/archives/a-synopsis-limits-to-growth-the-30-year-update)

In a recent interview with the *Guardian* newspaper (20 May 2021), primatologist Jane Goodall said: 'We have to reduce the unsustainable lifestyles of so many of us. We have so much more than what we actually need, and we have this crazy notion that we can have unlimited economic development on a planet with finite natural resources.' Yet how to tame our over-consumption remains unanswered.

Pretty et al. (2003: 6) highlight the importance of 'closeness to nature' for our physical and emotional well-being. Such closeness is beneficial not only to individuals but also to the society at large, including our environment. As our quality of life depends on our environment, living in harmony with the environment is essential. While national policies aimed at changing consumer behaviour or developing and protecting green spaces are necessary for maintaining harmony between our needs and the caring capacity of the planet earth, there is a general consensus on the important role that individuals and communities could play in promoting sustainable living. In fact, there are numerous examples of environmental actions, such as Chipko,[1] being initiated by individuals and community groups all over the world.

Small-scale initiatives such as growing fruit, vegetables and herbs on allotments and in back gardens, recycling and reusing, avoiding car journeys and promoting a sense of community can have a far-reaching effect on natural, as well as on human environments. In the following sections, I discuss how adult learning in a small-scale local project such as GO[2] can contribute to this wider debate on sustainable living.

Adult learning

Why and how do adults learn? Do they learn intentionally or accidentally or both? How much of the knowledge and skills learned is put into practice and retained for future use? How does adults' previous background impact their learning outcomes? I will begin this review by focusing on these key questions.

Adult learning has been conceptualized as a continuous process where 'learning and living are virtually synonymous' (Aspin et al., 2012: xlvi). Learning can take place in a formal, non-formal or informal environment. Formal learning takes place in an institution with specific learning objectives and assessment often leading to a degree or certificate, while non-formal learning though structured is not normally provided by educational and training institutions. In contrast, informal learning takes place at home or within society and community groups and is not structured with specific learning objectives and does not lead to any qualification.[2]

Rogers (2014: 19) argues, however, that such a neat categorization of different kinds of learning is problematic because informal learning may have some element of formal learning; likewise, informal learning can also take place in formal institutions such as schools – consciously or unconsciously. With regard to learning intentions, both formal and non-formal learning can be seen as intentional from the perspectives of both the learners and providers, while informal learning is mostly unintentional and unconscious from a learner's perspective (2014). As a result, most formal and non-formal learning is inclined to be instrumental, that is, considered as a means to certain ends such as employment, further education and so on, while informal learning can be both instrumental and intrinsic, that is, learning considered and valued as an end in itself. Rogers (2014: 8) further categorizes informal learning into 'self-directed learning (intentional), incidental learning, task-conscious learning and unintentional, unplanned and unconscious learning'.

Tuckett (2017) has highlighted the transformational potential of adult learning. He suggests that apart from adult learning as a tool for employment, it can open up new opportunities through social contacts, improve health and well-being and could have a positive impact on family and children. Here the focus of transformational potential appears still to be on instrumental outcomes. But what about the role of adult learning in facilitating social change?

In this context, Sen's notion of freedom – understood as 'our ability to get what we value and want but without the levers of control being directly operated by us' (Sen, 1992: 64) – is relevant in explaining the instrumental and intrinsic role of adult learning. Sen (1988: 270) argues that freedom needs to be seen as important in terms of its 'instrumental role', that is freedom as a means to an end, as well as in terms of its 'intrinsic value'. In the latter case, freedom is considered as important on its own, including aspects such as liberties and democratic rights. Similar views are expressed by Aspin et al. (2012: li): 'Individual and community welfare is protected and promoted when communities arrange for lifelong learning to be available to the widest range of constituents.' So irrespective of the outcomes of adult learning, including informal learning, to have the opportunity to learn is important on its own. Taking the concept of freedom as defined by Sen, the opportunity to learn is a necessary condition for individuals to take 'social responsibility' (Sen, 1999).

The importance of informal learning is now widely recognized; as summed up by Rogers (2014: 11): 'informal learning is both larger and more important than formal learning.' According to Aspin et al. (2012), both the Western and Eastern philosophies had long recognized the importance of informal learning. What has changed in recent years is the attitude of policymakers and academicians in recognizing the importance of informal learning in people's everyday lives. The following sections will investigate the role played by informal learning in the GO^2 project in promoting sustainable development.

Introducing Grow Our Own (GO^2) Initiative

In October 2004, I set up a pilot initiative in a Norwich City Council allotment[3] site where I already had an allotment. My intention was to encourage and support people to grow their own fruit and vegetables by offering mini plots,[4] tools, seeds, plants, practical help and advice for a small membership fee. As there were so many overgrown plots on the site, the aim was to nurture a 'grow our own' culture in Norwich so that allotments could be better utilized in producing fruit and vegetables.

Eight novice growers signed up for the pilot scheme and managed to grow vegetables successfully, some of them for the first time in their lives. The following year saw a big increase in the number of people to twenty-eight (see SLI Annual Report, 2005–6) wanting to join the scheme. This led to the set-up of a formal organization SLI, registered initially as a not-for-profit company and eventually as a charity. A sister project of GO^2, Marlpit Community Garden, was opened in 2013 in one of the more deprived areas of Norwich. In addition to the provision of mini plots for individuals, families, schools and community groups, this new site included an orchard, herb garden, forest garden, beehives and wildflower meadow.

With a view to make gardening enjoyable, accessible and inclusive, GO^2 project offers small manageable size plots for individuals, families and children, specially designed raised bed for people with mobility difficulties and plots for schools and community groups. Unlike the Council-managed allotment sites where there normally is a waiting list, GO^2 has never had a waiting list. Under the 'grow-at-home' scheme managed by GO^2, members can get seeds, plants, help and advice to grow fruit and vegetable in their own garden. In addition to this, both sites have an information centre, cycle stands, car parking facilities for blue badge holders only, communal meeting place with tea-making facility, a composting toilet, shared seeds, plants and tools stores providing social space for members. These are facilities which are not usually available in conventional allotments. To quote Saunders (1993: 15): 'By and large ... work on allotments is normally solitary and is not strongly motivated by social considerations.' In GO^2 in contrast, monthly and weekly food-sharing (when members bring meals to share or a meal cooked at the centre is shared) and volunteering events (when members carry out communal tasks collectively) are taking place on both sites. These sites are largely managed by volunteers.

Because of the help and support provided by GO^2 to its members and the facilities available on site for members to meet and socialize, the scheme has managed to attract a diverse range of people, including women and children, school and university students, wheelchair users, people with mobility difficulties, homeless people and people suffering from anxieties. By 2019–20, there were 175 members (growers including home growers, volunteers and members without a plot) and a couple of schools and community groups taking part in the scheme (SLI Annual Report, 2019–20). According to the SLI Annual report 2019–20, the majority of the members were women and over fifty-five years old, although the number of young people joining has been increasing in recent years; there is also greater ethnic diversity in GO^2 membership than in the general Norwich area. For example, according to the SLI Annual Report 2017–18, nearly 60 per cent of our members were white British which also reflects the ethnic composition of Norfolk. The rest of the members were Asian (8 per cent), European (6 per cent) and the remainder included Irish and mixed race.

The higher proportion of women in GO^2 scheme is in sharp contrast to the overall picture of Council-managed allotments where the majority (84 per cent; see Saunders, 1993: 1) of the members are men. Although the allotments initially were meant for the rural poor (The United Kingdom Parliament, 2004), they have now become a place for the urban middle class motivated by aspirations for a healthy lifestyle (Saunders, 1993), and the GO^2 scheme is not an exception. The general picture of allotments described in the national survey of allotment gardeners' views in England and Wales sharply contrasts with the following comments made by one of the GO^2 members:

> the scheme feels like a social club where I can get to know like-minded people.
> I love that this is about building a community, not just growing fruit and veg.
>
> (Rochelle, SLI Annual Report, 2006–07: 15)

There were a number of reasons as to why so many people joined the GO^2 scheme; for people living in flats without a garden, it was a way of getting access to land and to grow some food. For other members, the main attractions were learning skills and the opportunities for experimenting in growing fruit and vegetables with practical help and support from the scheme. Members also appreciated the social aspects of the scheme such as meeting new, like-minded people and companionship. For a small number of university students, it was their academic research interest (see SLI Annual Report, 2017–18). However, often growing food was only one of many reasons for deciding to join the scheme. A sample of personal comments made by members over a long period supports this point:

> I very much enjoy growing the food and it has saved me money. I don't have a garden at home, so this space is important to me. I like being outside in fresh air.
> (Joanna, SLI Annual Report, 2008/09: 9)

Since the large cohort of SLI members were retired or semi-retired women over fifty-five years, improving physical and mental well-being and avoiding isolation were the other main reasons for joining the scheme:

> I have been trying to improve my health both in a physical and emotional way after becoming disabled about 5 years ago and retiring from teaching due to ill health. With the invaluable support from the scheme, I have been able to grow wonderful produce on my own manageable plot of land and have met some remarkable, friendly and encouraging members of the scheme in the process.
> (Moira, SLI Annual Report, 2006/07: 15)

Members' sense of safety and security on site[5] and the provision of small, manageable-sized plots[6] along with tools, seeds and advice were the main reasons why so many women had joined GO^2:

> As a single woman, recently retired, the project is excellent for people on their own... There are often people nearby and this makes the allotment site feel a safe place to be.
> (Anonymous, SLI Annual Report, 2005/06: 11)

For a small number of members, other reasons such as an ethical lifestyle, care for the environment and the opportunity for learning from each other were behind joining the scheme:

> GO^2 brings together people from very different backgrounds and age groups, and gives us the possibility to learn from each other, share knowledge and

practical experience and have common events. It has a very warm and friendly atmosphere with so many great people passionate about the same thing, sharing similar interests and ideas.

(Alina, SLI Annual Report, 2010/11: 6)

To sum up, in addition to creating and supporting a learning environment for people to grow fruit, vegetables and herbs, GO² activities helped develop a sense of community. As observed by one of our trustees in her foreword to SLI's Tenth Anniversary Report, 'the project [GO²] has evolved from an allotment scheme to a fully-fledged community garden offering an important social space in which to bring people together' (Kim, SLI Annual Report, 2013–14: 3).

Understanding the concept of learning in GO²

When the pilot initiative was taking shape, I was trying to familiarize myself with the history of allotments in England and its development. I came across terms such as 'grow your own' and 'pick your own'. Without being pedantic, I chose the term 'grow our own' instead of 'grow your own' because I saw the former as giving a sense of collectiveness, that is – 'let us do it together', while the latter could appear individualistic, that is 'do it yourself'.

So, from the very beginning of the GO² scheme, the emphasis was on learning from each other, sharing skills, knowledge, tools, seeds and plants, promoting organic growing practices and cooperation between members. Additional activities such as regular volunteering to maintain the project site, a food-sharing lunch using seasonal home-grown produce and a grow-at-home scheme (to support members using their own home garden to grow fruit and vegetables) were added. Regular food events, open days and activities for family and children were aimed at raising awareness about 'farm to fork'; that is where the food comes from, where and how it is grown.

Since the opening of the new site, Marlpit Community Garden, additional activities such as regular non-formal training and workshops on growing fruit, vegetables and herbs, cooking simple meals using seasonal produce and food-preserving such as jam and chutney making have been organized for members as well as for non-members. Regular volunteers are also offered opportunities to attend external training on specific subjects such as bee-keeping and forest gardening; they in turn share the knowledge with other volunteers and help manage the community garden. This new site also offers opportunities for business organizations to bring their staff for volunteering.

Staff participating in this scheme learn about environment management, develop team building and provide valuable practical help needed to maintain the garden.

The publication of a monthly newsletter with gardening advice and resources available, a website with simplified gardening factsheets, training videos and a Facebook page for members to share their experiences all are aimed at encouraging members to learn how to grow fruit and vegetables, make good use of the produce grown on their plots and promote a sense of community.

To sum up, the learning space created by GO^2 offers opportunities to a diverse range of people in varied ways. Members learn to grow fruit and vegetables organically in a non-formal setting such as face-to-face training, workshops and one-to-one mentoring as well as through simple manuals available in hard copy on-site and online. Members also learn technical aspects of growing fruit and vegetables such as the use of organic and heritage seeds,[7] companion planting and ways of avoiding the use of chemical fertilizers and pesticides.

While carrying out a task or by observing fellow members' plots, members learn (informally and accidently) from fellow members. By taking part in communal activities such as tool cleaning, maintaining paths and tool sheds, members learn (unintentionally) about the importance of collective action. Such communal activities, including the food-share lunch, also provide opportunities to make new friends and avoid isolation. Students from the nearby university join as volunteers for their academic projects and end up learning about community and the environment.

Learning to grow our own: Learners' perspectives

What did members in GO^2 scheme learn? How was the learning process facilitated? In this section, I draw on the findings from the project's evaluation study and comments made by the members over a long period of time (from the annual reports).

The results of the evaluation carried out in 2017 suggest that the majority of the respondents were very positive about the benefits of the scheme in improving their health and well-being, in saving money and in learning new skills. For example, 81 per cent said they eat more fruit and vegetables as a result of the scheme, and 89 per cent said their mental health and well-being have improved as a result of joining the scheme. Apart from learning to grow fruit and vegetables organically (84 per cent), 63 per cent said they have learnt new skills (SLI Annual Report, 2017–18: 3). These results coming from a small sample[8] are corroborated by personal comments made by the members over a long period of time:

> So far we have been part of the Marlpit Community Garden for few months, yet the experience has been much more enriching than we had expected … being able to produce something from the land, learning about different seeding techniques and about how to take care of plants we didn't even know, have given us a lot of happy moments.
>
> (Sacnicté and Tristan, SLI Annual Report, 2015/16: 18)

> I've made new friends … and I feel part of the community through joining in some of the activities. I've enjoyed feasts of home grown food at the monthly food share, …. and learnt how to preserve produce for the winter in small, friendly groups. The project has prevented me from feeling isolated in my own garden.
>
> (Tish, SLI Annual Report, 2009/10: 6)

> I have never lost the thrill of planting seeds and watching them turn into vegetables. For instance, it had never occurred to me to grow garlic. I had thought that it came from hotter countries.
>
> (Rochelle, SLI Annual Report, 2013/14: 10)

> The other really pleasing thing about the scheme is that we are all trying to grow sustainably without chemicals and we recycle and compost and save seed and use old varieties of plants. We benefit from the communal expertise of the experienced growers.
>
> (Janet, SLI Annual Report, 2007/08: 5)

These comments made by the members highlight a number of important learning practices, particularly shared learning and outcomes such as learning new skills, avoiding isolation and connectedness to nature. For some members, the joy of learning new skills such as 'different seeding techniques and about how to take care of plants' (Sac and Tristan; Janet) was paramount. While for others, rediscovering and realizing gaps in their knowledge about growing vegetables (for instance, Rochelle's comment on garlic) were the main aspects of their learning experiences. Learning new skills, for example making jam, in a small friendly group (Tish) and learning from fellow members (Janet) had not only widened the learning space but also made learning sociable; members were making new friends which was important in avoiding isolation. Members experienced learning new growing techniques such as using home-made compost instead of using chemical fertilizer, using heritage seeds and seed saving. Members also feel connected to nature and experienced improved well-being (Sac and Tristan) as a result of joining the scheme.

From growing food to growing community

As discussed earlier, one of the challenges facing sustainable living is how to reduce our insatiable consumer culture. The sharing culture promoted by GO² could be seen as an example of 'concerted social efforts' (Jackson, 2005) in reducing personal consumption at a micro level. The importance of connectedness between people and the environment has now been well established for the well-being of people and the planet (Pretty et al., 2003). In this section, I am going to discuss the role played by informal shared learning in GO² in promoting sustainable living.

The scheme initially aimed at promoting a grow-our-own culture in Norwich. However, because of the evolutionary nature of the initiative, it was capable of adapting to its members' needs and aspirations in the project. For example, until so many women members demanded a toilet, saying they could not stay long on the site to look after their plot, we had not thought of providing this facility because it was so expensive and needed planning permission. Likewise, our original plan was to provide mentoring to novice growers for a maximum of two years and encourage them to get a council allotment after that. There were forty-one members at the end of the third year of the project, and they all wanted to stay on and be part of the organization. Unlike most externally funded projects, SLI did not have specific targets to fulfil, so it was possible to adapt to such changes. The result was to widen the learning space to accommodate a more diverse group of people.

Through informal, shared learning promoted by the scheme, members were able to grow food, make new friends and become more aware of ethical and environmental issues. These learning outcomes were not only instrumental in improving the well-being of the members but also in promoting participation of the members in the management of the scheme itself. This could be seen in terms of the concepts of 'positive social values' (Roche, 2018: 537) and 'public good' (Aspin et al., 2012: I). How far skills learned both intentionally and incidentally will be retained and for how long is questionable though. The comment made by one the volunteers indicates the possibility of 'delayed learning' (Rogers and Horrocks, 2010: 305):

> Gardening makes me feel more connected with nature which is extremely fulfilling and I know that I am storing up plenty of skills that I will be able to share with others and bring to my own garden one day.
> (Lucy, SLI Annual Report, 2008/09: 12)

As discussed earlier, apart from providing much-needed practical help, members played a significant role in shaping the direction of the project and its management. While a core group of committed members did the bulk of the work, others provided occasional help. On the progress made in the new site, one of the regular members commented:

> A small group of us meet every Tuesday morning weather permitting (and it usually does!) at Marlpit Community Garden in a work party of volunteers undertaking a number of tasks such as hoeing, digging, planting. In this way, in the space of two years, we have helped to establish on this beautiful site a fruit bush and rhubarb garden, communal plots, a border some hundreds of yards long of herbs of all kinds, a wild flower border, a bee sanctuary and an extensive forest garden. After an hour or two of hard work we are glad to break off and share the delicious hot food … The field, the food, the good company and the fresh air make these working Tuesdays a really enjoyable experience.
> (Mark, SLI Annual Report, 2014–15: 12)

This is an example of how the members are learning not only to grow food but in the process are learning to grow community. Members' increased sense of participation in the project could be seen as one of the incidental learning outcomes.

Learning to live sustainably

From the very beginning, GO^2 focused on growing food organically and sharing resources. The project attracted a large number of people from a range of backgrounds and aimed to promote a sharing culture. Members learned about organic practices and promoting bio-diversity. In this section, I discuss the contributions and limitations of informal learning in promoting sustainable living, focusing on personal consumption and care for nature.

Personal consumption

The GO² project's approach to encourage its members to grow and make good use of their own food and share seeds and tools was aimed at reducing personal consumption and waste. However, it was not aiming to achieve food self-sufficiency; food produced in a mini plot was never going to be adequate even for a single person, let alone a family. In addition to this, given the temperate climate of England, hardly anything grows at least for four to five months in a year unless expensive growing aids (such as a heated greenhouse) are used. So, the aim was to raise awareness about food. The food-sharing events, training workshops on cooking using seasonal produce and food preserving were aimed at minimizing food waste and encouraging healthy eating.

Views expressed by members in previous sections, including the results of the evaluation study, suggest they were practising cooking and using their own produce. I also observed that the sample of dishes brought by the members at the food sharing events was impressive. Quite a few members who had learned to make jam for the first time in their lives told me afterwards that they were not going to buy jam any more.

Despite these very positive learning outcomes expressed by the members, there were plenty of examples of gaps between learning and practice; members were encouraged to sow seeds in succession to avoid glut, share surplus produce with other members and let their friends know when they were going away. Regular advice was posted in the newsletter encouraging members to avoid wasting produce. Yet every year, there was so much food waste, mainly during the summer months when members were away on holiday.[9] Even simple advice on how to pick leafy vegetables to minimize waste was not practised by many growers. This may be due to the prevalent culture of food waste; according to various reports, up to 30 per cent food is thrown away in the UK annually (Smithers, 2020). There were a few families making good use of the produce from their plot, including preserving surplus food by making jam, chutney and bottling. These included families from eastern Europe who were used to the practice of preserving surplus produce from the garden. Here the importance of learner's prior practices in influencing the outcome of informal learning seems to have played a role.

Another key aspect of the GO² scheme was sharing resources such as tools, seeds and plants aimed at reducing personal consumption. In Council-managed allotments, members are allowed to have their own tool shed and they have to buy their own tools, seeds and plants. If GO² was a standard Council-managed allotment, all 138 GO² plot holders (see SLI Annual Report, 2019–20) would have 138 tool sheds and a whole set of tools; they would have to buy hundreds of packets of seeds for their personal use. Instead, GO² had a total of six tool sheds and about a dozen tool sets for 138 members. GO² buys organic seeds mostly in bulk, thereby avoiding packaging and shared with all members reducing seed waste.[10] Members appreciated the sharing of tools and seeds. Because of the availability of tools and plants on site, most members and volunteers were happy to walk, cycle or use public transport in visiting the project site thus reducing the use of car journeys. These are a few examples of attitudinal changes due mainly to the sharing ethos promoted by the project. It is interesting to note that most members were happy to share tools, seeds and knowledge, but not to share their produce nor share a plot to avoid food waste.

Care for nature

The organic growing practices promoted by the scheme, the waterless composting toilet, rainwater harvesting for watering plants, use of heirloom and heritage seeds, and using home-made compost all were aimed at conserving resources and promoting bio-diversity. The newly established orchard, herb garden, forest garden, beehives and wildflower meadow provide learning spaces and opportunities for members and visitors. If adult learning is a continuous process, members and visitors will continue learning from this extended learning space. As mentioned earlier, members expressed how their connectedness to the garden had impacted on their health and well-being.

As the project is mostly managed by volunteers, not all members have time, or skills or commitments, needed to keep the project going. So it relies on a small core group of committed members who have time, skills and aptitude to maintain the sites and to provide the horticultural and environmental expertise to sustain the learning practices. Keeping such a core group of committed members is a challenge because change in membership is a continuous process. In this respect it is important to continue promoting a learning environment where young members learn practical skills from the older members. Equally important is to continue initiating and promoting activities that bring members together.

Conclusion

Most people who joined the GO^2 scheme initially came to grow food and meet new like-minded people, so had certain specific learning aims and a wealth of knowledge and skills. In the process they also learned about organic practices, growing unusual, exotic vegetables and nature conservation, which could be related to the idea of incidental and task-based learning (Rogers, 2014). One of the main incidental learning outcomes of the project was 'growing community' along with growing food. For GO^2 members, this sense of community was pivotal in avoiding isolation. For SLI, the active participation of its members in managing the scheme and in providing practical help was crucial in sustaining the work of the organization. Corporate volunteers who came to our project sites to help maintain the garden and practise team building also ended up learning about gardening and nature conservation. Although it is hard to foresee how and when such task-based, incidental learning will be put into use, it will certainly add to their list of 'pre-existing knowledge' (Rogers, 2014) in future.

A note about my own learning experience is relevant at this point. I come from a tropical, mid-hill area of Nepal where my family used to grow food – fruit, vegetables and cereal – for subsistence. I grew up in a community where the culture of sharing surplus fruit and vegetables, seeds and tools was prevalent. When I started growing fruit and vegetables in Norwich, I not only had to learn to adapt to the temperate and variable weather pattern of England but also had to find out about plant species that I had never known. I remember when I first learned to grow chard and to make jam from reading a book. Eventually, I was not only making jam and growing fruit and vegetables for my family, but was running training workshops on making jam and writing fruit and vegetable growing manuals[11] for GO^2 members. After all these years running the project, I now can see where the idea about setting up a gardening scheme with a sharing ethos came from. It could have been incidental in the first instance, but my cultural values and prior knowledge of growing food in Nepal certainly played a role in developing the GO^2 project.

In previous sections, I discussed the learning experiences of GO^2 members. Although most people initially came to learn growing fruit and vegetables because that is what an allotment offers, slowly they started learning about sharing resources, building community and caring for the environment. However, putting these newly acquired learning skills and ideas into practice was a challenge for many. While the sharing of tools, seeds, plants and meals was widely accepted, not all members were committed to communal tasks or to maintaining communal areas. As mentioned earlier, a significant amount of produce was wasted in many members' plots despite repeated advice urging members to avoid such waste. Members were also not interested in growing fruit and vegetables communally, and as a result small communal growing areas were either neglected or abandoned.

For many members, the main purpose of growing fruit and vegetables seemed to be aesthetic; for example, growing one or two aubergines after five months of care and nurture instead of growing some leaf vegetables that grow easily and supplies food for a long time. The food-growing culture of the UK such as 'dig for victory'[12] promoted by the government during the Second World War, which according to some reports reduced the UK food imports by half, seems to have all but disappeared. In the age of ready-meals delivered to our doors, it is not surprising that growing fruit and vegetables has lost its functional significance.

I observed a parallel between the incidental individual and community learning goals. Regarding the individual goals, as discussed earlier, not all members practised what they learned about growing, using and preserving fruit and vegetables they grew. Likewise, with regard to community learning, not all members were committed to community values and ethos. These comments, however, should not undermine one of the key learning outcomes of the project, the aspect of growing community, a 'positive social value' (Roche, 2018: 537).

If we understand adult learning as a continuous process, it is hard to predict when and how the skills learnt and the knowledge acquired will be put into practice. My own personal experience discussed earlier provides a good example in this respect; when learning (informally) subsistence agriculture in Nepal, I never anticipated those skills and knowledge would be valuable later in life in such a different cultural context. This is a good example of how my own earlier learning opportunities enabled me to contribute to wider social goals, similar to Sen's argument about individual freedom and social responsibility (Sen, 1999). Projects like GO^2 offer examples of a small step towards sustainable living. The challenge though is how to sustain and scale up such initiatives, without losing their basic tenets.

Acknowledgements

I would like to acknowledge the role of the late Prof Alan Rogers for his valuable comments on an earlier version of this chapter. The support offered by SLI members and trustees in writing this chapter is much appreciated.

Notes

1. 'The Chipko movement was a non-violent agitation in India in 1973 that was aimed at protection and conservation of trees, but, perhaps, it is best remembered for the collective mobilisation of women for the cause of preserving forests, which also brought about a change in attitude regarding their own status in society. The name of the movement "chipko" comes from the word "embrace", as the villagers hugged the trees and encircled them to prevent being hacked'. https://indianexpress.com/article/what-is/what-is-the-chipko-movement-google-doodle-5111644/
2. For a detailed definition of formal, informal and non-form learning, see UNESCO, 2009a in Rogers, 2014: 7–8.
3. The word 'allotment' means a land allotted to an individual under the General Inclosure Act 1845 and subsequent Allotment Acts. Initially, up to a quarter of an acre land was made available to the landless rural poor to grow their own fruit and vegetables. The United Kingdom Parliament, 2004. www. Parliament.the-stationary-office.co.uk, 2004.
4. Each measuring 6 metres long and 1.20 metres wide.
5. Council-managed allotments in general have no meeting place and toilet facilities and are in closed places, not suitable for women and children; it is no wonder that the allotment occupants are overwhelmingly male (see Saunders, 1993).
6. As mentioned earlier, original allotment plots were large in size so that the landless rural poor could produce enough food for their family. Even now, the standard plot size in Council allotments is 250 square metres and only recently, Council in Norwich has started offering 125-square-metre plots.
7. 'The Heritage Seed Library (HSL) aims to conserve vegetable varieties that are not widely available. We are not a gene bank and all of our collection, once we have enough seed, will become available for our members to grow and enjoy.' https://www.gardenorganic.org.uk/hsl.
8. Of the total 125 questionnaires sent to members, 30 per cent responded.
9. It is unfortunate that, we, in England, have a six-week-long summer holiday when people go away; there is so much fresh produce on the allotment, as well in the wild, which could have been utilized well if we were around.
10. Producing seeds requires a lot of energy; when we buy a packet of seed, it has hundreds of seeds in it, and as an individual grower (not commercial), we only need a small quantity.
11. See https://www.grow-our-own.co.uk/grow.
12. 'The "Dig for Victory" campaign was set up during WWII by the British Ministry of Agriculture. Men and women across the country were encouraged to grow their own food in times of harsh rationing. Open spaces everywhere were transformed into allotments, from domestic gardens to public parks – even the lawns outside the Tower of London were turned into vegetable patches'. https://www.bl.uk/learning/timeline/item107597.html

References

Aspin, D., Chapman, J., Evans, K., and Bagnall, R. eds. (2012), Introduction and Overview, in *Second International Handbook of Lifelong Learning*, Springer International Handbooks of Education, vol. 26, Netherlands: Springer.

The Indian Express (2018), What is the Chipko Movement? March 26.

Jackson, T. (2005), Live Better by Consuming Less? Is There a 'Double Dividend' in Sustainable Consumption? *Journal of Industrial Ecology*, 9 (1–2), 1–19.

Max-Neef, M. A., Elizalde, A., and Hopenhayn, M. (1991), *Human Scale Development: Conception, Application and Further Reflection*, New York and London: The Apex Press.

Meadows, D., Meadows, D., Randers, J., and Behrens, William W., III (1972), *The Limits to Growth: A Report for the Club of Rome's Project on the Predicament of Mankind*, New York: Universe Books.

Ozturk, E., and Shah, H. (2005), *Wellbeing and the Environment: Achieving 'One Planet Living' and Maintaining Quality of Life*, London: New Economics Foundation.

Pretty, J., Griffin, M., Sellens, M., and Pretty, C. (2003), *Green Exercise: Complementary Role of Nature, Exercise and Diet in Physical and Emotional Well-Being and Implications for Health Policy*, University of Essex, CES Occasional paper 2003–1.

Roche, S. (2018), @What's the Score? Assessing the Impacts and Outcomes of Lifelong Learning, *International Review of Education*, 64, 535–42.

Rogers, A. (2014), *The Classroom and the Everyday: The Importance of Informal Learning for Formal Learning*. Available at: https://www.researchgate.net/publication/311419581.

Rogers, A., and Horrocks, N. (2010), *Teaching Adults*, Milton Keynes: OUP.

Saunders, P. (1993), *Towards Allotment 2000: National Survey of Allotment Gardeners Views in England and Wales*, Northampton: The National Society of Allotment and Leisure Gardeners.

Sen, A. (1988), Freedom of Choice: Concept and Content, *European Economic Review*, 32, 269–94.

Sen, A. (1992), *Inequality Re-Examined*, Oxford: OUP.

Sen, A. (1999), *Development as Freedom*, New York: Alfred Knopf.

Sherwood, H. (2021), *Goodall Wins Templeton Prize of Life's Work on Natural World*, The Guardian, May 20.

SLI Annual Report (2005/06). Available at: https://www.grow-our-own.co.uk

SLI Annual Report (2007/08). Available at: https://www.grow-our-own.co.uk

SLI Annual Report (2008/09). Available at: https://www.grow-our-own.co.uk

SLI Annual Report (2009/10). Available at: https://www.grow-our-own.co.uk

SLI Annual Report (2013/14). Available at: https://www.grow-our-own.co.uk

SLI Annual Report (2014/15). Available at: https://www.grow-our-own.co.uk

SLI Annual Report (2015/16), https://www.grow-our-own.co.uk

SLI Annual Report (2016/17). Available at: https://www.grow-our-own.co.uk

SLI Annual Report (2017/18). Available at: https://www.grow-our-own.co.uk

Smithers, R. (2020), UK Households Waste 4.5m tonnes of Food Each Year, *The Guardian*. 24 Jan 2020.

Taylor, M. C. (2006), Informal Adult Learning and Everyday Literacy Practices, *Journal of Adolescent and Adult Literacy*, 49 (6), 500–9. DOI: https://doi.org/10.1598/JAAL.49.6.5.

Tuckett, A. (2017), The Rise and Fall of Life-Wide Learning for Adults in England, *International Journal of Lifelong Education*, 36 (1–2), 230–49.

Concluding reflections

Alan Rogers and Jules Robbins

In this concluding chapter, we draw together some of the key themes from the studies contained in this book and try to identify some lessons to be learned in looking at different forms of adult education in relation to social change.

We are very mindful that these ten chapters cannot be taken as representative of all adult education in the UK. The volume is not intended to be a systematic collection, and many areas of adult learning are missing. These include vocational (work-related) training and continuing professional development, which may constitute some 75 per cent of all adult education (formal and non-formal) in the UK, and other major programmes such as recent mass health campaigns in the pandemic – as well as ongoing activities such as prison education, MOOCs, one-to-one tuition, adults undertaking formal qualifications such as GCSEs, Access and open and distance learning courses, trade union education, education/training provided to specific groups of people with disabilities, to name but a few.

What we have here is a collection of ten examples of adult learning activities in the UK which are related in one way or another to social change. Many people have held the view of 'adult education as a powerful source for social change' (Tuckett), which 'fosters people's capacity to deal with change and to build the future they want' (UIL, 2020: 10). It is perhaps going too far to assert (as the UNESCO report does) that 'Education has been the primary means of reducing gender violence and poverty' (UIL, 2020: 24), but undoubtedly adult education has the potential to help adults to cope with and – to some extent – to direct social change for the benefit of the individual and society at large.

What then do these studies reveal about our three themes – about adult education, about social change and about the development of effective adult learning programmes for social change?

Adult education

Sharon Clancy shows clearly the importance of adult education and learning to the individual, to the community, to the nation and to the economy, and Fairfax-Cholmeley and Meade cite Stanistreet's argument for the need for proactive education in periods of change:

> the purpose of education cannot be reduced to the creation of productive economic units. Its purpose is, rather, to foster the development of a better society – a learning society in which people are empowered to change the future instead of being prepared for a future they did not choose and cannot control.
>
> (Stanistreet, 2020)

Some of the chapters here highlight the fact that some form of adult learning, more than legislation, is the major means by which governments communicate with their people to inform them and to persuade them to adopt practices beneficial to the health and wealth of the nation – whether through targeted interventions or mass campaigns which are a form of planned, purposeful adult learning. The neglect of adult education by governments in the UK, then, in terms of resources and support which again these papers indicate, is difficult to explain. Harder still to explain is the way in which many educationalists – state and non-state – tend to ignore the adult dimension when talking about 'education'; even some of the bodies campaigning for inclusive education frequently focus exclusively on schools and colleges and fail to mention the adult dimension.

Perhaps one reason for this is that – as these chapters confirm – the world of adult education is messy. Clancy speaks of the 'huge breadth and range, ... myriad manifestations and ... protean quality' of adult learning programmes and of providers (especially voluntary bodies). Rennolds talks of 'the complexity of [adult] learning', Puttick of 'the diversity of adult learning activities'; she describes in some detail those adult education activities which fall 'below the radar ... small voluntary organisations, community groups and semi-formal and informal activities'. Others have said the same: for example, 'The adult education [field] is a particularly complex and multifaceted field because it is addressed to adult learners who have different needs, different experiences, different expectations and their own personal way of learning' (Papadima, 2021: 583).

This sense of the incoherence of adult education has been increased by the recent expansion of online adult learning, caused by the pandemic and other factors. As the project manager of a case study in Fairfax-Cholmeley and

Meade's chapter points out: 'If you do not operate in the techno world, you do not exist.' Added to this, throughout the pandemic, the internet allowed access to MOOCs (massive open online courses) and other courses, to guided tours of castles, cathedrals and museums, to TED talks and YouTube how-to guides on an endless arena of topics.

In adult education, all the boundaries which characterize 'education' are blurred. At one end of the spectrum, adult education slips imperceptibly into 'the caring end of the profession' (Scribbins in Tuckett) or activism (Tett and Puttick); at the other end, it passes into formal education and even perhaps indoctrination. Similarly, many of the distinctions *within* education are challenged in adult education. Rennolds speaks of 'the complexity of defining learning parameters … the blurring of the distinctions … learning which blurs temporal and spatial boundaries', and Clancy says that all boundaries are obscured. The categories used in schools, colleges and universities tend to become unclear, such as the distinction between formal and non-formal education. Are allotment support groups, reading circles and discussion groups among older residents forms of adult education, and if so, what kind of adult education?

Similarly, the distinction that has often been drawn between individual learning and social learning is often obscured (see e.g. Belanger, 2011). Adult education cannot be said to be solely individual learning or social learning – in many cases, it is both at one and the same time: Gordon cites Duncan (2012: 165) [making] 'the case for reading circles as contexts … which 'epitomize reading as being at once individual and communal'. Likewise, the distinctions between adult and youth and between teacher and learner may vanish – when, for example, a seventeen-year-old learner becomes an eighteen-year-old teacher (Rennolds). The adult teacher learns from the teaching of the adult learner; in adult education, the teacher–learner relationship is more horizontal than vertical.

Clancy describes how Raymond Williams categorized adult education into 'the old humanist' tradition, 'the industrial trainer' and 'the democratic educator', similar to what the 2019 Adult Education Commission referred to as the Vocational, the Humane and the Civic (Clancy). But such a distinction between adult education for personal development or for social development or for vocational purposes seems to disappear in the field. For example, as Welby (cited in Clancy) points out, vocational training can be at one and the same time personal development, just as personal interest studies can lead to new forms of livelihoods. Human motivations for learning are complex, fluid and often confused.

Similarly, the alleged polarization of adult learning programmes between those which lead to confirming the *status quo* and those which challenge existing inequalities (Freire; see Tuckett) does not always carry conviction, for (as some of these chapters show) UK adult education aimed at overcoming exclusion and disabilities and at assimilation can, and almost inevitably will, lead to challenging the integrity of the dominant. Even the distinction we have drawn between adult education designed to help people to cope with change and adult education designed to bring about different forms of desired change cannot be held rigidly – these aims can elide imperceptibly into each other. Much will depend on whose point of view is being justified.

These ten chapters show that it is not just that adult education is hard to define, to grapple with; rather, it seems to have a life of its own, a dynamic – which helps to account for the recent expansion of informal self-generated forms of adult learning, 'unfunded peer support groups', as John Mills recently described them in a webinar hosted by the UK Adult Education Commission. Clancy speaks of user-led groups and self-initiated organizations, Puttick of 'below the radar' learning activities. For many years, there have been self-help learning groups; but the expansion in recent times appears to have been extraordinary and needs further research.

It may be suggested that it is precisely this amorphous nature of adult education – like a mist drifting in from the sea – which makes it hard to define, to explore and to control; and it is perhaps this nature which makes many policymakers and educators blind to the *adult* dimension when talking about 'education'. Adult education is not just the 'poor cousin' (Newman, 1979); for many of those engaged in 'education', it just does not exist; it is too hard to grasp.

There is also some confusion between adult education and informal learning. Pant points out that 'What has changed in recent years is the attitude of policy makers and academicians in recognising the importance of informal learning in people's everyday lives'. When Lane spoke privately with three of the participants in the weekly discussion group, they confirmed that informal learning was taking place. She gives the example of two men planning a walking route into the city centre after learning – from others in the group – about the local riverbank's accessibility. The group's social setting allowed informal learning to take place; it 'could arise from the discussions in non-instrumental, if imperceptible ways, and typically was generated by older people tapping into and sharing their own experiences'. In Puttick's case study, many of the activities resulted in informal learning which contributed to the progress of the group. Informal learning contributes to the incoherence of adult education.

Social change

What do these papers suggest about social change?

Social change can be a tricky customer when it comes to proof. Generally speaking, we can't take a portion of it and weigh it against a serving of injustice. What social change feels like is debatable and to an extent unmeasurable. It depends partly on the individual's prior life experiences and their aspirations, both of which may be linked to their class, their dis/abilities, their ethnic background, their sexuality, their family life, their educational experience, their employment history, their social world and so forth.

This is not the place to engage in any lengthy discussion of social change, but some of its many forms are only too visible. The world is very different today from what it was when this project started. Day by day, new crises push earlier ones off the headlines of the media. The pandemic revealed clearly the growing inequalities of UK society, especially in poverty and the uses of technology and other issues: Fairfax-Cholmeley and Meade point out that

> A British Academy report in (2021) identifies nine areas of long-term societal impact thrown up by the pandemic, including: the increasing importance of local communities; renewed awareness of education and skills; worsened health outcomes and growing health inequalities; low and unstable levels of trust; rising unemployment and changing labour market. The report points to the 'pre-existing social deprivations and economic inequalities' which gave space for COVID-19 to thrive.

But then with COP 26 (Conference of the Parties, in 2021), climate change for a time took precedence, followed by migration into Europe generally and into the UK specifically – a crisis which seems to have taken many in the West by surprise despite years of warning by international aid agencies that the growing imbalance of wealth, technology, health and educational provision between the Western and the non-Western worlds has been for years unsustainable and would inevitably lead to some international readjustment. At the time of writing, the war in Ukraine and the atrocities reported daily by the media are increasing our sense that we live in a world which is unpredictable and unjust. Add to these factors the growing and visible forms of violence on our streets and in some of our homes: the need to reduce violence and to increase tolerance of diversity is one of the aims of adult education for social change; as the Sustainable Development Goals put it, to 'Promote peaceful and inclusive societies for sustainable development, provide access to justice for all and build effective, accountable and inclusive institutions at all levels' (SDG 16: UN, 2015: 28). All this creates a toxic mix to which different forms of adult learning need to be addressed. Adaptation to change cannot only be left to the formal schooling of the younger generation; it is too urgent; it requires urgent adult learning and changed behaviour.

But beyond these immediate and obvious crises lie other aspects of social change, dominant unchallenged assumptions which can be critiqued through adult learning programmes: as Gordon remarks, '[t]ogether the group achieve subtle readings, an analysis of the text as literature, in a manner quite different from what we find in formal literary studies in secondary and higher education.' Other forms of desired social change are visible to many. One enduring concern is with social justice and inequalities (see Tuckett); 'we can seek not only social change but social justice' (Rennolds).

As these chapters show, adult education in the UK has a particular role in overcoming the many forms of exclusion. For example, provision of learning for adults with physical and learning disabilities is an area which has only been lightly touched on in this volume. Pant notes that his participants included 'wheelchair users, people with mobility difficulties, homeless people and people suffering from anxieties', and his enterprise specifically ensured that there was on-site parking provision for blue badge holders (a type of parking permit for car users with disabilities) plus raised beds which meant that participants with mobility difficulties would be able to join in with the gardening activities. Equally, while some UK parents found themselves tied down by the constraints imposed by their children's lockdown online education, others have benefitted from it and gained an unprecedented window into their children's education while increasing their own digital literacy. Bouttell notes that online adult learning provision during the pandemic particularly suited certain groups of learners with 'some women feeling more able to go to class from home, because of child-care or other care responsibilities'. She indicates that while some learners were disadvantaged by the Covid-related switch to online learning, citing problems such as lack of technology in the home and lack of technical skills, others found it easier to fit their online learning in with other aspects of their lives. Fairfax-Cholmeley and Meade also indicate that specific groups benefitted from the move online, including 'people who are housebound through illness or childcare needs or have no transport to groups'. However, while the move to online learning has provided learning opportunities for learners and staff alike, those without technology, digital skills or literacy/language skills have been left even further behind, their disenfranchisement sealed.

But overcoming exclusion and marginalization into existing social structures may not be enough; as Tett points out, one aim is not just to increase access of adults to education but to increase access to *quality* education. Calls for open government, transparency, accountability all promote different forms of social change; and as Rennolds points out, these are inevitably linked to the greater crises (see, for example, PIMA, 2021).

Much social change, like adult education, is messy, unplanned and unintended (Rennolds); and the world of social change – like that of adult learning and education – is capable of developing its own spontaneous reactions to such forces in the growth and strength of social movements. It is strange that, while in many parts of the world, adult education (under whatever name it goes) and social movements are closely linked, in the UK, despite the exhortations of the 1919 Adult Education Commission that 'Democracy … meant ensuring voluntary agencies and social movements were central in shaping and delivering adult education' (Clancy), the two fields seem on the whole to stand apart, each perhaps suspicious of the other. Both Puttick and Tuckett comment on the few linkages with national and supranational social movements, yet Tuckett says such links are important: adult learning alone 'is a necessary but not sufficient component in social change, and where the formal structures of adult education can engage with external social forces it can play a constructive and dynamic role' (Bouttell, citing Tuckett, 2015: 248). While individual incidents, particularly of violence, can swiftly lead to new campaigns, in particular through social media, yet adult education rarely so reacts.

At the heart of social change in the UK are the Sustainable Development Goals, to which Clancy, among others, draws attention, and to which Britain is a signatory (McGrath et al., 2016). Some in the UK feel there is a misapprehension that the SDGs apply only to the so-called developing countries, the non-Western world, largely we suspect because the Millennium Development Goals which preceded them were aimed specifically at the Global South.

But the UK too is not only called by the international community but has itself signed up to reduce its own poverty and hunger, to increase gender and other forms of equality, to improve health provision and so on. There is also a misapprehension that 'education' (including adult education) is limited to SDG 4 ('Ensure inclusive and equitable quality education and promote lifelong learning opportunities for all'). But all the 17 SDGs with their 167 targets call for programmes of adult learning:

> Each of the 17 goals has a set of targets and each set has at least one target that deals with or implies learning, training, educating or at the very least raising awareness for one or more groups of adults. Goals 3 [health], 5 [women], 8 [economy], 9 [infrastructure], 12 [consumption] and 13 [climate] especially include targets that imply substantial learning for ranges of adults – and organised, programmatic learning at that.
>
> (John Oxenham pers. comm.)

The promotion of social change in the UK through the empowerment of adults is part of the agenda for adult education today.

In short, as Puttick writes, there are 'multi-layered forms of social change in the home, the family, access and knowledge of gender-related healthcare, and of advocacy, mediation, and empowerment operating at differing levels of society, much of which [is] invisible', and one of the aims of adult education for social change is to help to make the invisible visible.

Adult education and social change

What then do these papers tell us about adult learning programmes for social change?

Some of the adult learning programmes and enterprises described in these chapters are designed with social change in mind. But in others – and in adult education more generally – it would seem to be more usual for social change to develop organically. Sometimes what a neighbourhood needs is someone digging in their allotment with an idea in their head or for someone to walk into a residential care home willing to give a spare hour or two a month.

And, as these studies suggest, the scale of social change which takes place in many adult education and learning environments is not likely to make headlines, but it can change lives. Much social change resulting from adult education will be local and specific and will impact individuals rather than whole communities. Pant's GO^2 scheme was founded on environmental aims such as the sharing of resources, the practice of organic growing techniques and avoidance of non-organic pesticides and fertilizers. These aims were met and, in some respects, can be counted on fingers – just six tool sheds were needed for the 138 members, for example. Other aims of the scheme were attitudinal, with 'the emphasis ... on learning from each other, sharing skills, knowledge', and these were also met through the 'sharing ethos promoted by the project'. The environmental impact of the scheme was another positive outcome with the reduction of the waste of resources such as seeds, and journeys to the site taken on foot or by public transport. Lane points out that the need for individuals to adapt to social changes in their lives can lead to adult learning. In the case of her study, it was a change from living in independent housing to sheltered housing.

Gordon has shown the links between the individual's perception of themselves as a reader in school and the ways in which this can lead to 'an issue of social justice' when it affects 'how we think about what reading is for, what sort of reading we value, and who can engage in what types of reading and when'. Therefore, the individual's access to the writing of others could be curbed not only through lack of sufficient literacy skills but by one's view of oneself as a reader. He states that 'The consequences for social transformation are subtle but profound, touching on literacy, access, cultural value, voice and participation'.

The three domains of social change in adult education

The chapters point to three different groups affected by adult education programmes for social change: the learner-participants, the providing body and staff, and the wider community.

The first, of course, are the **learners or participants**. Most of the chapters focus on the learners – both the individual motivation to participate in adult education and the social changes brought about by the adult learning experience.

By its nature, adult learning often provides a resource for those who are less privileged in our society. Fairfax-Cholmeley and Meade have indicated that the majority of learners in their case studies were experiencing social inequalities: 'insecure work, English as an additional language, religious and cultural issues, issues of confidence and well-being'. The stakes – in terms of people's lives and futures – are high.

Some of the chapters are clear about the changes these programmes have brought to their participants. Fairfax-Cholmeley and Meade report that 'The Learning and Work Institute Adult Participation in Learning Survey (Aldridge, Jones and Southgate, 2020) found that the pandemic is widening social inequalities in particular for young people, women and people with no qualifications and those lacking effective essential skills, including online skills'. They cite the WHO's February 2020 warning about the 'infodemic' (Arts and Humanities Research Council, 2020) of misinformation regarding Covid-19, and point out that deciphering the constant bombardment of Covid-19 information 'requires not only literacy skills but also skills of logic, comprehension and reasoned argument'. They also cite Lopes and McKay's argument that in a time of national emergency, adult learning should help people to make well-informed decisions regarding their health. Additionally, adult learning's provision of skills in literacy, numeracy and ICT may lead to individuals taking political action (EAEA, 2020).

Pant sets out the social and cultural changes in the participants – 'awareness about food ... minimising food waste and ... healthy eating', seeing alterations in understandings, attitudes and practices among his allotment participants and also some of the limitations of these changes. Puttick remarks on the changes with her participants in their sharing of their experiences and skills. Gordon focuses on the changes in the identity of the reading group members in relation to their reading practices: 'adult readers collaborating in generating sophisticated readings of novels.' Lane saw significant changes 'among the residents, helping to increase inclusivity and the possibility of new links between them'; not just in awareness and knowledge but particularly in 'enhanced social connectedness ... opportunity to mix with many others with different backgrounds and listen to their experience'. For her, the programme was 'social change in action, the discussions providing a platform and apparatus for individuals to feel more agency in their lives and to feel connected to the community around them'. Indeed, the increase in social interaction among the learners is the most frequently mentioned social change – as we shall see below, the formation of a learning peer group was a key common ground of these programmes.

Increased sense of agency: One theme which appears in various guises across the chapters is that of the increased sense of agency which individuals have/believe that they have in their lives arising from the adult education intervention. Although in some cases, Covid-19 made a negative impact, with Fairfax-Cholmeley and Meade commenting that many people reported themselves as feeling 'in "limbo"[and] not really able to make any changes to their lives at this time – a feeling of waiting for the next thing to happen to them, rather than feeling a greater sense of agency'. Puttick's participants felt themselves empowered by engaging in creating their own teaching-learning materials. Lane discusses the 'increase in individual residents' agency in their everyday lives', referring to the changes she outlines as demonstrating 'a notable impact'. This sense of agency was encouraged and enabled by the discussions themselves as these provided 'a platform and apparatus' for participants' increased sense of agency and connectedness to their community. Pant's gardening scheme purposefully promoted participants' agency in the scheme by involving them directly in the management and decision-making.

Social connectedness: One key social change which almost all the chapters reflect is that of increased social connectedness. It can be argued that a sense of connection to the people around is a major factor in well-being, and that social engagement, being with others, allows the individual to state and validate their own thoughts while positioning themselves within the group. Gordon's chapter refers to research by Sam Duncan (2012) which 'epitomise[d] reading as being at once individual and communal' (165). Just as the participants in Lane's discussion group listened to, encouraged and occasionally 'chivvied' one another, participants in reading groups might 'prompt or organise the contributions of others in the conversation'.

In the community of the sheltered housing accommodation, one of Lane's intentions was to promote connectedness, 'to increase socialisation and links among residents'. Comments from the participants themselves revealed that not only was this intention realized, it was acknowledged and valued. Residents came to know each other better and to recognize one another's unexpected qualities, with 'Resident C' noting that 'still waters run deep' and that someone who seemed 'insignificant' could be revealed, through the discussions, to be 'quite unexpected'. The value of this was especially heightened for those who had 'little contact with family or friends'.

For many learners or participants involved in adult learning, the social aspect is on an equal footing with the learning itself. Pant indicates that 'Most people who joined the GO^2 scheme initially came to grow food and meet new like-minded people'. Many members were women over fifty-five, and the chance of improved mental and physical health plus the chance to '[avoid] isolation' were/was a welcome possible outcome.

The fact that Pant has reported that there was greater 'ethnic diversity in GO^2 membership than in the general Norwich area' highlights another benefit of adult learning in that it provides the opportunity for people to connect with others who might not otherwise come into their lives. The possibility for social cohesion at a wider level of the community is a likely outcome.

The second domain for social change is that of the providing bodies and staff. Tuckett talks about the way ILSCAE challenged some of the providing agencies and how it was academic researchers and the teaching staff who kept the vision alive. Clancy also talks about the challenges to the providers of such programmes. Tett notes the importance of the multiple staffing on her programmes. While Pant's gardeners tended to rely on one leader, there was 'a core group of committed members' who led the way for the whole allotment community.

Sometimes, it is the educator's prior knowledge and experience which is of significance. Lane's Norwich discussion group was formed partly from her previous experience of a similar group she facilitated in Cambridge. Pant has acknowledged that the development of the GO^2 project was informed by his 'cultural values and prior knowledge of growing food in Nepal'. His informal learning of subsistence agricultural practices in Nepal later became valuable in a completely different setting, leading him to reflect on how this enabled him 'to contribute to wider social goals, similar to Sen's argument about individual freedom and social responsibility' (Sen, 1999). Similarly, the corporate volunteers on the gardening scheme will have gained knowledge from the incidental learning they experienced and this knowledge may be disseminated in the future.

The study of Covid-19 and adult education revealed the ways in which the staff changed their practices very rapidly. As Cholmeley-Fairfax and Meade suggest, adult education providers of all sorts, whether county-wide with responsibility to thousands of learners or church hall-based with responsibility for a dozen, have all needed to improvise, move quickly and weigh up their priorities amidst an unanticipated and unwelcome change of circumstances. Arguably, at no time in the past have adult learning and education providers had to move more quickly than they did during the pandemic.

The effect of adult learning programmes on the teaching staff and volunteers forms the central theme of Bouttell's study, including 'an attempt [by the government] to annex ESOL teachers as an extension of the Home Office' which was resisted. She has shown that the volunteer ESOL teachers she interviewed felt unable to have an influence on the structural factors which impacted their learners, such as funding and immigration policy; however, through the act of volunteering itself, they were able to exercise agency. She indicates the scope of the support which providers offered to their learners prior to the pandemic: 'community meals, access to food banks and clothing and signposting to other local support services for refugees' (Dawson, 2017). Fairfax-Cholmeley and Meade, however, reported that although providers offered more support during the pandemic, some learners found it easier or preferable to turn to religious groups or to free courses online. The CIC case study they looked at extended its scope to include further opportunities for the ex-offenders it was working with. Another of the organizations they looked at in their chapter was working with a local Muslim community and in response to the various needs ensuing from the pandemic, offered guidance and education concerning the *halal* status of the Covid-19 vaccine and held an Eid party for the women on Zoom.

The flexibility called for from the providing bodies is also illustrated by Pant's GO^2 scheme. None of the forty-one members wanted to move to a council allotment at the end of the third year, and Pant indicates that 'Unlike most externally funded projects, SLI did not have specific targets to fulfil, so it was possible to adapt to such changes ... to widen the learning space to accommodate a more diverse group of people'.

Third, of course, is the domain of change in the wider community. Few of the chapters focused on social change outside the classroom. Puttick's programme had incidental effects on the community from which her participants came, and Pant with the community gardening scheme saw some changes among the homes of his participants but his 'big questions' expressed in the aims of the programme remained unanswered. Tett is the only writer here who consciously aimed to bring about social change in the local community through the work of the participants in her classes. There must be some lessons here for adult learning programmes for social change.

The factors for effective adult education programmes for social change

What then do these case studies tell us about the key factors for the development of effective adult learning experiences for social change, helping adults to increase awareness and understanding of social change and of their potential to direct it? Several of the case studies set out their prescription for the promotion of social change through adult learning.

The first thing to note is that – as both Tuckett and Clancy show – adult education for social change is difficult, fragile and hard to maintain. Tuckett sets it out clearly: 'Most adult education does not change society. It confirms the powerful in their positions of power (people with more initial education get more adult education and training) and confirms the powerless in their positions' (what has been called the Matthew effect, Stanovich, 1986). Clancy points to resistance even to reflection on inequalities. On the other hand, in adult education for social change, there is some resistance to what are seen as unjust provocations: Bouttell speaks of her programmes as 'actively resisting restrictive UK government policy through community-based

English classes ... the very act of volunteering as an ESOL teacher is an act of resistance to' the hostile environment which the government developed in relation to asylum seekers.

Active learning. Rennolds's prescription for effective adult education for social change highlights four factors – experience, resources, continuing support and facilitation. In this context, by experience what is meant is that in adult education for social change, the participants (facilitator and learners alike) need to experience the desired social change 'for real' – not just in artificially created classroom exercises but in direct community involvement – as Rennolds showed with the National Citizenship Service programme. The participants are encouraged to model the required changes – for example, directly to identify inequalities in the local community and develop collaborative concrete action to be implemented to address the perceived injustices. Health issues (as Tett shows) need to be confronted, not just through textbook examples but for real by the community of learners in the adult learning group: '[t]he group then worked with the tutor to identify how this issue [which the group had identified] might be tackled in the local community' (Tett). This is learning *through* doing rather than learning *for* doing.

From this basic principle spring the other factors listed here (in no order of priority).

The chapters by Tett and Rennolds both suggest that adult education for social change would seem to be more individualized and practical rather than institutionalized and standardized, and many of the other case studies confirm this overall impression. Lane, for example, observes: 'each person absorbed different meanings and associations from the activity'. We are reminded of the call from UNESCO to 'promote local-level initiatives' (*UIL*, 2020: 9). Fairfax-Cholmeley and Meade point to the particular significance of 'small grassroots organisations in enabling the most vulnerable learners to interpret crisis situations and to build skills of resilience leading to greater agency'.

Perhaps the most important result of this basic principle of active learning is that the 'deficit' approach to adult learners is inappropriate: 'the pedagogical approaches that are most effective are those based on the view that people have important "funds of knowledge" to contribute to education ... rather than denigrating their expertise' (Tett). Tuckett agrees that 'the basic starting point for any democratic education is a deep respect for learners' life experiences'. Adult education for social change is based on the belief that the learners *can* do things collaboratively – even if sometimes they themselves feel they are unable to act.

A deficit approach implies that there is some common norm, an agreed 'centre', to which the adult learners first need to conform. Adult education for social change calls for decentring, decolonizing of adult education programmes, and eventually to 'problematis[ing] the boundaried thinking of who is teaching and who is learning' (Rennolds). The experience of these – and many other programmes of adult education for social change – indicates that instead of such a common norm to which the learners are asked to conform, we need to see a wide range of diversity of goals among the adult participants and that they each bring not only prior experience but many capabilities (some of which they may deny) which can be harnessed to the learning programme, 'involving them in co-designing and delivering education and learning' (Tett). Tett goes on to point out the value of '"an inquiry method of teaching" (citing González et al., 2005: 19) ... where participants are actively involved in developing their lived experiences. ... [O]pportunities for participation and self-determination were taken up and participants' voices were heard'. Puttick's learners created their own teaching-learning materials in many languages – the prior learning and experience which each learner brings to the group were identified, valued and utilized in the group activities.

The deficit model of adult education has, quite rightly, slipped from favour with many academics, educators and providers in the UK. Most adult educators, whatever contemporary frameworks and policies may be in place, cannot fail to be aware of the life experience and prior knowledge of the learners they come across, built up through informal learning, the largely unconscious and unintended learning which takes place in everyday activities as well as in adult education programmes and which results in the development of tacit funds of knowledge and banks of skills (Tett, citing González et al., 2005). In some of the case studies in this volume, the facilitators have outlined their impression of the prior learning, both informally and through their educational and professional experiences, of their participants. Lane has commented that participants in her discussion groups were mostly lower-middle and middle class, mostly white British, with some having gained post-school qualifications in nursing and teaching. She recognizes that while her discussion groups were not designed to be reminiscent in nature, participants would 'very likely draw on their own experiences'; their prior knowledge would be 'welcome'. Experience, rather than expertise, would be valued, putting all on an equal footing. In the reading groups in Gordon's chapter, members achieved 'a range of analytic achievements akin to high level literary study' without their discussion including facets we might usually associate with the discourse of formal literary study. Not needing to meet the requirements of formalized assessment criteria, they were free to use different methods, 'adult reading practices of inherent value', to investigate novels together, to tell 'stories of different types' and to invoke intertextual interpretations of the literature.

Such active learning for social change requires a good deal of time; it 'took longer; ... the pace of learning' was that of the learners, not that of the curriculum (Tett). Such adult education cannot be achieved with a single-injection mode of teaching. Almost all these case studies stress this factor. Pant's allotment programme lasted for at least sixteen years.

This also calls for a very flexible curriculum. Almost every study here shows how the teacher/tutor/leader adapted the curriculum to the immediate circumstances of the particular group they were leading. 'The curriculum was based on the learners' concerns and aspirations' (Tett). Puttick talks of experimentation with her groups, making it up as they went along. Rennolds says that the projects specified by the curriculum they were given were supplemented by 'real community engagement; ... learning is not static, prescriptive or functional but dynamic, fluid and open-ended'. Fairfax-Cholmeley and Meade describe the flexibility Covid-19 required of the providers and staff, and Lane speaks of 'flexibility and adaptability'.

And it is a curriculum which intersects with many immediate and local dimensions – health, poverty, family needs, inequalities, exclusion, etc. Bouttell says that 'providers often need to be flexible and accommodating, offering a wide variety of services to encompass the complex and hectic lives of refugees and asylum seekers in the UK', citing such activities as 'community meals, access to food banks and clothing and signposting to other local support services for refugees'. Generalized curricula imposed from outside could lead to maintaining the *status quo*: 'what counts as important knowledge is one way in which inequalities of power are systematically reproduced' (Tett).

At the heart then is the role of the group leader(s), whatever title is given to these persons. The impact of the tutor is referred to in various chapters. Fairfax-Cholmeley and Meade cite a learner who recognizes that the tutor, along with delivering the course content, has also instilled 'a new-found confidence' in their own ability. The tutor's support also increased the learner's confidence in exploring 'other online learning opportunities and resources when classes were not available.' Whereas Lane has considered the discussion group participants' reluctance to take over the reins in the selection of topics, Gordon has noted that 'Where members of reading communities choose to guide or organise others, they influence (or attempt to influence) the reading positions of others.

This may have some resonance with what Duncan (2012) called participant-led differentiation.'

Some of these programmes found they needed multiple staff to provide adequately for the adult learners for social change: in Tett's programme, there were 'an advice worker, a rehabilitation worker, and a literacy tutor', but this is unusual. Nevertheless, whether one or more than one, 'it was the staff that made a difference' (Tett). As one of Lane's participants remarked: the facilitator had 'control of the conversation'. When asked what she meant, the respondent told the author that 'you instil a kind of discipline that helps the conversation to flow, that keeps things going smoothly'.

As we noted above, Bouttell reports that some of the volunteer teachers she spoke with positioned themselves very specifically, seeing their volunteering as 'an act of resistance to "hostile environment" policies for some volunteers'. She suggests that volunteering can therefore be viewed as an act of solidarity with the migrants who were their learners and whom 'some volunteers viewed as being mistreated by the UK government'. She further reports that volunteer teachers referred to 'inter-cultural learning' which they had gained from teaching and meeting people from other cultures. This suggests that 'it is possible for adult education to facilitate "integration" which is not simply one-sided'.

Many of the writers here speak of the commitment of the group leader(s) – the best results come from 'the creativity and personal risks taken by' the leaders (Tuckett citing Gelpi). Puttick sees the group leader as a *'bricoleur'*: she commented on 'my own multifaceted roles as volunteer, teacher, student, researcher and peer: always complicated by my place within deeply embedded historical and societal intersectional inequalities, in this case particularly racial and gender inequalities. ... Interwoven within their literacy activism was my own activism'. Several chapters here speak of the confidence of the 'teacher' and the critical reflection they bring to the learners' situations (Tett and other authors). An effective leader will create 'a safe, inclusive setting ... where trust was being built ... a social setting distinct from their usual activities' (Lane) and a positive learning environment (Tett); they will build up over time a strong relationship with the learning group (Tett, Pant, Puttick). Clancy indicates that 'Much depends on the way in which a given subject is taught, and the object with which it is taken by the individual student'. Without such leadership, some groups might never engage with the critical reflection on social change needed – for example, Gordon's reading circle might spend all their time on literary conventions without exploring differing views of social issues raised by their texts, such as, when studying the book *Daddy-Long-Legs*, issues of teenage angst and the appropriateness of adult patronage. Such roles of course create challenges for the tutor but they are likely to lead to 'reciprocal care' (Rennolds).

Such activities, of course, will also call for access to adequate resources – not just for the tutor but for the group as a whole. Trinity support was essential for the success of Puttick's programme, as was NCS for Rennolds. Tett was able to call on adequate resources. Here the role of the providing agencies and their underlying ideologies – as Tuckett shows – are vital; the failure of the programme he describes was not due to the disagreement between academics and practitioners (both were equally committed) but to the fact that the academics had access to resources, for example, to engage in international meetings and the practitioners did not. As Puttick says, 'I now recognise the privileged position my role in the university institution gives me.' The practitioners could 'duck and dive' to an extent and achieve much, but without the whole-hearted support of the providing bodies, this is not likely to be enduring. Thus with ILSCAE several of the agencies gave only half-hearted support to the cause – the University of Nottingham, for example, paid for one international meeting but refused to join the organization as an institutional member.

Funding. It is easy to be pessimistic, to lose heart when the plight of adult education in the UK seems to be always low down on any politician's list of priorities, when (as some of the chapters here demonstrate) the funding rules shift and morph while never seeming to be a cause for celebration, and when we still live in a society in which the functionally illiterate are made to feel ashamed and disenfranchised. For anyone who has been involved in UK formal adult education, the thorny issue of (lack of) funding is one with which they will be very familiar. As Bouttell has pointed out, the lack of funding to support learning for refugees and its precarity is frustrating for providers as well as for the refugees themselves. Calls for change have been numerous (Bouttell cites Refugee Action, 2016; 2019). A government which extols the value of integration should surely be providing English language classes for all new migrants, whether they have refugee status or not. Migrants' chances to become integrated into their new country are lessened because of the lack of ESOL provision and there are obvious knock-on implications for their children's progress at school. Bouttell (citing Simpson (2015)) has indicated that both Scotland and Wales take a less prescriptive and future employment-focused approach to ESOL.

Perhaps the feature emphasized by most of these case studies is that of the **group learning**. It is not so much a matter of developing and assessing individual competences as 'about building a community ... [who] learn from each other, share knowledge and practical experience and have common events ... active participation of its members in managing the scheme and in providing practical help was crucial' (Pant). It is full participation in a group of learners and teacher(s) who share their experiences, knowledge and skills; as Tett puts it, forming a group is essential 'so that they can join together for mutual support and act together ... [and with it, the] dialogue that took place'. Gordon speaks of his 'group's social interaction, a gentle and level peer-to-peer pedagogy', and Bouttell points out that 'opportunities for volunteer ESOL teachers to form networks and learn from one another and others in the organisations present themselves as important ways in which informal learning may occur'.

Many of the chapters stress the importance of dialogue among the group members – open, frank, tolerant dialogue leading to increased critical awareness. ILSCAE had as a key point the use of 'dialogue as an educational method ... To encourage all those involved in adult education to foster participation in dialogue on the critical social issues confronting humankind today, such as class inequality, environmental concerns, peace, racism, sexism and ageism'. The 2019 Adult Education Commission has a chapter on 'Fostering community, democracy and dialogue through adult lifelong education'. Tett says that 'Confidence increased, not only because of changing experiences but also because of the dialogue that took place around those experiences in ways that promoted social awareness and critique'; Puttick talks of 'a constant dialogue that is made visible and that strives to disrupt'; and Rennolds of 'the reciprocity of dialogue'.

Collaborative action: But as Rennolds puts it, not just dialogue as the 'sharing of learning and knowing together', but more importantly

> '**doing**' with and alongside each other – elements that exceed organisational aims or intentions, elements that are unplanned by any one agent but which happen in the thick of the assemblage, that offer learning opportunities and the building of relationships. These in turn widen perspectives and knowledge, and create new worlds.

Clancy talks of reflecting and *acting* together, Puttick of peer support and sharing. Collaborative social action lies at the heart of adult education for social change; Rennolds's criticism of the NCS programme was in part its emphasis on individualized learning.

The building of group activities for social change also calls for changes in the forms of assessment. In group learning, 'assessing what you have learned is challenging' (Rennolds). Tett points to what she calls 'authentic assessment' and what others have called 'performative assessment' of real-life learning (Chun, 2010; Palm, 2008; UIL, 2020). Such assessment is difficult, especially to provide the certification which many agencies and many learners call for: Clancy refers to the 'lure of courses with accreditation or which can be assessed on observable results [which] becomes more potent'. 'Methods used to determine impact' (Bouttell) in, for example, reading circles (Gordon), allotment-sharing groups (Pant) and discussion groups with older people (Lane) call for innovative approaches which carry conviction in the eyes of learners, providing agencies and funders, whatever the facilitators believe.

Such then are some of the factors which will make for effective adult education for social change programmes.

... but two caveats

Two final comments from the case studies:

First, adult education for social change will very rarely achieve its goals in full, even when supported and resourced. There will always be some short fall. Tuckett points to the difficulty of maintaining the impetus over time, Clancy to the resistance which critical adult education arouses from the dominant neo-liberal culture of the day. Pant is most clear on this – after a time, the participants in the allotment programme began to resent the limitations on individual freedoms imposed by shared tools and tasks, and shared seeds and sowing policies; atomization began to creep in. It is important for those engaged in adult education for social change to take part in critical reflection and be honest with themselves, the participants and others about what can be and how much has been achieved.

And this leads to the second caveat: adult education for social change begins with us – it challenges those who advocate and practise it. We need to be critically reflective about ourselves and our own ideologies. We cannot put it any better than John Payne cited by Tuckett:

> I still support the aims and am pursuing them in my own way. But I think our practice in ILSCAE did not, and perhaps could not, match the grand ambitions of the aims because we were all institutionally and individually part of the 'forces of oppression'. This is not a criticism so much as a sociological observation ... Really meeting these aims involves life challenges which are greater than most of us are honestly willing to accept.
>
> (Mohorcic Spolar and Payne, 2002: 69–70 cited in Tuckett)

References

Aldridge, F., Jones, E., and Southgate, D. (2020), Learning through Lockdown: Findings from the 2020 Adult Participation in Learning Survey, Learning and Work Institute. Available at: [online] https://learningandwork.org.uk/resources/research-and-reports/learning-through-lockdown/. Accessed 26 April 2022.

Belanger, Paul (2011), *Theories in Adult Learning and Education*, Opladen: Barbara Budrich.

Chun, M. (2010), Taking Teaching to (Performance) Task: Linking Pedagogical and Assessment Practices, *Change: The Magazine of Higher Learning*, 42 (2), 22–9.

Dawson, R. (2017), A Snapshot of English Language Teaching in Seven Voluntary Sector Organisations in 2017, [Report]. Merton Home Tutoring Services. Available at: https://www.natecla.org.uk/uploads/media/208/16729.pdf.

Duncan, S. (2012), *Reading Circles, Novels and Adult Reading Development*, London and New York: Continuum/Bloomsbury Academic.

Freire, P. (1972), *Pedagogy of the Oppressed*, Harmondsworth: Penguin.

González, N., Moll, L., and Amanti, C. (2005), *Funds of Knowledge: Theorizing Practices in Households, Communities, and Classrooms*, New Jersey: Lawrence Erlbaum Associates.

McGrath, S., and Powell, L. (2016), Skills for Sustainable Development: Transforming Vocational Education and Training beyond 2015, *International Journal of Educational Development*, 50, 12–19.

Mohorcic Spolar, V. and Payne, J. (2002), Adult Education and Social Purpose: The Work of the International League for Social Commitment in Adult Education 1984–1994, in J. Field (ed.), *Promoting European Dimensions in Lifelong Learning*, Leicester: NIACE, 66–77.

Newman, M. (1979), *The Poor Cousin: A Study of Adult Education*, London: Allen and Unwin.

Palm, T. (2008), Performance Assessment and Authentic Assessment: A Conceptual Analysis of the Literature, *Practical Assessment Research and Evaluation*, 13 (4). DOI: https://doi.org/10.7275/0qpc-ws45.

Papadima, G. (2021), Is There a Split between Adult Educator's Educational Philosophy in the Learning and Teaching Process? *International Journal of Instruction*, 14 (3), 583–96, Available at: https://www.e-iji.net/dosyalar/iji_2021_3_34.pdf.

PIMA (2021), Climate Justice and ALE, *PIMA Bulletin* 39. Available at: https://drive.google.com/file/d/1cWLBy65p3bl300Gqskv64pQE-qyvbkvT/view.

Sen, A. (1999), *Development as Freedom*, New York: Alfred Knopf.

Stanistreet, P. (2020), Resources of Hope: Towards a Revaluing of Education, *International Review of Education*, 66, 1–7. DOI: https://doi.org/10.1007/s11159-020-09827-0.

Stanovich, K. E. (1986), Matthew Effects in Reading: Some Consequences of Individual Difference in the Acquisition of Literacy, *Reading Research Quarterly*, 21, 360–407.

Tuckett, A. (2015), Adult Education, Social Transformation and the Pursuit of Social Justice, *European Journal of Education*, 50 (3), https://doi.org/10.1111/ejed.12135.

UIL (2020), *Embracing a Culture of Lifelong Learning: Report, a Transdisciplinary Expert Consultation*. Available at: https://unesdoc.unesco.org/ark:/48223/pf0000374112 Accessed 14 February 2022.

UN (2015), *The 2030 Agenda for Sustainable Development*. Available at: https://sdgs.un.org/goals Accessed 14 February 2022.

Index

Locators followed by "n." indicate endnotes

Aboriginal adult education (South Africa) 21
active learning 200, 202
activism 7, 29, 77, 88, 189
    community 78–80
    covert 78
    literacies 75, 80, 88, 203
    social change 71
adolescents/teenagers 8, 10–11, 204
The Adult Community Learning Services Service 152
adult education 1–2, 8, 11–12, 18, 27, 30, 35–6, 55–6, 59, 69, 72, 150, 162–3, 188–90, 192–4, 203. *See also* adult learning
    campaign 6
    Covid-19 and 198
    formal structures of 67
    forms of 187
    funding for 64–6, 71, 204
    global organization for 23–4
    overall spending 163
    pedagogical value 15
    permanent national necessity 2, 5, 148
    philosophy and vision 2–4
    purpose 43
    re-politicization 1, 17
    and social change 60, 187, 191, 194–7, 199–201, 205–6
    state and social movements 14–17
Adult Education and Lifelong Learning for 21st Century Britain 6
Adult Education Commission (1919 & 2019) 189–90, 193, 205
Adult Education Committee (AEC) 2
    and Centenary Commission 6–7
    farsighted and bold 4–5
    Final Report 1, 6–7, 12, 17
    Ministry of Reconstruction 2, 9, 13
    Report (1919) 1–3, 6–8, 10–12, 16
    vision 2
Adult Education Quarterly 150
adult educators/learners 6, 21, 25–8, 35, 67, 147, 188–9, 201, 203
    deficit approach 200–1
    literature 128
    radical 22, 24
adult learning 1, 5, 7, 16, 21, 36, 41, 55, 59, 67, 72, 78, 81, 88, 103, 116, 147, 155, 160–1, 163, 167, 169–71, 193, 200
    activities 187
    alleged polarization of 190
    community-based 55
    complexity 188
    and Covid-19 pandemic 148–9
    diversity of 76, 188
    grassroots 8
    instrumental and intrinsic role 170
    online 188, 192
    programmes 150, 188, 190, 192, 194, 198–9
    providers 147, 150–1, 198
    and social change 1, 75, 79, 107, 199
    and sustainable development 168
    transformational potential of 170
Adult Learning and Education (ALE) 55, 161–2, 193, 198
adult reading
    practices 144, 202
    and school experiences of literary reading 130–5
advocacy 76–7, 80–1, 88
    as affective and embodied 81–3
aesthetic orientation 136
affect 50, 52, 54, 100, 110–12, 120, 127, 195
affective literacy events 75–6

agency 44, 85, 103–4, 108, 111–12, 120, 147, 158, 161–3, 198, 200
  increased sense of 196–7
  of individuals and groups 78, 105, 196
  volunteer 66–7
agents of change 110
allotment 171–4, 177, 180–1, 183 n.3, 183 n.9, 194, 198–9, 202, 206
Amanti, C. 43
Anderson, D. 16
anecdotes 137–8
anti-establishment 13
anti-globalisation movement 17
Aspin, D. 170–1
assessment 45, 128, 130, 132, 170, 202, 205–6
asylum seekers 29, 59–62, 64–7, 69, 81, 202
  hostile environment 200
  impacts of pandemic 70–1
Atkinson, K., *Life after Life* 141–3
Australian Journal of Adult Learning 23
authentic assessment 45, 206

Barad, K. 108
'below-the-radar' (BTR) sector 77, 81
Benseman, J. 29
Beresford, P. 55
Berlin, A. 87
Big Society 7, 76, 78
bio-diversity 178, 180
Black
  and anti-racist studies 23
  Britons 29
  and minority ethnic community learners 152, 161
Boal, A., Theatre of the Oppressed 32, 34
Board of Education 6, 8
Boeren, E. 150
book groups 127, 130, 132, 135
  by intertext proxies 141–3
  literary reading achievements 135–8
  positioning readers and reading 138–40
  shared process of reading 138
Bouttell, L. 192, 198–9, 202–5
Briggs, W. 9
British Academy 130, 148–9, 191
British Association for International and Comparative Education (BAICE) 161

British Medical Council 86
British Ministry of Agriculture 183 n.12
Bron, M. 28
Burke, P. J. 43
Butler, J. 112

Cable, V. 16
Cameron, D., 'Big Society' initiative 76
case studies (Covid-19)
  digital learning and training for staff 154–5
  face-to-face learning 156–7
  health and well-being, learning for 158–9
  learning through new methods, response 151–4
  needs of learners, response 155–6
  opportunities for learning 157–8
Castles, S. 71
Cave, G. 13, 18 n.3
Centenary Commission on Adult Education Report 6–7, 16, 148
Central Labour College 22
children 8–11, 44–6, 64, 66, 83, 85–6, 111, 149, 152, 154, 170–2, 174, 183 n.5, 192, 204
Chipko movement 169, 183 n.1
citizenship 2, 4–5, 9, 18, 55, 65, 78, 85, 107, 112–13, 116
City Council, Swansea (Wales) 149
civic education 1, 5, 14, 148, 189
Civic University Commission 16
Clancy, S. 188–90, 193, 197, 199, 203, 205–6
Clarke, C. 17
classroom teaching 136
climate change 191
Cohort Leader 117
Cole, G. D. H. 22
colonialism 23, 29, 69, 83
communication 30, 32, 44, 50, 77, 80, 83, 104, 129, 132, 136, 160
community 2, 5, 14, 23, 28, 35, 37, 41, 47, 55, 67, 77, 81, 101, 104, 132, 153–4, 156, 159, 169–72, 174–5, 196, 199, 205
  activism 7, 29, 78–80
  bricoleur 82
  education 6, 8, 17

ESOL 60, 65–6, 71
  gardening scheme (Norwich) (*see*
    Grow Our Own (GO²) initiative)
  growing food to 177–8, 181–2
  HIIC 50–2
  international 193
  learning 8, 55, 77–8, 88, 148, 158, 160, 175, 182, 200
  sheltered-housing 93, 103, 197
  and well-being 160
Community College 154–5
Community Hub 52
Community Inc 108
Community Interest Company (CIC) case study 156, 159, 162, 198
Conrad, J., *The Nigger of the Narcissus* 133
conspiracy theories 149
contemporary schooling system 14
conversation analysis 128, 132, 135. *See also* book groups
Cooke, M. 65
council-managed allotments 171–2, 179–80, 183 n.5, 183 n.6
Covid-19 pandemic 1, 55–6, 61, 63, 80, 93, 147, 162
  and adult education/learning 148–9, 198
  case studies, key themes 151–9 (*see also* case studies (Covid-19))
  challenges of responding to 149–50
  digital learning 149–51
  and ESOL 70–1
  flexibility 202
  infodemic 149, 195
  lockdowns 150, 152–7, 160
  methodology 150–1
  staff development 160
  vaccine, *halal* status 199
Crooks, S. R. 83
cultural capital 128, 130
cultural diversity 41–2, 53
cultural heritage 83–5
cultural studies 22–3

Deci, E. L. 68
Declercq, C. 82
deficit model 43, 200–1
deficit school-based literacy 83
De Genova, N. P., legal production of migrant illegality 61

delayed learning 178
democracy 2, 4, 6–8, 24, 55, 193, 205
democratic education/educator 3–5, 17, 21, 189, 200
Deshler, D. 34
"Dig for Victory" campaign 182, 183 n.12
digital learning/pedagogy 71, 149, 151, 160–1
  opportunities for 154–5
  platforms 86, 155, 160–1
disability 32, 159, 187, 190, 192
discussion(s)/discussion groups 31, 34, 50–2, 84, 93, 96, 189–90, 197–8, 201–2, 206
  analysis and 101–5
  Christmas 103
  critical reflection on 96–7
  gendered differences 94
  ground rules 95–6
  informal learning 97–8
  Norwich-based 97
  participatory ageing and social change 101
  participatory nature of 102
  purposeful conversation and social connection 104–5
  reflections from residents 98–101
  sheltered-housing scheme 93–4, 96, 105
  social patterns as 100
  topics 95
diversity 41–2, 47, 53–4, 76, 78, 80, 96, 104, 109, 129, 172, 188, 191, 201
Dowling, W. 32
Duncan, S. 127–8, 189, 197
  participant-led differentiation 136, 203

ecology, learning 76, 87–9
economics 7, 10, 14, 16, 25, 42–3, 77, 84, 160, 163, 169
educación popular. *See* popular education
Education ('Fisher') Act (1918) 8–9, 12
El-Metoui, L. 70
emancipatory 2, 4
English 29–30, 78, 85, 148, 152, 195
  classes 60, 62, 70, 200, 204
  flexible, non formal classes 67–8

integration 59
learning 59, 62–3, 69, 71
as Second Language 23, 29, 32
English as a Second or Other Language (ESOL) 56, 151–3, 204
   classes 67–8, 71, 81, 83–4, 153
   Covid-19 and 63, 70–1
   and family literacy 83
   funding 59–60, 62, 64–6, 71
   Scottish Executive Strategy for 62
   study 63–4
   Trinity 81
   in the UK 62–3
   volunteer teachers 59, 64, 66, 68–70, 198, 200, 205
environment 14, 35, 46, 49, 83, 87–8, 93, 107, 111, 119, 129, 141, 155–7, 160, 167–70, 173–5, 177, 180–1, 194, 203
equality 14, 44, 53, 55, 193. *See also* inequality/inequalities
   of decision-making 47, 53–4
   and pedagogy 42–4
Equality Act (2010) 77
Erel, U. 85
ethnicity 32, 36, 96, 154
ethnography 75, 80, 82, 107
Euro-Centrism 69
European Association for the Education of Adults (EAEA) 148
extrinsic and intrinsic motivations 68

FaceTime 152, 161
face-to-face learning/teaching 55, 150–2, 155–7, 159–62, 175
Fairfax-Cholmeley, K. 188, 191–2, 195–6, 198, 200, 202
Falk, I. 77
family literacy 41, 44–7, 81–3, 85
family-literacy worker (FLW) 44–5
Federici, F. M. 82
feminism 23, 29, 109
First World War 1, 7
Folklander High School (American South) 21
food growing 167, 169, 171–9, 181–2, 183 n.3, 183 n.12, 197–8
food-growing culture (UK) 182
Fordham, P. 27

formal learning/reading 67, 69, 75, 81, 127–8, 130–2, 134–7, 140, 143–4, 147, 149–50, 170–1, 189, 192, 201, 204. *See also* informal learning
Fraser, N. 42–3, 53. *See also* social justice
Freire, P. 23, 29–30, 51
functional skills 65, 118, 152, 158
funding 6–8, 11, 16, 31, 64–6, 70, 81, 149–50, 162–3, 198, 204
   for ESOL 59–60, 62, 64–6, 71
   ring-fenced 64
   for Trinity 81, 83
funds-of-knowledge pedagogy 43–5, 53, 200–1

gay rights 32
GCSE English Literature 128–9, 131, 134, 187
Gedalof, I. 85
Gelpi, E. 26–7
gender 32
   differences 94
   dynamics 96
   equality/inequalities 87–8, 193, 203
   issues 31, 36
General Inclosure Act (1845) 183 n.3
Godfrey-Smith, P. 107
González, N. 43
Goodall, J. 169
Google Classroom 155
Gordon, J. 137–8, 189, 192, 195–7, 201–3, 205
   Researching Interpretive Talk around Literary Narrative Texts: Shared Novel Reading 132
Graham-Brown, N. 70
grammar school 133–4
Greenwood, A. 17
Griffiths, D. 77
Griffiths, N. 15
group learning 16, 46, 152, 159, 161, 190, 200, 203–5
Grow Our Own (GO²) initiative 167, 169, 171–4, 194–5, 197–9
   care for nature 180
   concept of learning in 174–5
   council-managed allotment 180, 183 n.5, 183 n.6
   environment, learning 173–4

food-sharing 172, 174–5, 179
'grow-at-home' scheme 171, 174
growing food to community 177–8
informal shared learning 177
learners' perspectives 175–7
learning experiences of 181
live sustainably, learning to 178
personal consumption 179–80
safety and security 173
sense of community 169, 174–5
volunteering events 172, 174–5
women in 172–3
Gutiérrez, K. D. 88

Harré, R. 136
Harrison, L. 77
Haugan, E. 87. See also language ecology
health and well-being 35, 41, 104, 114, 151, 168–9, 170, 175, 177, 180
family literacy 44–7
HIIC 50–2
homelessness project 47–50, 53
impact of pandemic 161
inequalities 41, 51, 53
learning for 158–9
sense of control 47, 50
and social change 105
social determinants 41
socio-economic risk conditions 50–1
Health Issues in the Community (HIIC) 41, 50–2, 54
Heath, S. 80
Heinemann, A. M. B. 69
The Heritage Seed Library (HSL) 183 n.7
higher education 132, 140, 192
literary studies in 129
programmes 23
historical 6, 15, 78, 80, 88–9, 95, 103, 203
History Workshop 29
Hoggart, R. 22
homelessness project 47–50, 53
Home Office 60–1, 66, 68, 198
Horton, M. 21
hostile environment 60, 63, 66–7, 71, 200, 203
hostile policy 59, 66
humane adult education 1, 5, 11, 13–14, 189
human motivations for learning 189

illegal migration 60–1
Immigration Acts (2014 & 2016) 60
immigration policy 59, 63, 66–8, 71, 198
incidental learning 170, 177–8, 181–2, 198
inclusion for disabled adults 32
Independent Commission on Lifelong Learning 16, 18 n.6
individual learning 114, 154, 167, 182, 205
and social learning 189
industrial trainer 3–4, 189
Industrial Training Boards 23
inequality/inequalities 17, 37, 43, 56, 162, 190–1, 199–200
economic 148, 162, 191
health 41, 51, 53, 55, 82, 148, 191
of power 41, 55, 202
racial and gender 88, 203
social 79–80, 147–9, 162, 191, 195
infodemic 149, 195
informal learning 16, 49, 78, 100, 102–3, 105, 114, 147, 152, 159, 161–2, 170–1, 178–9, 190, 198, 201, 205
formal and 75, 81, 147, 150
initial reflections 97–8
and integration 69–70
opportunities 152, 162
shared learning 177
information gaps 77
Inner London Education Authority (ILEA) 23, 29–30
inquiry method of teaching 43, 201
integration 59, 62, 65–6, 69–70, 77, 203–4
intellectual landscape 22–3
inter-cultural learning 69, 71, 203
international 21, 23–4, 26–8, 30, 32, 42, 76, 86–7, 89, 193
international co-operation 26, 28
International Council for Adult Education 34, 37
International English Language Testing System (IELTS) 81, 86–7
The International League for Social Commitment in Adult Education (ILSCAE) 21–2, 24–37, 197, 204–6
Bergen conference 33
dominant education ideologies, dissatisfaction 26
environmental concerns 35

Gelpi's challenges 26–7
international dialogue 37
migration 29
preamble and objectives (Valentine) 25–6
Slovenian conference 36
Toronto conference 34
translators 31
tyranny of dominant languages 30
women's education 31
intertextual 138, 144, 202

Jackson, T.
  concerted social efforts 168, 177
  consumer behaviour 168
Johnson, B. 59, 62
Johnson, M. 14–15

Kane, l., beliefs 4
knowledge-rich curriculum 130
Kuk, H. 2

Lane, K. 190, 195–8, 200–3
language ecology 87
languages 27, 31, 67, 76, 82, 84–5, 89, 153, 201. *See also* English
learner-centred education 56
learners/participants 11, 22, 43, 47–8, 50, 53, 55–6, 63–6, 68, 70–2, 147, 151, 153, 158, 195, 197, 202
  community 14, 51–2, 160–1, 200
  face-to-face learning 156–7, 160
  ICT skills 154
  as meaning-makers 44
  needs of, adapt provision 155–6
  perspectives 175–7
  tutor and 45–6, 49, 54, 189
The Learning and Work Institute Adult Participation in Learning Survey 149, 195
legal migration 61
liberal arts education 3
liberals and radicals 22–4
lifelong learning 7, 16, 18 n.6, 55–6, 127, 144, 170
Lifelong Loan Entitlement 162
Limits to Growth 168–9
literacy(ies) 23, 29, 32–4, 75, 83–4, 87, 160, 192, 196

activism 75, 88, 203
adult 127–8, 131
deficit school-based 83
event 80
family 41, 44–7, 82–3
health 162
and literature 127
meaningful activist 79–81
theories of 87
transitory 83
tutor 47–8, 203
literariness 129–30
literary-critical works 136
literary forms 136
literary reading
  adult reading and school experiences 130–5
  book groups (*see* book groups)
  evaluation of aesthetic merit 129
  institutionalized practice 136, 139, 143
  quality 133
  and reading development 128
  vernacular method 144
literary study 127
  discipline of 136
  formal 135, 137, 140, 143–4, 192, 201
  Literature's Lasting Impression 130, 131
  in schools 128, 131, 135
literate valuation 84
literature 76, 78–9, 127–32, 135, 140, 167, 192
  as community bricoleur 82
  patterns of reading 134
  studying 5, 9 (*see also* literary reading)
Literature's Lasting Impression 130, 131
Lit in Colour 129–30
Local Authority Adult Community Learning Service 151
Local Education Authorities (LEAs) 8–10, 11–12
Localism Act (2011) 76
Lopes, H. 148–9, 196
Lorimer-Leonard, R. 84
Lorna Doone 134
Lovett, T. 27, 29
  'Adult Education and Social Change in Northern Ireland' 27–8
  typology of initiatives 28

Mansbridge, A. 2, 18 n.1, 22
Marlpit Community Garden 171, 174, 176, 178
Marmot, M. 41, 47, 50
mass health campaigns (pandemic) 187
massive open online courses (MOOCs) 189
Max-Neef, M. A., fundamental human needs 168
May, T. 60
McCabe, A. 77
McKay, V. 148–9, 196
Meade, C. 188–9, 191–2, 195–6, 198, 200, 202
mental health 15, 47, 61, 113–14, 152, 156, 159, 161–2, 175. *See also* health and well-being
Mezirow, J. 29
migrants 23, 59, 62–3, 66, 68–9, 82, 203–4
  integration 59, 69
  multilingual 84
  parenting 83
migration 29, 32, 60, 65–6, 79, 84, 191
  legal and illegal 60–1
  statuses 60, 65–6, 71
Millennium Development Goals 193
Mills, J. 190
missionary approach 4
Modern Languages 8
Mohorcic Spolar, V. 32–4, 36
Moll, L. 43
Morton, J., 'Notes on Industry and Education' 12–13
multilingual 83–4, 88
multiliteracies 88

National Citizen Service (NCS) programme 107–13, 117
  challenges 112
  function of 110–11
  logistical issues 112
  'Seasonal Staff Guide' (fieldwork document) 110–11
  social cohesion 111
  social engagement 111
  social mobility 111
  structural framework 111
  Summer Evaluation 114
  Trust 110
  vision of social change 122

National Health Service (NHS) 86–7
Nationality and Borders Bill (2021, UK) 59, 61, 72, 78
National Lottery 63
National Skills Fund 162
negative experiences of reading 133
neoliberal 24, 42, 110–14, 122, 206
New Management practices 36
New Plan for Immigration 61, 71
Nieto, S., 'Puerto Rico, Adult Education, and the U.S. Education System' 29
non-formal learning 174–5
  flexibility 67–8, 71
  and informal learning 114, 149–50, 167, 170, 189
non-government organizations (NGOs) 63, 70, 77
non-retired teachers 68–9
non-vocational education 5, 7–12. *See also* vocational education
Nottingham University 6, 29, 204

objective-led teaching 144
Occupy movement 17
Office of Communications (Ofcom) 150
OFSTED 130
older people 98, 103–5, 159, 190
  discussion groups with 93–4, 206
  informal learning for 98
  sheltered-housing 101
old humanist tradition 3–5, 189
online adult learning 150, 152, 156, 158–61, 188, 192, 202
online information sharing 149
Ontario Institute for the Study of Education 34
organic practices 178, 180–1
Oxford University 6, 23
Ozturk, E., 'one planet living' 168

Pahl, K. 79–80, 87
Paine, T. 4
Palestine Liberation Organization (PLO) 35
Palestinian National Authority 36
Pamoja (Action Aid) 23
Pant, M. 190, 192, 194, 196–9, 202, 206. *See also* Grow Our Own (GO^2) initiative

participation 27, 29, 42, 50, 101–2, 104, 112, 155, 177–8, 181, 205
   in decision-making 42, 53–4
   discussion group 99
   participant-led differentiation 136, 203
   and self-determination 47, 201
Payne, J. 32–4, 36, 206
   'The Language Question' 30
pedagogy/pedagogical 2, 4–5, 10, 15, 42–4, 49, 88, 127–8, 137, 200
   adult literacy 128
   digital 71
   ethnography 75
   of family literacy 83, 85
   funds of knowledge 45, 53
   peer-to-peer 140, 205
   reading 127–8, 134, 144
peers, exchange 133
peer-to-peer pedagogy 6, 140, 205
performative assessment 206
performing 85
Peutrell, R. 65
policies 7, 42–4, 60, 62, 71, 88, 128–30, 144, 148, 162, 169, 190, 201, 206
   hostile environment 60, 66, 71, 203
   immigration 59, 63, 66–7, 71, 198
   US foreign 34
popular education 4, 17, 21, 51
portfolios 45
positioning theory 136–7
   affordances of spoken quotation 137
   appreciate aesthetic qualities 137
positive learning environment 179, 203
positive social values 102, 177, 182
postcolonial theory 109
posthumanism 108, 111, 113
   centres 122
   ethico-onto-epistem-ological premise 110, 120
   and social change 109–10
poverty 31, 41, 50, 52, 61, 187, 191, 193
power 5, 14–15, 29, 42, 50, 54, 75–6, 109, 114, 120, 136, 199
   dynamics 110, 153
   inequalities 41, 55, 202
Pretty, J., 'closeness to nature' 169
primary schools 86, 132
prior learning 201
privilege memorization 130

providers 43, 47, 62, 86, 108, 111, 117, 123, 147, 150–1, 155–6, 160–2, 170, 188, 197–8, 201–2, 204
Public Knowledge and Public Education 4
purposeful discussions 94, 97, 101, 104
Puttick, M-R. 188, 190, 193–4, 196, 199, 201–5

qualification(s) 86, 96, 154–6, 158, 170, 187, 201

racism 66, 79, 87
radical/radicalism (adult education) 22, 24
   alternatives 28
   ILSCAE (*see* The International League for Social Commitment in Adult Education (ILSCAE))
   liberals and 22–4
   social movements 6
Rahim, A. A. 21
Rasool, Z. 79–80, 88
reading 45, 47, 181, 192, 195
   groups 132, 135–6, 196–7, 201
   literary (*see* literary reading)
   negative experiences of 133
   pedagogy 127–8, 134, 144
   small stories 138, 140
Refugee Action 77
refugee community organizations (RCOs) 77, 79, 89
Refugee Convention 59–60
refugees 27, 29, 34, 81–2, 86–7, 198, 202, 204
   challenges 87
   impacts of pandemic 70–1
   organization 75, 77–8, 89
   Palestinian communities 35
   third sector (*see* third sector (refugee))
   in the UK 60–4, 66–7
regular/irregular migration 61
rehabilitation worker 47, 203
Rekindling commitment in adult education 24
relationships 1, 6–8, 14, 46–7, 55, 122–3, 128, 205
   adult education and social change 60
   adult reading habits and school experiences 130–5
   learning 107

learning and living sustainably 167
social 104
tutor-learner 45–6, 49, 54, 189
relevant adult education movement 1, 22, 30, 44, 105, 109, 170, 181
Rennolds, N. 188–9, 193, 199–200, 202, 204
  National Citizenship Service programme 200, 204–5
  reciprocity of dialogue 205
research context 108
Rogers, A., kinds of learning xiii, 69, 114, 119, 170–1, 178, 181
Rombalski, A. 88
Rose, J., *The Intellectual Life of the British Working Classes* 16
Rowsell, J. 87
Roy, A. 162
Royal Charter 110–12
Ruskin College 22
Rustin, M. 3
Rutgers University (New Jersey) 24
Ryan, R. M. 68

sanctuary 59, 71, 178
Satchwell, C. 127
Saunders, P. 172
Scribbins, J., 'Gender issues – A perspective on the ILSCAE conference 1986' 31
secondary schools 132, 140, 192
second-wave feminism 23, 29
self-directed learning 170
self-help learning groups 190
Sen, A., notion of freedom 170–1, 182, 198
Shah, H., 'one planet living' 168
Shah, S. 79
shared learning 176–7
sheltered-housing 93–4, 96–7, 99–101, 103, 105, 195, 197
Sibieta, L. 163
Skills for Jobs: Lifelong Learning for Opportunity and Growth 3
skills of resilience 162–3, 200
small stories 138–9
  Daddy-Long-Legs (Webster) 138–40, 203–4
  personal 138
  reading 138, 140
  recasting 138, 140
  text-generated/given 138–40
Smith, A. L. 2
social change 1, 3–4, 17, 22, 25–7, 37, 60, 67, 71, 75–7, 93, 103–4, 108, 116, 119, 147, 160–2, 187, 191–4
  active learning 200–4
  adult education and 60, 187, 191, 194–7, 199–201, 205–6
  adult learning for 1, 75, 79, 107, 199
  collaborative action 205–6
  domains of 195–9
  effective adult learning programmes 187, 199–206
  funding 204–5
  future thinking for 88–9
  posthumanism and 109–10
  reflections from residents 98–101
  refugee third sector (*see* third sector (refugee))
  tales of learning and (*see* tales (learning and social change))
  volunteer agency and 66–7
social cohesion 77, 111, 197
social connection/connectedness 97, 100–1, 103–5, 196–7
Social Development Goals (SDGs) 193–4
social engagement 94, 101, 104, 111, 197
social inequalities 25, 79–80, 147–9, 195
social justice 21, 25, 27, 37, 42–3, 108, 116, 127, 130–2, 192, 195
  participatory parity 42, 53–4
  recognition 42–3, 53–4
  redistribution 42, 53–4
social mobility 111
social movements 1–2, 5, 8, 17, 21, 79, 193
  radical 6
  state and 14–17
social networking 46, 87, 104
social transformation 67, 71, 128, 144, 195
Society for Educational Studies (SES) 6–7, 14
socio-economic adversity 42
Soteri-Proctor, A. 76, 78
Southampton University 27
Spanish flu pandemic 1
spiritual 1, 3–5

Standing Conference of University Teaching and Research in the Education of Adults (SCUTREA) 33
Stanistreet, P., need for education 148–9, 188
state 3, 6, 8–9, 11, 76, 188
   and civil society 2, 7
   funding 8, 11
   and social movements 14–17
status model of recognition 42–3
status quo 29, 190, 202
Stevenson, R. L., *Dr Jekyll and Mr Hyde* 134
Sustainable Development Goals 191, 193–4
sustainable living 167–9, 177, 182
   learning to 178
   non-formal and informal learning 167 (*see also* Grow Our Own (GO^2) initiative)
Sustainable Living Initiative (SLI) reports 167, 171–2, 174
sustainable/sustainability 63, 68–9, 71, 167–8, 171, 191
sympoiesis 109–10

Tahir, I. 163
tales (learning and social change) 108, 123
   doing 113–16
   entanglement 110, 119–22
   national programme (*see* National Citizen Service (NCS) programme)
   octopuses and challenges 107
   young adults as team leaders 116–19
Tarlau, R. 2
task-based learning 181
task-conscious learning 170
Tawney, R. H. 2, 4
teacher-researcher affective reflections 75, 80–7
teaching-learning materials 196, 201
technical education 10
technology 70, 95, 99, 149, 152, 155, 162, 191
Tett, L. 193, 197, 199–201, 203–6
Thatcherism 24
Thematic Analysis (Braun & Clarke) 64
theory and practice (education) 43
third sector (refugee) 75–6

collective activism 78
learning ecology for social change 76, 87–8
to social change 76–9
Thompson, E. P. 22
Education and Experience 14
time-limited funding 76
The Time Traveller's Wife 142
tools (learners) 152
transformational learning 29
transitory literacies 83
Traveller community 45–6, 53
Trinity Centre 79–81, 204
   advocacy as affective and embodied 81–3
   expanding repertoires and preserving cultural heritage 83–5
   instigating international dialogue 86–7
Troup, E. 13
Tuckett, A. 67, 170, 193, 197, 199–200, 204, 206
tutor(s) 10, 45–6, 48–9, 50–3, 130, 135–6, 200, 202–4
   and learners 45–6, 49, 54, 189
   literacy 47–8, 203
   peer and 48–9
   staff development 160
Tutorial classes and Summer Schools 18 n.2

Ulmer, J. B. 109
UNESCO 148, 200
   Futures of Education initiative 163
unintentional, unplanned and unconscious learning 170
Union Learning Fund 17
United Nations High Commissioner for Refugees 61
Universal Basic Income 69
Universal Declaration of Human Rights 61
university 22, 82, 88, 117, 130, 141, 173, 189, 204
   education 3, 63, 117, 130, 172
   extramural provision 22–3
   students as volunteers 175
University of Glasgow 63
University of Nottingham 204
utilitarian 10
utopianism 24

Valentine, T. 25
van der Veen, R. 30
van Langenhove, L. 136
vernacular storying 130, 144
virtual learning opportunities 150
vocational education 1, 3, 8–10, 187, 189
voluntary organizations/sector 5, 7–8, 11, 16–17, 36, 77, 147, 188
volunteers/volunteering 60, 63–6, 71–2, 80, 172, 174–5, 178, 203
   agency and social change 66–7
   corporate 181, 198
   ESOL teachers 59, 64, 66, 68–70, 198, 200, 205
   flexible, non-formal classes 67–8
   sustainability of 68–9, 71

Walker, A. 104
'Walk of Life' activity 115, 121
Waltmann, B. 163
Webster, J., *Daddy-Long-Legs* 138–40, 203–4
Welby, L. 189
well-being. *See* health and well-being
White, R. 15
White Paper 3, 162–3
Williams, R. 1, 4, 22, 189
   The Long Revolution 3
   An Open Letter to WEA Tutors 3
Windrush scandal 60
women 31, 35, 84–5, 94, 98, 100, 149, 152–4, 172, 183 n.1, 183 n.12, 195, 197, 199
   affective literacy events 75
   capacity building of 88
   discussion group 97
   in GO^2 scheme 172–3
   health 86
   learning ecologies 88
   at Trinity Centre 80
women's education 23, 31, 36
   and refugee provision 34
   second-wave feminism 23
Women's Educational Centre (Ramullah) 36
work and education 12–13, 151, 158, 162–3, 199
Workers' Educational Association (WEA) 2, 16, 18 n.1, 22–3
working class people 5, 23, 120
   appetite for adult education 16
   social movements 5
workshop groups 15–16, 181
World Association for Adult Education 23
World Conference on Adult Education 36
World Health Organisation 149
World Social Forum 37
The World Transformed, Arts Emergency 6

young adults 7, 114
   learning environment and relationships 107
   NCS 122
   as team leaders 116–19

Zoom (digital learning) 70, 152–4, 159, 161–2, 199

www.ingramcontent.com/pod-product-compliance
Lightning Source LLC
Chambersburg PA
CBHW062215300426
44115CB00012BA/2070